HUMAN
SECURITY
NOW

COMMISSION ON HUMAN SECURITY

New York

2003

Editing, design and production by Communications Development Incorporated in Washington, DC, with art direction by its UK partner, Grundy & Northedge.

Photos on front cover and chapters 1, 2, 3 and 5 by UNHCR. Photo in chapter 4 by PhotoDisc. Photos in chapters 6 and 7 by Curt Carnemark, World Bank Photo Library.

ISBN 0-9741108-0-9

Members of the Commission on Human Security

Foreword

When the idea of an independent Commission for Human Security was launched at the 2000 UN Millennium Summit, there was general agreement on the importance of "freedom from want" and "freedom from fear". Today, three years later, the fears are larger and the apprehensions greater. This report is an attempt to respond to both old and new worries and also to the underlying reasons for concern.

In addition to the persistent problems and vulnerabilities with which the world has long been familiar, there is a new wave of dramatic crises at the turn of the millennium related to terrorist attacks, ethnic violence, epidemics and sudden economic downturns. There is also a fear that existing institutions and policies are not able to cope with weakening multilateralism, falling respect for human rights, eroding commitments to eradicate poverty and deprivation, outdated sectarian perspectives in education systems and the tendency to neglect global responsibilities in an increasingly interrelated world.

At the same time, the opportunities for working towards removing insecurity across the world are also larger now than ever before. Globalization, despite its challenges, creates new opportunities for economic expansion and, if properly aligned, can reach peoples and countries that were previously excluded. Democratic principles and practices are continuing to gain ground and to attract stronger support. There has also been a massive increase in the role of civil society and of community organizations. Further, the Millennium Development Goals represent a major initiative aimed at removing deprivations, on which efforts to improve human security can build.

This report should be seen in the light of the increased challenges the world faces and the enhanced opportunities. Human security is concerned with safeguarding and expanding people's vital freedoms. It requires both shielding people from acute threats and empowering people to take charge of their own lives. Needed are integrated policies that focus on people's survival, livelihood and dignity, during downturns as well as in prosperity.

The demands of human security involve a broad range of interconnected issues. In its work, the Commission has concentrated on a number of distinct but interrelated areas concerned with conflict and poverty, protecting people during violent conflict and in post-conflict situations, defending people who are forced to move, overcoming economic insecurities, guaranteeing the availability and affordability of essential health care, and ensuring the elimination of illiteracy and educational deprivation and of schools that promote intolerance. The recommendations of the Commission involve policies aimed at both empowerment and protection, and focus on what can be done in the short and the long run to enhance the opportunities for eliminating insecurities across the world.

This report can, of course, be no more than a beginning, but it is, we believe, extremely important to move rapidly in the right direction. The task demands leadership and vision as well as commitment from the world community.

****

The independent Commission on Human Security was an initiative of the Government of Japan. We are grateful for the support and encouragement of UN Secretary-

General Kofi Annan and the active engagement and commitment to human security of successive Prime Ministers of Japan: Keizo Obuchi, Yoshiro Mori and Junichiro Koizumi. The continuing support of Ruud Lubbers, UN High Commissioner for Refugees, and Mark Malloch-Brown, Administrator of the United Nations Development Programme, made possible the establishment of the Commission Secretariat and implementation of its research programme. We would like to express our deep appreciation for their cooperation and advice. We plan to carry forward their ideas as well as the outcomes of the Commission's work into a new Advisory Board for Human Security.

The work of the Commission received generous financial support from the Ministry of Foreign Affairs of Japan. It also received support from the Government of Sweden, the World Bank, the Rockefeller Foundation, and the Japan Center for International Exchange. The United Nations Office for Project Services efficiently managed the administrative arrangements. We are grateful for their generosity and confidence in our work.

The commissioners each brought unique contributions to the Commission's work, reflecting their wide-ranging professional expertise and personal commitment. Their insights contributed enormously to the richness of this report. We are now counting on them to assist in translating the concept of human security into concrete policy programmes in their regions of the world.

Finally, we would like to thank those—indeed a great many—who have shared their understanding, fears and hopes about human security with the Commission in many parts of the world. We count on everyone's continuing support to advance human security around the world.

Sadako Ogata   **Amartya Sen**

Contents

Human security
now

1

Today's global flows of goods, services, finance, people and images spotlight the many interlinkages in the security of all people. We share a planet, a biosphere, a technological arsenal, a social fabric. The security of one person, one community, one nation rests on the decisions of many others—sometimes fortuitously, sometimes precariously. Political liberalization in recent decades has shifted alliances and begun movements towards democracy. These processes opened opportunities for people but also new fault lines. And political and economic instabilities, some involving bitter conflicts with heavy casualties and dislocations, have broken out within states. Thus people throughout the world, in developing and developed countries alike, live under varied conditions of insecurity.

Institutions have gradually responded. The United Nations completed more peacekeeping operations in the 1990s than ever in its history. It also negotiated new international agreements to stop some threats. Transnational corporations, working in many countries, have transformed scientific and informational advances into practical applications. They regularly navigate diverse markets and cultures, facilitating the exchange of goods and services. Regional entities are finding appropriate avenues of coordinated action. And civil society organizations are flourishing, relying on low-cost electronic communication to keep expenses down.

This report's call for human security is a response to new opportunities for propelling development, for dealing with conflict, for blunting the many threats to human security. But it is also a response to the proliferation of menace

in the 21st century—a response to the threats of development reversed, to the threats of violence inflicted. With so many dangers transmitted so rapidly in today's interlinked world, policies and institutions must respond in new ways to protect individuals and communities and to empower them to thrive. That response cannot be effective if it comes fragmented—from those dealing with rights, those with security, those with humanitarian concerns and those with development. With human security the objective, there must be a stronger and more integrated response from communities and states around the globe.

Security centred on people—not states

The international community urgently needs a new paradigm of security. Why? Because the security debate has changed dramatically since the inception of state security advocated in the 17th century. According to that traditional idea, the state would monopolize the rights and means to protect its citizens. State power and state security would be established and expanded to sustain order and peace. But in the 21st century, both the challenges to security and its protectors have become more complex. The state remains the fundamental purveyor of security. Yet it often fails to fulfil its security obligations—and at times has even become a source of threat to its own people. That is why attention must now shift from the security of the state to the security of the people—to human security (box 1.1).

Human security complements state security, enhances human rights and strengthens human development. It seeks to protect people against a broad range of threats to individuals and communities and, further, to empower them to act on their own behalf. And it

Box 1.1 Rethinking security: An imperative for Africa?

Traditional notions of security, shaped largely by the Cold War, were concerned mainly with a state's ability to counter external threats. Threats to international peace and security were also usually perceived as threats from outside the state (see, for example, chapter 7 of the United Nations Charter). More recently, thinking about security has shifted. In Africa, for example, such shifts can be traced to the internal struggles of African people against colonial rule and occupation, whether in Algeria, Angola, Cape Verde, Kenya, Mozambique, Namibia, South Africa or Zimbabwe.

Views on security were shaped by the experiences of colonialism and neocolonialism and by the complex processes through which internal and external forces combined to dominate and subjugate people. The enemy came from within the state, and the conditions under which people lived every day placed them in chronic insecurity. These experiences introduced into the debate such issues as whose security matters and under what conditions, and what are the moral, ethical and legal bases for what is now termed a "just war".

These experiences and perceptions were important in shaping such disparate-seeming issues as how the women's movement mobilized against oppression and what form reconstruction, development and reconciliation would take in newly independent countries. Notable in Africa was the way the women's movement linked struggles for national independence and security to the struggle for equality and social equity. The persistent marginalization of countries in Africa from processes of economic growth and development, however, reinforced perceptions of exclusion and vulnerability. For these reasons, development, poverty eradication and greater social equality were increasingly linked to conflict resolution, peace-building and state building in Africa.

Thinking about security broadened from an exclusive concern with the security of the state to a concern with the security of people. Along with this shift came the notion that states ought not to be the sole or main referent of security. People's interests or the interests of humanity, as a collective, become the focus. In this way, security becomes an all-encompassing condition in which individual citizens live in freedom, peace and safety and participate fully in the process of governance. They enjoy the protection of fundamental rights, have access to resources and the basic necessities of life, including health and education, and inhabit an environment that is not injurious to their health and well-being. Eradication of poverty is thus central to ensuring the security of all people, as well as the security of the state.

This understanding of human security does not replace the security of the state with the security of people. It sees the two aspects as mutually dependent. Security between states remains a necessary condition for the security of people, but national security is not sufficient to guarantee peoples' security. For that, the state must provide various protections to its citizens. But individuals also require protection from the arbitrary power of the state, through the rule of law and emphasis on civil and political rights as well as socio-economic rights.

Significantly, such thinking on security takes place alongside the development of renewed initiatives focusing on regional and continental cooperation and regeneration. A convergence in how we understand issues of security and how we view the effects on the lives of people is already evident in the founding documents of the African Union, the New Partnership for Africa's Development, the Conference on Security, Stability, Development and Cooperation in Africa, and the reformed Southern African Development Community, including its Organ on Politics, Defence and Security.

But, of course, this does not mean an end to the debate about the role of the state in security management. Rather, it reinforces the point that without popular participation in shaping agendas on security, political and economic elites will go it alone in a process that will further marginalize and impoverish the people of Africa. It is against this background that the idea of human security must become a tool and instrument to advance the interests of humanity, particularly in Africa. Rethinking security in ways that place people and their participation at the centre is an imperative for the 21st century.

Frene Ginwala

Note: Based on a presentation at the "Parliaments Uniting for African Unity Conference", Cape Town, June 2002.

seeks to forge a global alliance to strengthen the institutional policies that link individuals and the state—and the state with a global world. Human security thus brings together the human elements of security, of rights, of development.

The Commission on Human Security's definition of human security: to protect the vital core of all human lives in ways that enhance human freedoms and human fulfilment. Human security means protecting fundamental freedoms—freedoms that are the essence of life. It means protecting people from critical (severe) and pervasive (widespread) threats and situations. It means using processes that build on people's strengths and aspirations. It means creating political, social, environmental, economic, military and cultural systems that together give people the building blocks of survival, livelihood and dignity.

The vital core of life is a set of elementary rights and freedoms people enjoy. What people consider to be "vital"—what they consider to be "of the essence of life" and "crucially important"—varies across individuals and societies. That is why any concept of human security must be dynamic. And that is why we refrain from proposing an itemized list of what makes up human security.

As UN Secretary-General Kofi Annan points out, human security joins the main agenda items of peace, security and development. Human security is comprehensive in the sense that it integrates these agendas:

Human security in its broadest sense embraces far more than the absence of violent conflict. It encompasses human rights, good gover-nance, access to education and health care and ensuring that each individual has

opportunities and choices to fulfil his or her own potential. Every step in this direction is also a step towards reducing poverty, achieving economic growth and preventing conflict. Freedom from want, freedom from fear and the freedom of future generations to inherit a healthy natural environment—these are the interrelated building blocks of human, and therefore national, security.[1]

Human security also reinforces human dignity. People's horizons extend far beyond survival, to matters of love, culture and faith. Protecting a core of activities and abilities is essential for human security, but that alone is not enough. Human security must also aim at developing the capabilities of individuals and communities to make informed choices and to act on behalf of causes and interests in many spheres of life. That is why human security starts from the recognition that people are the most active participants in determining their well-being. It builds on people's efforts, strengthening what they do for themselves.

Human security and state security
Human security complements "state security" in four respects (box 1.2):[2]

- Its concern is the individual and the community rather than the state.
- Menaces to people's security include threats and conditions that have not always been classified as threats to state security.
- The range of actors is expanded beyond the state alone.
- Achieving human security includes not just protecting people but also empowering people to fend for themselves.

Box 1.2 Human security and state security

Security is facing new challenges. In the past, security threats were assumed to emanate from external sources. State security focused mainly on protecting the state—its boundaries, people, institutions and values—from external attacks.

Over the last decades, our understanding of state security and the many types of threats has broadened. In addition to securing borders, people, values and institutions, we have come to understand the dangers of environmental pollution, transnational terrorism, massive population movements and such infectious diseases as HIV/AIDS. Most significant, there is growing recognition of the role of people—of individuals and communities—in ensuring their own security.

This broadening of security reflects the changing international and national environments. Internal conflicts have overtaken interstate wars as the major threats to international peace and security. The globalization process has deeply transformed relationships between and within states. Although more people than ever have access to information and essential social goods, the gaps between rich and poor countries—and between wealthy and destitute people—have never been greater than today. The exclusion and deprivation of whole communities of people from the benefits of development naturally contribute to the tensions, violence and conflict within countries.

To achieve peace and stability in today's interdependent world, preventing and mitigating the impact of internal violent conflicts are not sufficient. Also important are upholding human rights, pursuing inclusive and equitable development and respecting human dignity and diversity. Equally decisive is to develop the capability of individuals and communities to make informed choices and to act on their own behalf.

In many respects, human security requires including the excluded. It focuses on the widest possible range of people having enough confidence in their future—enough confidence that they can actually think about the next day, the next week, and the next year. Protecting and empowering people are thus about creating genuine possibilities for people to live in safety and dignity. Seen from this angle, human security reinforces state security but does not replace it.

At the start of the 21st century, we are at a dangerous crossroads. In response to the threat of terrorism and the spread of weapons of mass destruction, states may revert to a narrower understanding of state security—rather than foster human security. The credibility and legitimacy of the multilateral institutions and strategies are being questioned, and long-standing alliances among states are eroding. Under the guise of waging a war against terrorism, human rights and humanitarian law are being violated. Even commitments to earlier international agreements are being reviewed.

Humanitarian action now also seems to be in crisis. Few situations better reflect these new developments than the ongoing Palestinian-Israeli conflict. The denial of access to humanitarian actors to reach civilians, the closing off of whole communities, the willful destruction of civilian properties, as in the Jenin refugee camp in 2002—all imply that people are being held hostage to protect state security needs. Too little attention, as in the case of Iraq, is given to the impact on civilians and the possible implications for maintaining the principles of impartiality, neutrality and independence guiding humanitarian action. The provision of life-saving humanitarian assistance should not be used as a bargaining tool in weapons issues, as in the case of the nuclear armament of the Democratic People's Republic of Korea.

In a world of growing interdependence and transnational issues, reverting to unilateralism and a narrow interpretation of state security cannot be the answer. The United Nations stands as the best and only option available to preserve international peace and stability as well as to protect people, regardless of race, religion, gender or political opinion. The issue is how to make the United Nations and other regional security organizations more effective in preventing and controlling threats and protecting people, and how to complement state security with human security at the community, national and international levels.

It is frightening today that the dangers of war loom as large as ever—that hundreds of millions of people do not feel secure enough to rebuild their houses or plow their fields or send their children to school. The agenda, vast and complex, must be tackled starting from the pervasive and critical threats confronting people today. Now, more than ever, human security is essential.

Sadako Ogata

Human security broadens the
focus from the security of
borders to the lives of people
and communities inside and
across those borders

People-centred. State security focuses on other states with aggressive or adversarial designs. States built powerful security structures to defend themselves—their boundaries, their institutions, their values, their numbers. Human security shifts from focusing on external aggression to protecting people from a range of menaces.

Menaces. State security has meant protecting territorial boundaries with—and from—uniformed troops. Human security also includes protection of citizens from environmental pollution, transnational terrorism, massive population movements, such infectious diseases as HIV/AIDS and long-term conditions of oppression and deprivation.

Actors. The range of actors is also greater. No longer are states the sole actors. Regional and international organizations, nongovernmental organizations (NGOs) and civil society are involved in managing security issues—as in the fight against HIV/AIDS, the ban against landmines and the massive mobilizations in support of human rights.

Empowerment. Securing people also entails empowering people and societies. In many situations, people can contribute directly to identifying and implementing solutions to the quagmire of insecurity. In post-conflict situations, for example, bringing diverse constituents together to rebuild their communities can solve security problems.

Human security and state security are mutually reinforcing and dependent on each other. Without human security, state security cannot be attained and vice versa. Human security requires strong and stable institutions. Whereas state security is focused, human security is broad.

Human security's distinctive breadth

Human security thus broadens the focus from the security of borders to the lives of people and communities inside and across those borders. The idea is for people to be secure, not just for territories within borders to be secure against external aggression. And unlike traditional approaches that vest the state with full responsibility for state security, the process of human security involves a much broader spectrum of actors and institutions—especially people themselves.

Human security is concerned with violent conflict. For whatever form violence takes, whether terrorism or crime or war, violence unseats people's security. More than 800,000 people a year lose their lives to lethal violence—and in 2000, nearly 16 million lived as refugees.[3] The catastrophic effects of war persist for generations. The memory of conflict and loss lives on, affecting people's ability to live together in peace.

Human security is also concerned with deprivation: from extreme impoverishment, pollution, ill health, illiteracy and other maladies. Catastrophic accident and illness rank among the primary worries of the poor—and accurately, for their toll on human lives—causing more than 22 million preventable deaths in 2001. Educational deprivations are particularly serious for human security. Without education, men and especially women are disadvantaged as productive workers, as fathers and mothers, as citizens capable of social change. Without social protection, personal injury or economic collapse can catapult families into penury and desperation. All such losses affect people's power to fend for themselves.

Each menace, terrible on its own, justifies attention. Yet to address this range of insecurities

6

Focusing on human security adds an important perspective to today's global challenges

effectively demands an integrated approach. That approach would keep the full range of human deprivation in view, for all people. It would attend not only to the protection of refugees from ongoing violence—but also to their health and livelihoods. It would concentrate on the provision of basic education to the poor—but also on basic education that is safe, that strengthens civil society and that creates tolerant societies. It would not focus on peace to the exclusion of development or on the environment to the exclusion of security. Instead, it would have a spectrum of basic variables in full view.

Not only are peace and development both important. They are also interconnected. The chain from poverty and deprivation to violent conflict—and back—has to be followed carefully. Deprivation persists in countries that do not flare up in conflict, and conflicts flare up in relatively well-off countries. Deprivation and unequal treatment may not generate an immediate revolt, but they can remain in people's memory and influence the course of events much later. And while the leaders of conflicts often come from the more prosperous parts of society, poverty can provide rich recruiting grounds for the "foot soldiers" of violent engagements.[4]

Wars destroy human lives and scar survivors. They destroy homes, economic assets, crops, roads, banks and utility systems. They destroy habits of trust that form the basis of market transactions and broad-based political associations. Poverty rises in wartime, often significantly. During conflicts, gangs, mafias and black market activities can increase insecurities. Governments may cut social expenditures, and economic growth may slow or even contract. After conflict, countries face the enormous expense of rebuilding their assets and

markets, usually from a reduced tax base and with unpredictable foreign assistance. And conflicts are prone to recur, deepening poverty even more.[5]

Economic injustice and inequality also polarize communities. The tolerance of conflict by an otherwise peaceful population is a peculiar phenomenon in many parts of the contemporary world, particularly where a large part of the populace feels badly treated or left behind by global economic and social progress. Many who find violence utterly unacceptable in their personal lives provide remarkably little opposition to political violence seen as part of a fight against injustice—whether for their ethnic group or their nation or their faith.

In transitions, too, each aspect of human security must be kept in view to maintain balance while moving forward. That balance can be tenuous. In post-conflict situations, if countries focus too much on consolidating political stability, they may be destabilized by economic retreats (or any number of other factors). In the transition from communism to an open economy, there was cause for celebration in the countries of the former Soviet Union. Yet in Tajikistan per capita incomes fell 85%, plunging four-fifths of the population below the poverty line. In Latin America, the transition from authoritarian rule to democracy has often been impeded by slow or negative growth, weak institutions, corruption and reversal of social protection, leading people to question why democratic forms of governance do not deliver promised benefits.

Human security and human rights
Focusing on human security adds an important perspective to today's global challenges. But the

Box 1.3 Development, rights and human security

Human security is concerned with reducing and—when possible—removing the insecurities that plague human lives. It contrasts with the notion of state security, which concentrates primarily on safeguarding the integrity and robustness of the state and thus has only an indirect connection with the security of the human beings who live in these states.

That contrast may be clear enough, but in delineating human security adequately, it is also important to understand how the idea of human security relates to—and differs from—other human-centred concepts, such as human development and human rights. These concepts are fairly widely known and have been championed, with very good reason, for a long time, and they too are directly concerned with the nature of human lives. It is thus fair to ask what the idea of human security can add to these well-established ideas.

Human development and human security
The human development approach, pioneered by the visionary economist Mahbub ul Haq (under the broad umbrella of the United Nations Development Programme, UNDP), has done much to enrich and broaden the literature on development. In particular, it has helped to shift the focus of development attention away from an overarching concentration on the growth of inanimate objects of convenience, such as commodities produced (reflected in the gross domestic product or the gross national product), to the quality and richness of human lives, which depend on a number of influences, of which commodity production is only one.

Human development is concerned with removing the various hindrances that restrain and restrict human lives and prevent its blossoming. A few of these concerns are captured in the much-used "human development index" (HDI), which has served as something of a flagship of the human development approach. But the range and reach of that perspective have motivated a vast informational coverage presented in the UNDP's annual *Human Development Report* and other related publications that go far beyond the HDI.

The idea of human development, broad as it is, does, however, have a powerfully buoyant quality, since it is concerned with progress and augmentation. It is out to conquer fresh territory on behalf of enhancing human lives and is far too upbeat to focus on rearguard actions needed to secure what has to be safeguarded. This is where the notion of human security becomes particularly relevant.

Human security as an idea fruitfully supplements the expansionist perspective of human development by directly paying attention to what are sometimes called "downside risks". The insecurities that threaten human survival or the safety of daily life, or imperil the natural dignity of men and women, or expose human beings to the uncertainty of disease and pestilence, or subject vulnerable people to abrupt penury related to economic downturns demand that special attention be paid to the dangers of sudden deprivation. Human security demands protection from these dangers and the empowerment of people so that they can cope with—and when possible overcome—these hazards.

There is, of course, no basic contradiction between the focus of human security and the subject matter of the human development approach. Indeed, formally speaking, protection and safeguarding can also be seen as augmentations of a sort, to wit that of safety and security. But the emphasis and priorities are quite different in the cautious perspective of human security from those typically found in the relatively sanguine and upward-oriented literature of the human focus of development approaches (and this applies to human development as well), which tend to concentrate on "growth with equity", a subject that has generated a vast literature and inspired many policy initiatives. In contrast, focusing on human security requires that serious attention be paid to "downturns with security", since downturns may inescapably occur from time to time, fed by global or local afflictions. This is in addition to the adversity of persistent insecurity of those whom the growth process leaves behind, such as the displaced worker or the perennially unemployed.

Even when the much-discussed problems of uneven and unequally shared benefits of growth and expansion have been successfully addressed, a sudden downturn can make the lives of the vulnerable thoroughly and uncommonly deprived. There is much economic evidence that even if people rise together as the process of economic expansion proceeds, when they fall, they tend to fall very divided. The Asian economic crisis of 1997–99 made it painfully clear that even a very successful history of "growth with equity" (as the Republic of Korea, Thailand, and many other countries in East and Southeast Asia had) can provide very little

1

protection to those who are thrown to the wall when a sharp economic downturn suddenly occurs.

The economic case merely illustrates a general contrast between the two perspectives of *expansion with equity* and *downturn with security*. For example, while the foundational demand for expanding regular health coverage for all human beings in the world is tremendously important to advocate and advance, that battle has to be distinguished from the immediate need to encounter a suddenly growing pandemic, related to HIV/AIDS or malaria or drug-resistant tuberculosis.

Insecurity is a different—and in some ways much starker—problem than unequal expansion. Without losing any of the commitment that makes human development important, we also have to rise to the challenges of human security that the world currently faces and will long continue to face.

Human rights and human security

There is a similar complementarity between the concepts of human rights and human security. Few concepts are as frequently invoked in contemporary political debates as human rights. There is something deeply attractive in the idea that every person anywhere in the world, irrespective of citizenship or location, has some basic rights that others should respect. The moral appeal of human rights has been used for varying purposes, from resisting torture and arbitrary incarceration to demanding the end of hunger and unequal treatment of women.

Human rights may or may not be legalized, but they take the form of strong claims in social ethics. The idea of pre-legal "natural" or "human" rights has often motivated legislative initiatives, as it did in the US Declaration of Independence or in the French Declaration of the Rights of Man in the 18th century, or in the European Convention for the Protection of Human Rights and Fundamental Freedoms in the 20th century. But even when they are not legalized, affirmation of human rights and related activities of advocacy and monitoring of abuse can sometimes be very effective, through the politicization of ethical commitments.

Commitments underlying human rights take the form of demanding that certain basic freedoms of human beings be respected, aided and enhanced. The basically normative nature of the concept of human rights leaves open the question of which particular freedoms are crucial enough to count as human rights that society should acknowledge, safeguard and promote. This is

where human security can make a significant contribution by identifying the importance of freedom from basic insecurities—new and old. The descriptive richness of the considerations that make security so important in human lives can, thus, join hands with the force of ethical claims that the recognition of certain freedoms as human rights provides.

Human rights and human security can, therefore, fruitfully supplement each other. On the one hand, since human rights can be seen as a general box that has to be filled with specific demands with appropriate motivational substantiation, it is significant that human security helps to fill one particular part of this momentous box through reasoned substantiation (by showing the importance of conquering human insecurity). On the other, since human security as an important descriptive concept demands ethical force and political recognition, it is useful that this can be appropriately obtained through seeing freedoms related to human security as an important class of human rights. Far from being in any kind of competition with each other, human security and human rights can be seen as complementary ideas.

One of the advantages of seeing human security as a class of human rights is the associative connection that rights have with the corresponding duties of other people and institutions. Duties can take the form of "perfect obligations", which constitute specific demands on particular persons or agents, or of "imperfect obligations", which are general demands on anyone in a position to help. To give effectiveness to the perspective of human security, it is important to consider who in particular has what obligations (such as the duties of the state to provide certain basic support) and also why people in general, who are in a position to help reduce insecurities in human lives, have a common—though incompletely specified—duty to think about what they can do. Seeing human security within a general framework of human rights can, thus, bring many rewards to the perspective of human security.

To conclude, it is important, on one side, to see how the distinct ideas of human security, human development and human rights differ, but also to understand why they can be seen as complementary concepts. Mutual enrichment can go hand in hand with distinction and clarity.

Amartya Sen

question arises: How does human security relate to other approaches already in use in the United Nations?

The idea of *human security* fits well with human development and human rights, but it also adds something substantial (box 1.3). Human security and human development are both fundamentally concerned with the lives of human beings—longevity, education, opportunities for participation. Both are concerned with the basic freedoms that people enjoy. But they look out on shared goals with different scopes. Human development "is about people, about expanding their choices to lead lives they value".[6] It has an optimistic quality, since it focuses on expanding opportunities for people so that progress is fair—"growth with equity". Human security complements human development by deliberately focusing on "downside risks". It recognizes the conditions that menace survival, the continuation of daily life and the dignity of human beings. Even in countries that have promoted growth with equity, as in some Asian countries, people's lives are threatened when economic downturns occur.[7] The recent downturn in Argentina similarly threatened the lives of many in that country.

Any notion of development is, in some ways, inescapably "aggregative". But when it comes to insecurity, there is an important need to keep the individual at the centre of attention. Why? Because any larger unit—an ethnic group or a household—may discriminate against its own members. This is especially so for women—within the household and, more generally, in society.

Respecting human rights is at the core of protecting human security. The 1993 Vienna Declaration of Human Rights stresses the universality and interdependence of the human rights of all people. Those rights have to be upheld comprehensively—civil and political, as well as economic and social—as proclaimed in the legally binding conventions and protocols that derive from the 1948 Universal Declaration on Human Rights.

Human rights and human security are therefore mutually reinforcing. Human security helps identify the rights at stake in a particular situation. And human rights help answer the question: How should human security be promoted? The notion of duties and obligations complements the recognition of the ethical and political importance of human security.

Protection and empowerment for human security

Human security naturally connects several kinds of freedom—such as freedom from want and freedom from fear, as well as freedom to take action on one's own behalf. Ensuring human security expands "the real freedoms that people enjoy".[8] So how can we protect the basic freedoms people need? And how can we enhance people's capabilities to act on their own behalf? *Protection* strategies, set up by states, international agencies, NGOs and the private sector, shield people from menaces. *Empowerment* strategies enable people to develop their resilience to difficult conditions. Both are required in nearly all situations of human insecurity, though their form and balance will vary tremendously.

Protecting people's security requires identifying and preparing for events that could have severe and widespread consequences. Critical and pervasive conditions cut into the core activities

To protect people—the first key to human security—their basic rights and freedoms must be upheld

People's ability to act on their own behalf—and on behalf of others—is the second key to human security

of people's lives. Risks and threats may be sudden—such as conflict or economic or political collapse. But they need not be, for what defines a menace to human security is its depth, not only its swift onset. And many threats and disastrous conditions are pervasive—affecting many people, again and again. Some causes of human insecurity are deliberately orchestrated, and some are inadvertent, the unexpected downside risks. Some, such as genocide or discrimination against minorities, threaten people's security directly. Others are indirect threats: when military overinvestment causes under-investment in public health, when the international community does not provide sufficient resources to protect refugees in a deprived area. But these menaces must be identified and prioritized in an empowering way.

Protection
Human security is deliberately protective. It recognizes that people and communities are deeply threatened by events largely beyond their control: a financial crisis, a violent conflict, chronic destitution, a terrorist attack, HIV/AIDS, underinvestment in health care, water shortages, pollution from a distant land.

To protect people—the first key to human security—their basic rights and freedoms must be upheld. To do so requires concerted efforts to develop national and international norms, processes and institutions, which must address insecurities in ways that are systematic not makeshift, compre-hensive not compartmentalized, preventive not reactive. Human security helps identify gaps in the infrastructure of protection as well as ways to strengthen or improve it. People must participate in formulating and implementing these strategies. The

infrastructure of protection may be imperfect, but it can help to counter threats, mitigate their force, support people threatened and create a more stable environment.

Empowerment
People's ability to act on their own behalf—and on behalf of others—is the second key to human security. Fostering that ability differentiates human security from state security, from humanitarian work and even from much development work. Empowerment is important because people develop their potential as individuals and as communities. Strengthening peoples' abilities to act on their own behalf is also instrumental to human security. People empowered can demand respect for their dignity when it is violated. They can create new opportunities for work and address many problems locally. And they can mobilize for the security of others—say, by publicizing food shortages early, preventing famines or protesting human rights violations by states.

Supporting people's ability to act on their own behalf means providing education and information so that they can scrutinize social arrangements and take collective action. It means building a public space that tolerates opposition, encourages local leadership and cultivates public discussion. It flourishes in a supportive larger environment (freedom of the press, freedom of information, freedom of conscience and belief and freedom to organize, with democratic elections and policies of inclusion). It requires sustained attention to processes of development and to emergency relief activities, as well as to the outcomes. The primary question of every human security activity should not be: What can we do? It should be: How does

People protected can exercise many choices. And people empowered can avoid some risks and demand improvements in the system of protection

this activity build on the efforts and capabilities of those directly affected?

Protection and empowerment are thus mutually reinforcing. People protected can exercise many choices. And people empowered can avoid some risks and demand improvements in the system of protection.

Interdependence and shared sovereignty
This report is testimony to our living in a world more interdependent than ever before. All societies depend much more on the acts or omissions of others for the security of their people, even for their survival. This reality is evident in every aspect of life—from sustaining the environment, to relieving poverty, to avoiding conflict. Given our moral obligations to others, and given our enlightened self-interest, we need to develop institutions that allow us to meet our responsibilities to others in today's interdependent world.

It is no longer viable for any state to assert unrestricted national sovereignty while acting in its own interests, especially where others are affected by its actions. There has to be an institutional system of external oversight and decision-making that states voluntarily subscribe to. Why? Because nobody has a monopoly on being right (particularly when defending one's own interests), and the assertion of unilateral rights of action inevitably leads to conflicting claims by others. Unilateral action does not contribute to the peaceful resolution of differences. The creation of an independent adjudication authority for disputes in the World Trade Organization provides an example of a recent advance in the regulation of interdependence. A renewed commitment to such multilateralism is crucial for the future of human security.

It is particularly in arms proliferation and armed conflict that multilateral authority should be respected to the utmost because of the devastating consequences of war. If oversight in these areas is to work effectively, the decision-making processes must work, and be seen to work, fairly—with integrity and consistent with the constitution of the institution in question.

It was during the inspired period of institution-building after World War II that the principles and instruments of multilateralism were largely created and incorporated in many organizations of the UN system. Others, such as the World Trade Organization, were created later, but all are dedicated to fostering proper interdependence. Some of these institutions require reform, renewal and adaptation to deal with today's challenges. But they are an indispensable requirement for a better world. And they demand respect and support.

***

The following chapters delve into the implications of a human security approach for current work in conflict and in development. Chapters 2, 3 and 4 explore conflict-related aspects of human security: violent conflict, people on the move and post-conflict situations. Chapters 5, 6 and 7 explore poverty-related aspects of human security: economic insecurity, ill health and lack of knowl-edge. Each chapter suggests further action. Chapter 8, returning to the overarching question of how to create a human security initiative, proposes concrete actions.

This report has had to select a few topics to explore human security. The treatment is thus incomplete, suggestive rather than exhaustive. The hope is that others will develop some of the many issues reluctantly left aside (see the feature on special issues of human security on pages 14–19).

Notes

1. Annan 2000.
2. This section draws on Ogata 2001 and 2002 as well as background materials for the Commission.
3. WHO 2001.
4. Sen 2002.
5. Stewart and FitzGerald 2001.
6. UNDP 2002, p.13.
7. It was precisely the impacts of the financial crises on the lives of people in South East Asia that led the late Japanese Prime Minister Keizo Obuchi to emphasize the importance of human security as a way of comprehensively addressing the menaces that affect people's survival, livelihood and dignity.
8. Sen 1999, chap. 10.

References

Annan, Kofi. 2000. "Secretary-General Salutes International Workshop on Human Security in Mongolia." Two-Day Session in Ulaanbaatar, May 8-10, 2000. Press Release SG/SM/7382. [www.un.org/News/Press/docs/2000/20000508. sgsm7382.doc.html].

Drèze, Jean, and Amartya Sen. 2002. *India: Development and Participation*. New Delhi: Oxford University Press.

Ogata, Sadako. 2001. "State Security—Human Security." UN Public Lectures, the Fridtjof Nansen Memorial Lecture, UN House, Tokyo, 12 December. [www.unu.edu/hq/public-lectures/ogata.pdf].

———.2002. "From State Security to Human Security." The Ogden Lecture, Brown University, Providence, Rhode Island, 26 May.

Sen, Amartya. 1999. *Development as Freedom*. New York: Anchor Press.

———. 2002. "Global Inequality and Persistent Conflicts." Paper presented at the Nobel Awards Conference, Oslo.

Stewart, Frances, and Valpy FitzGerald. 2001. *War and Underdevelopment*. Oxford: Oxford University Press.

UNDP (United Nations Development Programme). Various years. *Human Development Report*. New York: Oxford University Press.

WHO (World Health Organization). 2001. *World Health Report*. Geneva.

Feature: Special issues in human security

Hunger

As many as 800 million people in the developing world and at least 24 million people in developed and transition economies do not have enough food.[1] These people suffer daily hunger, malnutrition and food insecurity even though most national food supplies are adequate. The problem is a lack of entitlement to food and access to an adequate food supply.[2]

Improved nutrition increases the capacity to earn and produce, and the income earned provides the means to buy food. Having access to adequate food affects people's ability to participate in all spheres of economic, political and social life and to move out of chronic poverty.

People's access to food is affected by a number of factors, including inequitable distribution of food, environmental degradation, natural disasters and conflicts. Land degradation in some areas has severely impaired land productivity. In 1977, 57 million people failed to produce enough food to sustain themselves as a result of land degradation. By 1984, this number had risen to 135 million.[3] Natural disasters such as droughts can also have terrible multiple impacts on people. Droughts in the Horn of Africa in the 1970s, 1980s and 1990s triggered famines and civil wars in a region that was already food-insecure. The famine in Ethiopia in the 1980s highlighted the importance of a political commitment to respond to food insecurity and the need for early warning monitoring systems on malnutrition and food availability.[4]

War and conflict can also lead to reduced food production as well as income losses and limited or no access to food for many people, with the most serious impact on the poorest households. A new dimension of food insecurity in situations of conflict is the use of hunger as a weapon and food insecurity as a constant threat.[5] The world's 35 million refugees and internally displaced persons are among those who experience conflict-induced hunger. Food supplies are seized and cut off; food aid is hijacked; crops, water supplies, livestock and land are destroyed and often households and families are stripped of assets. In some regions where food might otherwise have been available, conflict made people food-insecure and affected their access to adequate food as well as their ability to lead healthy and productive lives. In southern Sudan, violence in November 2000 is said to have left some 2.6 million people in need of emergency food assistance.[6]

Food insecurity and hunger undermine a person's dignity and well being. A country's ability to produce and procure enough food for its people to avoid hunger and malnutrition is critical to human security. The question in addressing issues of food insecurity and its results is not only how to maintain an adequate national supply of food but also how to place an existing adequate supply of food at the disposal of those who need it most. Given the desperate nutritional status of many people, what is urgently required is direct and immediate intervention as well as longer term development policies.

Food security to ensure people's survival demands a dual focus on practical strategies in the immediate term for the direct transfer of food to desperate people to improve their food security, and longer term capacity-building initiatives that can gradually improve sustained production and access to food. The emphasis should be on creating and maintaining viable avenues of access to food, enhancing entitlement to food and transfering food to people living in critical or pervasive food insecurity. In an increasingly fragmented world, with ongoing conflict and poverty, it is more important than ever to ensure that food programmes and development assistance are administered in ways that do not fuel further conflict, but instead encourage peace negotiations and an end to fighting.

Water

Without water, survival, human or otherwise, is impossible. The relatively little freshwater on our planet in accessible form is unevenly distributed. One in five people lack access to safe water,[7] and almost half the world's population lacks access to adequate sanitation. More than 1.7 million people die every year from illnesses linked to poor water and sanitation.[8] One in three people live in countries that are moderately to severely water deprived.[9] The resulting water scarcity has significant effects on many aspects of human health, agriculture and species diversity. Inevitably, in water-scarce situations it is poor women who bear the burden of carrying water long distances to their homes.

The growing concern about the availability and usage of water focuses on issues of access, equity and ever-increasing needs for water. Meeting these needs for water—particularly in developing economies—imposes difficult choices on governments. Failure to respond carries human costs as well as significant economic and political risks. Food security, power blackouts and empty water taps are among the most immediate and sensitive public service issues for which societies hold governments accountable. This places considerable strains on the relationships:

- Within and between countries.
- Between rural and urban populations.
- Between upper and lower river interests, affecting people's survival and livelihoods.
- Among agricultural, industrial and domestic users.
- Between human need and the requirements of a healthy environment.[10]

Water scarcity is not only about quantity but also quality. Some 90% of sewage and 70% of industrial waste in developing countries is untreated, often contaminating already scarce freshwater supplies.[11] More than half the world's major rivers are seriously depleted and polluted as a result of sewage, chemical discharges, petroleum leaks, mine and agricultural runoff and other pollutants.[12] The simple act of bathing in many developing countries can bring life-threatening misery. Washing in polluted seas, for example, is estimated to cause some 250 million cases of gastroenteritis and upper respiratory disease every year.[13] Children are particularly vulnerable to such conditions, and 4,000 children a day die from diseases that can be prevented by clean water and good sanitation.[14]

Most freshwater is not, however, used for either drinking water or sanitation. Over 70% of freshwater is used for agriculture, and 40% of all food is now raised on irrigated land.[15] The explosive growth in irrigation—water for irrigation has increased 60% since 1960—has increased food productivity.[16] But poor management and irrigation design have led to the salinization of nearly 20% of irrigated land.[17] Poor techniques cause much of the water to be lost to evaporation, often returning to the water table contaminated by pesticides and waste, with harmful effects on people.

Water scarcity may also escalate tensions between nations. While the last outright war over water occurred 4,500 years ago, historical precedent may not be an absolute guide in the case of water scarcity. Water consumption has increased six-fold in the last century, over twice the rate of population growth.[18] In just over two decades, more than 5 billion people could be living in water-stressed nations.[19] Moreover, 40% of the world is served by one or more of 261 international river basins. And while most international interactions over shared basins have been cooperative, tensions exist in many areas.[20] For example, Turkey's massive dam projects in the Tigris-Euphrates basin have strained relations with its downstream neighbors.[21]

Yet water scarcity cannot be permitted to lock people, regions and nations in a fierce, competitive struggle. The challenge is not to mobilize to compete for water but to cooperate in reconciling competing needs. Water resource management is therefore an important element in efforts to build a socially and environmentally just society. Recognizing the global threat posed by water scarcity, the United Nations has declared 2003 the International Year of Freshwater and, through its Millennium Development Goals, called for reducing by half the proportion of people without sustainable access to safe drinking water by 2025. In a few decades, the growing world population will require 20% more water than today. Any comprehensive view of human security must address this vital scarce resource, which is integral to our very survival.

Population

The number of people in the world is projected to increase from 6.3 billion people in 2000 to 8.9 billion by 2050, or at a rate of 77 million a year.[22] The good news is that this projected increase is considerably less than estimated previously— some 0.4 billion less—because of expected declines in fertility rates. The bad news is that the number of projected deaths will be much higher because of the HIV/AIDS epidemic.

Population structures will be undergoing important changes in the future. Half the world's projected population increase will be concentrated in eight countries: India, Pakistan, Nigeria, the United States, China, Bangladesh, Ethiopia and the Democratic Republic of Congo. Considerable differences in longevity will continue, with the lowest life expectancy at birth in developing countries. The median age of people is expected to rise by 10 years to 37 by 2050. The median age in 17 developed countries will be 50 or older in 2050, whereas in many developing countries it will be 23 years.

The United Nations Population Division projects that at some point in the 21st century fertility rates in three of four developing countries will likely fall below 2.1 children per woman, the rate needed to ensure long-term replacement of the population. Consequently, the number of people 60 years old or older is expected to triple, from 606 million in 2000 to around 1.9 billion in 2050. Although the debate about ageing populations has focused primarily on developed countries, the number of older people in developing countries is expected to rise from 8% in 2000 to nearly 20% in 2050.

These changing population structures will have major implications for human security. They will affect people's ability to move out of poverty and cope with crises, especially for households with a high number of young dependents, as in Sub-Saharan Africa. In developed countries, the ageing population is straining health care provision and retirement plans. In developing countries, the HIV/AIDS crisis is having a devastating impact on the most productive segments of the population, leading to profound changes in household composition. Years of investments in education and skills training are being lost, and the number of orphans and households headed by women is increasing. Much of the burden falls on women, further eroding any sense of security and dignity.

When designing human security strategies, these longer term shifts in population structures need to be taken into account.[23] As populations age, more emphasis will need to be placed on protection and empowerment strategies benefiting older people. This will have major implications for health and education strategies, and for the resources needed for creating a minimum social safety net. Keeping the most productive segments of the population healthy will be among the biggest challenges.

Environment

"In Africa there is no food security, a result of ecological instability or ecological insecurity. One of the root causes of human insecurity is ecological or resource degradation….without ecological stability we cannot have food security. We need to promote community-based natural resource management … to address this."
—Sudanese participant at the Commission on Human Security's Public Hearing in Johannesburg, August, 2002.

The relationship between human security and the environment is most pronounced in areas of human dependence on access to natural resources. Environmental resources are a critical part of the livelihoods of many people. When these resources are threatened because of environmental change, people's human security is also threatened. This relationship is captured in the promotion of sustainable development. And at the centre of sustainable development is the delicate balance between human security and the environment.

For those who live in rural areas, many of whom are among are the poorest, economic and household security are intimately connected to the natural environment. Families rely on forests for fuel and on subsistence agriculture for food. Survival of the biosphere has a determining influence on human survival. In Sub-Saharan Africa and Asia, 75% of the poor live in rural areas.[24] Most are heavily reliant on common lands for necessities such as wood for fuel and fodder. For example, in some states in India, the poor obtain 66%–84% of fodder for their animals from common lands.[25] When these resources are degraded, the effect is direct and immediate: poor families are forced to migrate to ever more marginal lands; household income falls as non-timber forest products become depleted.

The unchecked consumption of fossil fuels can lay a suffocating blanket of pollution over cities. Whether from smokestacks and car exhausts or from cooking and heating, pollution from the burning of fossil fuels causes health problems and premature deaths on a massive scale. In developing countries, for instance, an estimated 1.9 million people die annually from exposure to high concentrations of small particulate matter in the indoor air in rural areas. And some 500,000 people die each year from the effects of outdoor exposure to particulate matter and sulphur dioxide.[26] These impacts highlight the risks to people of excessive and improper use of fossil fuels and the need to provide more efficient, sustainable and safe alternatives that are accessible to poor people.

Among the more intractable and costly environmental problems is land degradation, including salinization from poorly planned irrigation systems, erosion from deforestation and agriculture, and heavy metal and other pollutants from industrial runoff. Pollution and land degradation have extensive health impacts in addition to impairing people's ability to grow food.[27] Creeping desertification may also undermine the ability of a traditional rural community to subsist. In addition, more than 70% of the world's commercially important fish stocks are said to be either fully fished, overexploited, depleted or slowly recovering.[28]

The sheer diversity and breadth of environmental crises have an enduring impact on human security across generations and time. The stresses on the Earth's ecosystem and their effects on the human security of its inhabitants are multiple and severe. Emissions from the consumption of fossil fuels also contribute directly to the build-up of greenhouse gases that envelope our planet and threaten widespread climate change. An enormous cloud of soot, acids, and other particles over Asia may be having a substantial impact on the climate of Western Asia by changing the monsoon pattern, causing droughts in some areas and flooding in others.[29] Such environmental impacts have a tremendous effect, especially on poor people and their food security, contributing to hunger and famine.

Governments and other stakeholders are increasingly aware of the relationship between ecological stability and human security. Civil society has mobilized strongly to promote sustainable development and increase awareness of its importance. The emphasis of governments, however, is more on improved environmental management. There has been little concrete action at a local level to ensure the participation of affected communities and people in such management. There have been some encouraging recent exceptions. Strategies designed by Burkina Faso, Mozambique and Nicaragua have sought to give poor people and local communities greater access to and control over natural resources.[30]

The crucial links between the environment and human survival require more commitment to effective regulation, management and sustainable use of natural resources. Critical to this is the need to explicitly link plans for improved environmental management and sustainable development to disaster prevention and preparedness.

Notes

1. FAO 1999b and United Nations, Department of Economic and Social Affairs 2001.
2. Sen 1981. See also Drèze and Sen 1989, Eide 1995 and Blyberg and Ravindran 2000, p. 222.
3. UNEP 1992.
4. Messer, Cohen and Marchione 2002.
5. Messer 1996.
6. FAO 1999a.
7. WHO 2002, p. 68.
8. WHO 2002, p. 68.
9. CSD 1997.
10. World Commission on Dams 2002, p. xxix.
11. United Nations, Department of Public Information.
12. World Commission on Water 1999.
13. GESAMP 2001.
14. WHO 2002, p. 68.
15. UNEP 2002a, p. 151.
16. United Nations, Department of Public Information.
17. FAO. [www.fao.org/ag/AGL/agll/spush/intro.htm].
18. United Nations, Department of Public Information.
19. CSD 1997.
20. World Water Assessment Program. [www.unesco.org/water/wwap/targets/facts_and_figures.pdf].
21. Jacques 2000.
22. United Nations Population Division 2003.
23. Raymond 2003.
24. Pinstrup-Andersen and Padya-Lorch 2001, p.109.
25. Jodha 1986.
26. WHO 1999.
27. UNEP 1992.
28. FAO 1999a.
29. UNEP 2002.
30. Marcus and Wilkinson 2002.

References

Blyberg A., and D.J. Ravindran, eds. 2000. *A Circle of Rights. Economic, Social and Cultural Rights Activism: A Training Resource.* International Human Rights Internship Program/Asian Forum for Human Rights and Development.

CSD (Commission on Sustainable Development). 1997. *Comprehensive Assessment of the Freshwater Resources of the World.* Report of the Secretary-General.

Drèze, Jean, and Amartya Sen. 1989. *Hunger and Public Action.* Oxford: Clarendon Press.

Eide, A. 1995. "The Right to an Adequate Standard of Living Including the Right to Food." In A. Eide, C. Krause and A. Rosas, eds., *Economic, Social and Cultural Rights. A Textbook.* Dordrecht: Marthinus Nijhoff.

FAO (Food and Agriculture Organization). "Global Network on Integrated Soil Management for Sustainable Use of Salt-affected Soils." [www.fao.org/ag/AGL/agll/spush/intro.htm].

———. 1999a. "Assessment of the World Food Security Situation." Report CFS: 99/2. Prepared for the 25th Session of the Committee on World Food Security, Rome, 31 May–2 June. [www.fao.org].

———. 1999b. *State of Food Insecurity in the World 1999.*

GESAMP (Joint Group of Experts on the Scientific Aspects of Marine Environmental Protection). 2001. *Protecting the Oceans from Land-Based Activities: Land-based Sources and Activities Affecting the Quality and Uses of the Marine, Coastal and Associated Freshwater Environment.* GESAMP Reports and Studies 71. [http://gesamp.imo.org/no71/index.htm].

Jacques, Leslie. 2000. "Running Dry: Water Scarcity." *Harpers Magazine* July 1, 37.

Jodha, N.S. 1986. "Common Property Resources and Rural Poor in Dry Regions of India." *Economic and Political Weekly* 21(27): 1169–81.

Marcus, Rachel, and John Wilkinson. 2002. "Whose Poverty Matters? Vulnerability, Social Protection and PRSPs." Working Paper 1. CHIP, London.

Messer, Ellen. 1996. "Food Wars: Hunger as a Weapon in 1994." In Ellen Messer and Peter Uvin, eds.,

The Hunger Report: 1995. Amsterdam: Gordon and Breach.

Messer, Ellen, Marc J. Cohen and Thomas Marchione. 2002. "ECSP Report." Issue 7. Woodrow Wilson International Center for Scholars, Washington, D.C.

Pinstrup-Andersen, Per, and Rajul Padya-Lorch, eds. 2001. *The Unfinished Agenda: Perspectives on Overcoming Hunger, Poverty and Environmental Degradation.* Washington, D.C.: International Food Policy Research Institute.

Raymond, Susan. 2003. "Foreign Assistance in an Aging World." *Foreign Affairs* March/April: 91–105.

Sen, Amartya. 1981. *Poverty and Famines: An Essay on Entitlement and Deprivation.* Oxford: Oxford University Press.

UNEP (United Nations Environment Programme). 1992. *Global Environmental Outlook 2.* New York.
———. 2002a. *Global Environmental Outlook 3.* New York.

United Nations, Department of Public Information. "Water: A Matter of Life and Death." Fact Sheet. [www.un.org/events/water/factsheet.pdf].

United Nations, Department of Economic and Social Affairs. 2001. *Report on the World Social Situation 2001.* New York.

United Nations Population Division. 2003. *World Population Prospects: The 2002 Revision.* ESA/P/WP.180. New York.

WHO (World Health Organization). 1999. *Air Quality Guidelines.* Geneva.
———. 2002. *World Health Report 2002.* Geneva.

World Commission on Dams. 2002. *Dams and Development: A New Framework for Decision-Making.* London: Earthscan Publications.

World Commission on Water. 1999. *World's Rivers in Crisis—Some Are Dying; Others Could Die.* [www.worldwatercouncil.org/Vision/].

World Water Assessment Program. "Challenges," and "Facts and Figures." [www.unesco.org/water/wwap/targets/facts_and_figures.pdf].

People caught up
in violent conflict

2

Numerous positive developments offer new opportunities to prevent violent conflicts and mitigate their impact on people

Wars between states, internal conflicts and transnational terrorism pose major risks to people's survival, livelihoods and dignity—and thus to human security. An estimated 190 million people were killed directly or indirectly as a result of the 25 largest violent conflicts in the 20th century, often in the name of religion, politics, ethnicity or racial superiority.[1] In many societies, violent conflict suffocates daily life, adding to pervasive feelings of insecurity and hopelessness. During conflict, groups may engage in gross violations of human rights and war crimes, including torture, genocide and the use of rape as a weapon of war.

Despite this gloomy picture, numerous positive developments offer new opportunities to prevent violent conflicts and mitigate their impact on people. An important qualitative shift has occurred as the understanding of state security has widened to include the protection of people in conflict. The creation of the international criminal court is raising hopes that the slaughter and massive displacement of civilian populations will no longer occur with impunity. The production and use of landmines, which cause indiscriminate harm to civilian populations, are being banned, and pressure to halt the spread of illicit small arms is growing. More efforts are preventing violent conflicts through confidence-building and attention to underlying causes. The added value of the human security paradigm is that it places people at the centre, not states.

Changes in violent conflict
War and conflict have surged in the last decade. Between 1990 and 2001, there were 57 major

armed conflicts in 45 countries (box 2.1).[2] The highest number of conflicts occurred in 1990–93 and the lowest in 1996–97.[3] In 2001 there were 24 major armed conflicts, most in Africa. Of these, 11 had lasted for eight or more years. Of the 20 countries with the lowest scores on the human development index in 2002, 16 are in conflict or just out of it. The large majority of these conflicts have been internal.

Among the key factors that cause violent internal conflict:

- Competition over land and resources.
- Sudden and deep political and economic transitions.
- Growing inequality among people and communities.
- Increasing crime, corruption and illegal activities.
- Weak and instable political regimes and institutions.
- Identity politics and historical legacies, such as colonialism.[4]

The consequences of these violent internal conflicts are devastating, from the collapse of states and their institutions to surging poverty.[5] Another consequence is the high proportion of civilian casualties. The distinction between combatants and civilians in such conflicts is often murky, and control over people is often an objective of the fighting. This led to massive forced population movements in the 1990s—and to the mass killing, even genocide, of civilians.

Although officially classified as internal, many internal conflicts are in fact also "international". Several countries on all sides have been engaged in the internal conflict in the Democratic Republic of Congo. And in West Africa, the rebel parties in

Box 2.1 Conflict data are state-centred, not people-centred

Violent conflict is defined as a situation in which armed force is used to resolve issues of government or territory, at least one of the parties is the government of a country and there are at least 25 battle-related deaths. Because data collection is based on this definition, current conflict data sets do not provide a complete picture of violent conflicts confronting people (Mack 2002).

First, the requirement that at least one actor be a state party leads to serious omissions. For example, the 1994 Rwandan genocide and the attacks of armed rebels on refugee settlements are not included in some data sets, despite the high level of civilian casualties, because so-called government agents were not officially involved in the armed conflict. Yet according to data from the Minorities at Risk Project analyzing communal conflicts, 275 groups were in conflict from 1990 to 1998 (Gurr 2002, pp. 46–47).

Second, estimates of the number of people killed as a result of violent conflict usually reflect only battle-related deaths. From 1945 to 2000 more than 50 million people are estimated to have died in wars and conflicts. But many more die from the consequences of conflict—from the destruction of infrastructure, the collapse of essential health services and the lack of food. But those data are not available or included (Ghobarah, Huth, and Russett 2001).

These omissions have far-reaching policy implications. Violent conflicts often remain hidden because they do not fit the state-centric criterion. Nor do policy strategies aimed at preventing and mitigating violent conflict adequately address the impact on people. Conflict prevention and capacity-building strategies target mainly official authorities, not the communities (and community leaders) at risk. This also means that protecting and assisting people in internal conflicts is seen primarily from the perspective of national sovereignty—and the principle of non-interference—instead of from a perspective of responsibility shared by states.

Guinea, Sierra Leone and Côte d'Ivoire receive tacit support from neighbouring countries. No internal conflict can be seen apart from its historical and regional dimensions, such as colonialism and geo-strategic interests, and the impact of global economic and political processes, such as globalization.

Borders are no longer an obstacle. A key global process affecting violent conflicts is the rise of transnational organized crime—trafficking in people, laundering funds, smuggling drugs, diamonds and arms. Criminal groups link with local warlords, rebel groups and even government authorities illegally exploiting natural resources, as in Colombia, the Democratic Republic of Congo and Liberia. Violence and insecurity are often exploited to gain control of economic and political resources while crowding out the provision of essential public and social services to people, such as health and education, with the worst impacts felt by the poorest. A consequence of this increase in general insecurity is an increase in interpersonal violence, intensifying the dangers people face (box 2.2).

Terrorist organizations are also a major threat to people's security and international peace. Terrorism is not a new phenomenon. It has been used by states and violent movements to attain political objectives. But transnational networks—often linking crime syndicates—with potential access to weapons of mass destruction have changed its nature.

The existing international security system is not designed to prevent and deal effectively with the new types of security threats

---

Box 2.2 Conflict and interpersonal violence

In and immediately following conflict, crime rates soar. So do incidents of gender-based and sexual violence, abuse of the elderly and children, and suicides. The increases arise from the trauma of conflict and its impact on interpersonal relations and community networks, and from the broader issues of the breakdown of law and order, the police and judicial systems and health and education services, as well as the loss of legitimacy of social and ethical norms.

But the influence works both ways. High levels of interpersonal violence also appear to affect the likelihood for violent conflict. High rates of communal violence may reflect growing inequalities among communities as well as the manipulation of identity politics. The surge in high crime rates following the sudden political and economic transitions in the former Soviet Union reflected not only the breakdown of law and order but also the struggle for control over resources, along with spreading corruption and weakening government institutions. Increases in gender-based and sexual violence may mark a rise in poverty and the collapse of social safety nets. And although by itself interpersonal violence will not lead to conflict, combined with other factors it leads to a widespread sense of insecurity easily manipulated along identity lines.

What is now being described as the "war on terrorism" dominates national and international security debates. In addition to military actions, it has increased attention to other tools to fight terrorism, such as tracking (and blocking) flows of funds, information and people. It has also given rise to new areas of multilateral cooperation, such as the sharing of intelligence. Yet these actions focus on coercive, short-term strategies aimed at stopping attacks by cutting off financial, political or military support and apprehending possible perpetrators. Equally, state-sponsored terrorism is not being addressed, while legitimate groups are being labeled as terrorist organizations to quash opposition to authoritarian government policies. And fighting terrorism is taking precedence over protecting human rights and promoting the rule of law and democratic governance.

What do these changes in violent conflict mean for peace and security? It is still too early to tell. But the understandings and principles of the international security system, in place for more than 50 years, are being challenged, weakening the established safeguards aimed at preventing and resolving violent conflicts. The objective of the international system, designed after World War II, was to help protect states—and the people, institutions and values inside their boundaries—from threats beyond their borders. The international peace and security system maintained "collective security" by limiting the rights of states to use force to self-defence after an attack, following a UN Security Council resolution. By stopping aggression, the drafters of the UN Charter envisaged that wars would belong to the past—that wars would no longer be an acceptable method for resolving international disputes.

But the existing international security system is not designed to prevent and deal effectively with the new types of security threats. New multilateral strategies are required that focus on the shared responsibility to protect people. Considerable progress has been made in the 1990s—as exemplified by the prominence given to human rights and humanitarian action, as well as the efforts to deploy peacekeeping operations and rebuild conflict-torn countries. But the "war on terrorism" has stalled that progress by focusing on short-term coercive responses rather than also addressing the underlying causes related to inequality, exclusion and marginalization, and oppression by states as well as people. A multilateral approach must respond to the full range of human security concerns and requires the active support of all states—especially the five permanent members of the Security Council.

Adopting a human security approach
What, then, can be done to protect people in violent conflict? Five policies are essential:
• Placing human security on the security agenda.
• Strengthening humanitarian action.
• Respecting human rights and humanitarian law.
• Disarming people and fighting crime.
• Preventing conflict and respecting citizenship.

Placing human security on the security agenda
Putting human security on the security agenda of states, regional organizations and the United Nations would inspire concern for vulnerable groups during conflict and amplify support for protecting all human rights. Civil society, humanitarian actors and the media have drawn the attention of policymakers to the suffering of people in internal conflicts. The debate has been dominated by questions about intervening in the internal affairs of a country on humanitarian grounds.

Shifting the focus of the discussion, the International Commission on Intervention and State Sovereignty emphasized the responsibility of states and the international community to protect people—militarily if necessary—in situations resulting in a "large scale loss of life, actual or

apprehended, with genocidal intent or not, which is the product of either deliberate state action, or state neglect or inability to act, or a collapsed state situation; or large scale 'ethnic cleansing', actual or apprehended, whether carried out by killing, force expulsion, acts of terror or rape".[6] This emphasis on responsibility was prompted in part by the Rwanda genocide, perhaps the most shocking human security failure in the last decade.

Among the key actors, the UN Security Council has gradually broadened its understanding of security to include the protection of people by recognizing the links between security and women, children, refugees and HIV/AIDS.[7] And to promote consistency, the Council adopted an aide memoire on the protection of civilians, focusing on four themes: protection of civilians in conflict; women, peace and security; children in armed conflict; and conflict prevention.[8]

In reality, however, few mechanisms can be invoked to protect the security of people in violent conflict.[9] Organizational mandates and mechanisms draw heavily from state security assumptions, which are inadequate for responding to security issues in internal conflicts. In many instances, there are no cease-fire arrangements to uphold, and it is often hard to distinguish combatants from civilians. Many of the reforms of the UN peace operations recommended in the Brahimi Report still need to be implemented— strengthening conflict prevention and peace-building, developing rapid deployment capacities and improving management.[10]

Also important is incorporating human rights specialists and strengthening civilian police by extending their mandate to the reform and

The last decade's significant progress in developing normative frameworks to protect women and children shows what is possible

2

restructuring of local police forces. By emphasizing public safety—not military security—civilian police can help prevent abuses and corruption among local law and order officials. They can also assist in building capacity and rebuilding trust and legitimacy in the new national law and order institutions. Based on the experiences in Cambodia, the former Yugoslavia, and Timor-Leste, a framework for the transition from conflict to peace and development should be prepared from the outset of a peace operation (chapter 4).

Regional security organizations can also do much for human security:

- The Organization for Security and Co-operation in Europe is focusing on human rights training, support for independent media, reintegration of former combatants, election monitoring, and training and capacity-building.
- The peace and security agenda of the New Partnership for Africa's Development links political, security and development issues at the regional, national and community levels. It can form the basis for developing comprehensive strategies that place human security at the centre.[11]
- The launch of the African Union in mid-2002 presents new opportunities to invigorate conflict prevention mechanisms. Through recent institutional innovations, such as a Pan African Parliament and a Peace and Security Council made up of 15 prominent members, people will participate more directly in the management of regional concerns in Africa.[12] Unlike for the UN Security Council, specific provisions are included facilitating opportunities for civil society to participate in the work of the Peace and Security Council.[13]

But the main challenge is dealing with the security of people at the national and local levels. Unless there are clear links between the deteriorating security of people and threats to international peace and security, the international community is unlikely to adopt preventive strategies or to respond. For refugees, for example, the Security Council recognized in resolution 1296 (2000) the threat that massive forced population movements pose to international peace and security and the need to adopt specific measures to create a safe environment. In the same resolution, the Security Council asked to be informed of situations where such a threat may occur. In practice, however, the Council is seldom in a position to propose and authorize any specific steps.

What alternative arrangements might strengthen the security of people? The last decade's significant progress in developing normative frameworks to protect women and children shows what is possible. For the first time ever, in a Special Session on Children in 2002, the UN General Assembly focused on children in conflict and formulated recommendations on how to protect and empower them more effectively.[14] National commissions for children in conflict-affected countries could do just this, augmented by awareness-building and capacity-building.[15]

Women and girls are also particularly vulnerable in conflict situations.[16] Gender-based violence in conflict often carries a political and symbolic message. Rape, enforced prostitution and trafficking are included in the definition of war crimes and crimes against humanity. The International Tribunals for Rwanda and the former Yugoslavia issued indictments and convictions on grounds of sexual violence. It is important that future peace agreements not grant amnesties for such crimes.

The big challenge, then, is to translate these normative developments into concrete policies and actions at the state, regional and international levels. For example, the mandate of peacekeeping operations should include specific references for combating the trafficking in women and girls and for policing communities. And women should have bigger roles in peace negotiations and settlements.

In addition to women and children, several other groups should receive greater attention:

- *The elderly.*[17] During the conflicts in Rwanda and Bosnia and Herzegovina, the elderly and the very young made up whole villages, with all others having fled or been killed. Few humanitarian actors have protection guidelines and policies for the elderly, despite their specific needs, including better community care and access to essential services.

- *The disabled.* Violent conflict leads to high numbers of disabled people, with physical and psychological needs. These needs are attracting growing attention and are contributing to preventive measures, such as banning the use of landmines that continue to produce victims long after the fighting ceases. But more physical and mental rehabilitation services are required.

- *The indigenous.* The suffering of indigenous people is often disproportionally high as warring factions seek control over their land and natural resources, as in Colombia, Guatemala, Mexico, and Myanmar. Protection strategies need to take into account their unique characteristics and traditions, as well as their rights to land and resources.[18]

- *The missing.*[19] Disappearances during violent conflict are one of the most contentious issues in peace processes and in truth and reconciliation efforts. Public and constructive discussions on "disappearances" are under way at the international level. A planned international convention will initiate a new instrument to provide preventive measures, such as training law enforcement personnel. It will also protect the rights of the disappeared and their families, recognizing the rights to know the fate of missing people and to receive reparation.

Strengthening humanitarian action

In conflict and emergency situations, humanitarian action rapidly protects people by addressing their most essential needs for food, water, sanitation, basic health care and shelter. In the 1980s such action had a narrow and distinctive framework. Today, its scope has broadened in response to the changing nature of conflicts and to the increase in famines and natural disasters.

Broader—and intertwined. Humanitarian action has become intertwined with the political, military and development dimensions of violent conflict— an uneasy relationship. Without the prospect of political solution, providing relief and protecting civilians and refugees in conflict are untenable. But the principles of impartiality, neutrality and independence are supposed to guide humanitarian action. These principles are easily compromised when humanitarian action is combined with political and military interventions. So while a broader approach is constructive, humanitarian action should not be an alternative to finding

The cross-fertilization between approaches with different time horizons and methods of operation could be fruitful

political solutions, nor should its principles be compromised to further political goals.

In a similar vein, humanitarian actors often depend on military and police forces to reach and assist civilian populations in need. But as with political action, this close relationship can also compromise humanitarian action, because force is inconsistent with neutrality. Military action is often masked by humanitarian intervention, as the debate on the Kosovo war shows. A sad consequence of such involvement in conflict situations: humanitarian workers come under attack and are killed or taken hostage, as in Chechnya, the Democratic Republic of Congo, and Afghanistan.

The fight against terrorism is also affecting humanitarian action, with security issues taking precedence over humanitarian concerns. Suspected of having terrorist sympathies, some victims of violent conflict are being denied humanitarian relief. Some leaders justify the threat of military action by arguing that the impact on the civilian population will be minimal, because humanitarian emergency relief will follow immediately behind military action. In a sense, humanitarian action has become a victim of its success and effectiveness in recent years. For some, it has reduced the cost of waging war, and they view humanitarian action as a tool available to minimize the impact on civilians—and mute international criticism.

The relationship between humanitarian and development action is often equally complex, particularly if effective humanitarian aid weakens the incentive to develop sustainable political and development solutions. More humanitarian actors—accustomed to rapid, short-term engagements—are now involved in areas normally the domain of development assistance, as in post-conflict

situations. And more development actors such as the World Bank—accustomed to long-term and more participatory institution-building approaches—are working in conflict rather than around it. The cross-fertilization between approaches with different time horizons and methods of operation could be fruitful. Recognition of the relationship between conflict and development challenges the strongly ingrained view that conflicts are aberrations of the progress towards development rather than inherently related to it.

Rights-based approaches. The growing prominence of human rights has also had a significant impact on humanitarian action. Humanitarian action can help realize rights by translating them into policies and programmes—and by building up institutional capacities to implement them.[20] Rights-based approaches to humanitarian assistance demonstrate the potential synergies.[21]

In conflict situations, a rights-based approach, like a human security approach, reorients humanitarian strategies towards enhancing people's capabilities, choices and security. It stresses the right to life, health, food, shelter and education. It also emphasizes non-discrimination policies, equality and equity, as well as the rights of specific groups, such as women, children, the elderly, the disabled and refugees. This leads to new policy options, such as making access to humanitarian assistance in conflict situations conditional on progress on certain rights. In Bosnia and Herzegovina, for example, communities accepting the return of minorities, restoring their properties and respecting their human rights and security, were given priority in the rehabilitation of water and electricity services and the reconstruction of buildings under the "Open Cities" programme.

But the rights-based approach has limitations.[22] Some humanitarian agencies have shied away from active promotion of human rights, fearing that it would politicize their actions and compromise their access to victims. Nor does a rights-based approach always provide answers when instant choices need to be made between two fundamentally bad options. The human security approach, with its broader emphasis, may be able to inform the decision-making by identifying the least objectionable option. In the former Yugoslavia, all parties to the conflict practiced ethnic cleansing. Serbs, Muslims and Croats were expelled from their homes and frequently sought the protection and intervention of the Office of the UN High Commsioner for Refugees (UNHCR). On occasion, the UNHCR was accused of assisting ethnic cleansing by helping people to flee enclaves surrounded by armed groups. But upholding their right not to be forcibly relocated could have meant letting them face harassment, sexual violations, torture and death.

Striking a balance. There is thus a need to strike a balance among humanitarian, political, military, human rights and development strategies. Humanitarian action cannot be an alternative to peace settlements or to development assistance—or the pretext for military intervention. Rather than letting efforts to address different kinds of human insecurity compete with each other or push in opposite directions, their interlinkages must be recognized, and comprehensive approaches developed that do not smother their distinctiveness. The human security paradigm provides such a framework, emphasizing the protection and empowerment of people, a concern shared by all the different strategies.

To protect people in conflict, sustained and predictable funding is essential, based on the needs of people rather than on donor priorities and interests. But compassion fatigue sets in quickly and diverts attention to other issues and emergencies (box 2.3).

Respecting human rights and international humanitarian law

Protecting human rights and upholding humanitarian law are essential to human security in conflict situations.[23] Like most international law, the protection of human rights has been approached mainly from a state-centric perspective—the obligations and duties of states towards individuals. So the focus of human rights has been on monitoring violations by governments.

Human security examines human rights not only in relation to states, which have the primary obligation to uphold them, but also in relation to other actors, such as armed non-government elements and corporations. Equally, human security focuses on enforcing humanitarian law for all parties to the conflict, including armed non-state actors such as warlords and rebel groups.[24] Enhancing their responsibility and capacity to respect human rights and humanitarian law is a major human security priority in conflict situations. The role of such institutions as the International Committee of the Red Cross is critical in this.

In *Strengthening of the United Nations: An Agenda for Further Change,* UN Secretary-General Kofi Annan suggested ways to strengthen the Office of the UN High Commissioner for Human Rights.[25] The human rights machinery should be improved, particularly the treaty bodies and committees. And the investigation of country

Regional human rights mechanisms can address state obligations

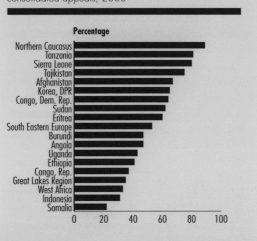
situations and issues should be streamlined. Including human rights principles and mechanisms in peace agreements provides the basis for rebuilding communities and countries.

Regional human rights mechanisms—for individuals to turn to in times of conflict—can address state obligations, as did the Inter-American Commission and Court for Human Rights during the civil conflicts in Guatemala, El Salvador and Nicaragua. The Organization for Security and Co-operation in Europe promotes protection of human rights through its "Human Dimension" programme, which links multilateral security issues with growing respect for domestic human rights and democratization. Its High Commissioner on National Minorities addresses the relationships between ethnic groups in conflict situations. Similar approaches on behalf of minorities in other regions would be a helpful step forward.

In Africa the Charter for Human and People's Rights and the Court on Human and People's Rights provide the normative and institutional framework for protecting people. But the lack of institutional capacity has hampered implementation. The newly created African Union offers opportunities for protecting human rights and addressing abuses in conflicts. And in Asia, civil society is actively working towards placing human rights on the regional conflict agenda.[26]

Many initiatives are under way to overcome the weak capacity of national institutions, but coordination and sustained effort are often lacking. The UN High Commissioner for Human Rights can assist in the development of national human rights offices, mechanisms and capacities.

Civil society and communities can promote respect for human rights and humanitarian law by pressuring governments and international actors to negotiate and sign international human rights instruments. In countries with weak or non-existent human rights machinery, support for a national human rights mechanism is an important step, acknowledging the risks and dangers that human rights advocates face.

Disarming people and fighting crime

Of an estimated 640 million firearms, three in five are held by civilians.[27] Some 500,000 people are killed with these weapons each year, and many more are intimidated, coerced and displaced. The easy availability of small arms permits the build up of armed forces at low costs, facilitates violent crime and threatens safety.

Programmes to curtail the spread of small arms and disarm civilians and combatants have had only limited success. Few of the weapons collected are destroyed. So linking such programmes with strategies to advance human security may prove more effective. Coupled with education, changes in attitudes about the role of small arms in societies are a priority and may reduce interpersonal violence and lessen the impact of violent conflicts.

But the demand for small arms and light weapons cannot be effectively addressed without examining the supply side. Four permanent members of the UN Security Council are responsible for 78% of global exports of conventional weapons. In a political climate that urges more military spending for the war against terrorism and greater protection of state security, reinvigorating efforts towards preventing and stopping the illicit trade and use of small arms is a priority.

How? Through arms embargoes, monitoring mechanisms and export controls.[28] But there are only

a few examples of successful efforts. The 1999 European Code of Conduct on Arms Transfers establishes principles and criteria for the approval of arms exports to countries where they might be used for internal repression—or to provoke or prolong conflicts in which serious human rights violations have been documented. The 1996 Wassenaar Arrangement controls exports of conventional arms and dual-use goods and technologies. The convention banning antipersonnel landmines is one of the most successful human security achievements in recent years.[29] In the first four years the convention was in force, it has resulted in the destruction of almost 30 million mines by 55 countries that agreed to eliminate them from their arsenals.

Also to be addressed are related problems of international crime and the illegal trade in arms, drugs, natural resources and people.[30] In some 30 countries, armed groups depend on conflict commodities to finance their arms purchases and pay their troops. In the Democratic Republic of Congo, the illegal exploitation of coltan, gold, copper, cobalt and diamonds has fueled the conflict. Transnational criminal networks offer their services in selling conflict commodities and providing finances to armed rebel groups.

The 2000 UN Convention against Transnational Crime provides the legal framework for criminalizing money laundering, corruption and the obstruction of justice—and for seizing goods and funds. Special provisions against the trafficking and smuggling of people have also been adopted (chapter 3). The challenge is to implement these provisions, particularly in countries with weak institutions and widespread corruption.

Businesses, recognizing their responsibilities for fighting illegal activities, are producing some

30

Preventive strategies should give higher priority to the protection of people in collapsed states and contested regions

innovative approaches. The certification of rough diamonds under the Kimberley process points the way towards greater cooperation, transparency and accountability in business practices. The Kimberly process recognized the importance of a reciprocal responsibility of both suppliers and buyers of rough diamonds to prevent the trade in conflict diamonds.

Preventing violent conflict and respecting citizenship

The responsibility to protect people in conflict, as argued by the International Commission on Intervention and State Sovereignty, includes a responsibility to prevent violent conflict. Conflict prevention is a strategy—or a culture—that builds on the interlinkages among the various issues causing conflict.[31] It is a lens for examining different actions and assessing their potential impact on conflict (box 2.4).

Preventive strategies are high on the agenda of states and multilateral organizations, according to an in-depth study by the Carnegie Commission on Preventing Deadly Conflict.[32] Tools include early warning mechanisms, targeted sanctions, fact-finding and diplomatic missions and preventive deployment of peacekeeping operations.[33] To meet the shifting challenges, attention to peaceful measures to prevent threats is a priority.

Preventive strategies should give higher priority to the protection of people in collapsed states and contested regions, whose citizenship is often at risk. The long-lasting Palestinian-Israeli conflict shows the dangers that contested territories pose for the human security of all people in conflict—and to international peace and security. Rather than targeting collapsed states and

contested territories as hotbeds of violence and criminal networks, the international community should seek negotiated settlements and build the capacities of states to protect human security—and thereby prevent violent and criminal networks from gaining ground.

Linked to the collapse and creation of states is the protection of citizenship. With the collapse of the former Soviet Union and the former Yugoslavia, citizens became aliens nearly overnight, without leaving their homes—such as the ethnic Russians living in the newly independent Baltic states. Having a nationality and being recognized a citizen of a country is a key element of human security, because citizens enjoy the benefits offered by responsible states. Having a nationality is a fundamental human right, and citizenship is "the right to have rights".[34] Without citizenship, people are often unable to attend school, receive health care, find employment, own property, participate in politics or travel abroad. Authorities may consider them illegal residents and force them to flee. Once abroad, they are denied the right to return home—or to stay where they are.

Citizenship can also be ineffective. Many countries have degrees of citizenship, giving more or fewer rights to ethnic or religious minority communities, creating inequalities that lead to grievances and possibly to conflict. The objective of these discriminatory policies is to exclude communities from political, social and economic power. In one of the worst forms of state-based violence and injustice, the apartheid regime in South Africa used race-based identities to disenfranchise the majority of its people. Exclusion from land on the grounds of citizenship leads to marginalization, poverty and possible conflict, as

There is a legitimate
multilateral interest in
preventing the downside
impacts of citizenship denied

Box 2.4 Civil society and conflict in multiethnic societies

Scholars of ethnic conflict routinely face an enigma: Why do some ethnically diverse communities experience violence while others do not? Rural India, for instance, is home to two-thirds of Indians but accounts for only 4% of Hindu-Muslim violence; eight urban centers account for the largest share of ethnic carnage. Most riots in India can be traced to intercommunal economic rivalry, polarized party politics and segregated neighbourhoods. Yet many cities displaying similar traits avoid riots. In a study of three pairs of Indian cities with similar Hindu-Muslim ratios, one in each pair riot-prone and the other not, Ashutosh Varshney concluded that the structure of local civil society is not unrelated to the amount of ethnic violence a region faces.

Intercommunal relationships can take two forms: associational and quotidian. The associational includes business associations, trade unions, reading clubs and similar bodies, and the quotidian involves every day activities such as playing or eating meals together. Both kinds of relationships can bind different groups of people together and promote peace. But the associational forms of engagement display more resistance to attempts by politicians to polarize ethnic communities. This suggests that networks of civic life that promote the self-interest of individuals actually create bonds between diverse people.

Of the pairs of cities studied—Aligarh and Kolkata, Hyderabad and Lucknow, Ahmedabad and Surat—the first of each pair is prone to intercommunal violence, while the second, even in the face of similar provocation, is not. The cities were selected from across India. Hindus and Muslims in each of the peaceful cities have strong associational relationships. Varshney suggests that these relationships, by promoting communication between members of different religious groups, help maintain peaceful neighbourhoods. They also aid the formation of temporary "peace committees" to patrol neighbourhoods and investigate and quash rumours during times of heightened tension. Thus while Hindus and Muslims have had casual contact over centuries in both Ahmedabad and Surat, for example, Muslims have few associational relationships with Hindus in Ahmedabad, whereas in Surat, many Muslim traders share strong business ties with Hindu traders. Apparently, these business associations built mutual trust and respect, and Surat remained free of the carnage that wracked Ahmedabad.

The recent riots in Gujarat that killed nearly a thousand Muslims in 2002 bear out Varshney's thesis. Clearly, what ensures peace is the existence of mechanisms that can diffuse tensions before they erupt in violence.

Source: Varshney 2002.

with the Banyarwanda in the Democratic Republic of Congo.

Some countries are reluctant to recognize certain communities as citizens and to allow them to enter or re-enter the country because of the possible economic burden. In other instances, preferential citizenship policies permit the return of descendents of former nationals. More than 3.5 million German descendents,

Aussiedler, have gained citizenship in Germany since 1980.[35]

The willful denial of citizenship for whole communities has major implications for other states, due to the potential large-scale population movements and the spread of conflict and poverty. Therefore, there is a legitimate multilateral interest in preventing the downside impacts of citizenship denied. And in a world with growing migrations of

Human security should be mainstreamed in the agendas of international, regional and national security organizations

populations across borders (chapter 3), multilateral approaches towards citizenship may be warranted.

The current multilateral provisions for citizenship are inadequate, largely because they date to the immediate post-World War II period and are not effectively implemented. Moreover, the primary focus has been on statelessness, not citizenship. Few states have acceded to the 1954 Convention Relating to the Status of Stateless Persons and the 1961 Convention on the Reduction of Statelessness. The UNHCR promotes state accession to these conventions and provides technical and advisory services, but it needs a clearer and more effective mandate.

At the national level, many issues relating to the denial of citizenship can be resolved by revising legislation, correcting administrative procedures (issuing birth registration cards) and promoting a culture of respect. The problems are more complex when they relate to access to political, social and economic resources. The lack of effective citizenship is also a poverty issue. People denied equal access to education, health services or employment opportunities on citizenship grounds should be explicitly included in development and poverty reduction strategies.

Policy conclusions

Human security focuses on the protection of people, not borders or territories. The added value of human security is its focus on a broader range of violent threats facing people, including war and internal conflict, but also communal conflicts and serious criminality. It also broadens understanding of the causes of violent conflict by emphasizing the links with poverty, the inequalities among communities and the impact of sudden downturns and risks. To

protect and empower people in conflict, a broad range of interconnected policies is required:

- Human security should be mainstreamed in the agendas of international, regional and national security organizations.
- Respect for the principles guiding humanitarian action is essential when developing comprehensive strategies linking the political, military and humanitarian dimensions of protecting people in conflict.
- Upholding human rights and humanitarian law is essential in protecting and empowering people in conflict.
- Concerted efforts are required to disarm people and fight crime.
- Violent conflict must be prevented and mitigated in collapsed states and contested territories, while fully upholding all rights.
- The right of each person to a nationality should be respected, and measures are needed to ensure effective citizenship, a condition for attaining human security.

Notes

1. Rummel 1994.
2. The significance of violent conflict is measured by the number of "battle-related" deaths, with the threshold generally at 1,000 deaths or more a year. Some data sets have lowered the number of deaths to 25 a year (see box 2.1).
3. SIPRI 2002.
4. Coletta 2002.
5. Sen 2001.
6. ICISS 2001, p. xii.
7. The Security Council has also paid increasing attention to the development of smart sanctions for activities such as the trade in raw materials (diamonds,

coltan) that fuels conflicts and the proliferation of small arms and landmines.

8. Security Council, 4492nd, SC/7329, 15 March 2002. Based on Security Council resolutions and presidential statements adopted in recent years, the aide memoire identified 13 core objectives: access to vulnerable populations; separation of civilians and armed elements; justice and reconciliation; security, law and order; disarmament, demobilization, reintegration and rehabilitation; small arms and mine action; training of security and peacekeeping forces; effects on women; effects on children; safety and security of humanitarian and associated personnel; media and information; natural resources and armed conflicts; and the humanitarian impact of sanctions.

9. In a report to the Security Council, the Secretary-General has proposed a "roadmap" outlining actions aimed at implementing the aide memoire on the protection of civilians (United Nations, Security Council 2002b).

10. United Nations 2000.

11. InterAfrica Group/Justice Africa 2002.

12. The New Partnership for Africa's Development (NEPAD) [www.avmedia.at/nepad/indexgb.html].

13. [www.africa-union.org/en/home.asp].

14. United Nations 2002b. In addition, the Special Session focused on issues such as health and education, the spread of HIV/AIDS and the protection of children from abuse and exploitation.

15. Harvard Program on Humanitarian Policy and Conflict Research 2002.

16. United Nations, Security Council 2002b.

17. United Nations, Second World Assembly on Ageing, Madrid, 8–12 April 2002. The Madrid Plan of Action on Ageing focuses on the development dimension, and limited attention is given to ageing populations in conflict situations.

18. 1993 UN Declaration on the Rights of Indigenous People [http://www.treatycouncil.org/section_211611.htm].

19. ICRC 2003.

20. UNDP 2000.

21. The rights-based approach has also been extended to other areas, such as poverty reduction and human development: OHCHR 2002.

22. Rieff 2002.

23. Ramcharan 2002.

24. United Nations Economic and Social Council 2001.

25. United Nations, General Assembly 2002.

26. Chulalongkorn University and Commission on Human Security 2002.

27. Graduate Institute of International Studies 2002.

28. The Programme of Action to Prevent, Combat and Eradicate the Illicit Trade in Small Arms and Light Weapons, adopted following a UN Conference in July 2001. United Nations, Security Council 2002.

29. [www.wassenaar.org/docs/IE96.html]. The 1997 Convention on the Prohibition of the Use, Stockpiling, Production and Transfer of Anti-Personnel Mines and Their Destruction. As of February 2003, 131 states have ratified the convention.

30. Naim 2003.

31. Lund 2002.

32. Carnegie Commission on Preventing Deadly Conflict 1997.

33. Hampson and Malone 2002.

34. U.S. Supreme Court Chief Justice Earl Warren in *Trop v. Dulles,* 1958, as quoted in ICIHI 1988, p. 107.

35. United Nations, Population Division 2002a, p. 27.

References

Aleinikoff, Alexander T., and Douglas Klusmeyer. 2002. *Citizenship Policies for an Age of Migration.* Washington D.C.: Carnegie Endowment for International Peace.

Arias, Oscar. 1998. "Globalization and the Challenges of Human Security." University of San Diego, California. [http://peace.acusd.edu/Arias/AriasTalk.html].

Armstrong, Andrea C. 2002. "Being Recognized as Citizens: A Human Security Dilemma in Central Asia and the Caucasus." Paper prepared for the Commission on Human Security. [www.humansecurity-chs.org].

Bach, Robert L. 2002. "Global Mobility, Inequality and Security: Reflections on a Human Security Agenda." Paper prepared for the Commission on Human Security. [www.humansecurity-chs.org].

Bajpai, Kanti. 2000. "Human Security: Concept and Measurement" Occasional Paper 19. The Joan B. Kroc Institute for International Peace Studies, University of Notre Dame, Notre Dame, Indiana.

Barton, Frederick D., John Hefferman and Andrea Armstrong. 2002. "Being Recognized as Citizens: A Human Security Dilemma in Sub-Saharan Africa, South, Central, and Southeast Asia, the Caucasus and Central and Eastern Europe: Lessons Learned and Policy Recommendations." Paper prepared for the Commission on Human Security. [www.humansecurity-chs.org].

The Brookings Institution–CUNY Project on Internal Displacement. 2002. *Recent Commentaries about the Nature and Application of the Guiding Principles on Internal Displacement.* Washington, D.C.

Bruderlein, Claude. 2001. "People's Security as a New Measure of Global Stability." *International Review of the Red Cross* 83: 353–66.

Butenschon, Nils A., Uri Davis and Manuel Hassassian. 2000. *Citizenship and the State in the Middle East: Approaches and Applications.* Syracuse: Syracuse University Press.

Canada Department of Foreign Affairs and International Trade. 2003. *Freedom from Fear: Canada's Foreign Policy for Human Security.* Ottawa. [www.humansecurity.gc.ca].

Carnegie Commission on Preventing Deadly Conflict. 1997. *Preventing Deadly Conflict: Final Report.* New York: Carnegie Corporation.

Carothers, Thomas. 2003. *Promoting the Rule of Law Abroad: The Problem of Knowledge.* Working Paper 24. Washington, D.C.: Carnegie Endowment for International Peace.

Chudoba, Johannes. 2002. "Being Recognized as Citizens: A Human Security Dilemma in Central and Eastern Europe." Paper prepared for the Commission on Human Security. [www.humansecurity-chs.org].

Chulalongkorn University and Commission on Human Security. 2002. "White Paper on Human Security." International Public Symposium on "Challenges to Human Security in a Borderless World," Bangkok, 11 December.

Coletta, Nat J. 2002. "Conflict, Human Security and Poverty: Implications for IFI Reform." Paper prepared for the Commission on Human Security. [www.humansecurity-chs.org].

Collins, Kathleen. 2002. "Human Security in Central Asia: Challenges Posed by a Decade of Transition 1991–2002." Paper prepared for the Commission on Human Security. [www.humansecurity-chs.org].

Commission on Global Governance. 1995. *Our Global Neighbourhood.* Oxford: Oxford University Press.

Edson, Sara. 2001. "Human Security: An Extended and Annotated International Bibliography." Center for History and Economics, King's College, University of Cambridge.

Forman, Shepard, Stewart Patrick and Dirk Salomons. 2001. "Recovering from Conflict: Strategy for an

International Response." Center for International Cooperation, New York University.

Ghobarah, Hazem, Paul Huth and Bruce Russett. 2001. "Civil Wars Kill and Maim People—Long After Shooting Stops." Draft. [www.hsph.harvard.edu/hpcr/events/hsworkshop/russet.pdf].

Graduate Institute of International Studies. 2002 *Small Arms Survey 2002.* Oxford: Oxford University Press.

Gurr, Ted Robert. 2002. "Containing Internal War in the Twenty-First Century." In Fen Osler Hampson and David M. Malone, eds., *From Reaction to Conflict Prevention: Opportunities for the UN System.* Boulder, Colo.: Lynne Rienner Publishers.

Hampson, Fen Osler. 2001. *Madness in the Multitude: Human Security and World Disorder.* Ottawa: Oxford University Press.

Hampson, Fen Osler, and David M. Malone. 2002. *From Reaction to Conflict Prevention: Opportunities for the UN System.* Boulder, Colo.: Lynne Rienner Publishers.

Haq, Mahbub Ul. 1998. "Human Rights, Security and Governance." *Peace & Policy.* Journal of the Toda Institute for Global Peace and Policy Research. Dialogue of Civilizations for World Citizenship 3(2).

Harvard Program on Humanitarian Policy and Conflict Research. 2002. "Children and Armed Conflict: A Symposium on Implementing UN Security Council Resolution 1379," New York, 8 November.

Hefferman, John. 2002. "Being Recognized as Citizens: A Human Security Dilemma in South and Southeast Asia." Paper prepared for the Commission on Human Security. [www.humansecurity-chs.org].

ICIHI (Independent Commission on International Humanitarian Issues). 1988. *Winning the Human Race.* London: Zed Books.

ICISS (International Commission on Intervention and State Sovereignty). 2001. *The Responsibility to Protect.* Ottawa.

ICRC (International Committee of the Red Cross). 2003. "The Missing: The Right To Know." International Conference of Governmental and Non-Governmental Experts, Geneva, 19–21 February.

InterAfrica Group/Justice Africa. 2002. "The African Union and Peace and Security." Paper prepared for the African Development Forum (ADF III), Economic Commission for Africa, Addis Ababa, Ethiopia.

Kirby, Kay. 2002. "Displacement as Policy." Paper prepared in cooperation with the Internally Displaced Persons Project, Norwegian Refugee Council, for the Commission on Human Security. [www.humansecurity-chs.org].

Klugman, Jeni. 1999. *Social and Economic Policies to Prevent Complex Humanitarian Emergencies: Lessons from Experience.* Policy Brief 2. UNU/Wider.

Leaning, Jennifer, and Sam Arie. 2000. "Human Security in Crisis and Transition: A Background Document of Definition and Application." CERTI Project, New Orleans, Payson Center for International Development and Technology Transfer, Tulane University. [www.certi.org/publications/policy/human security-4.htm].

Lodgaard, Sverre. "Human Security: Concept and Operationalisation." [www.hsph.harvard.edu/hpcr/events/hsworkshop/lodgaard.pdf].

Lund, Michael S. 2002. "Operationalizing Lessons from Recent Experience in Conflict Prevention." In Hampson, Fen Osler, and David M. Malone, eds., *From Reaction to Conflict Prevention: Opportunities for the UN System.* Boulder, Colo.: Lynne Rienner Publishers.

MacFarlane, Neil S., and Yuen Foong-Khong. "A Critical History of the UN and Human Security." Paper prepared for the UN Intellectual History Project. [www.unhistory.org/Research/Human.Security. Outline.htm].

Mack, Andrew. 2002. "Report on the Feasibility of Creating an Annual Human Security Report." Program on Humanitarian Policy and Conflict Research, Harvard University.

Martin, Susan. 2001. "Remittance Flows and Impact." Paper prepared for the Regional Conference on Remittances as a Development Tool. Multilateral Investment Fund and the Inter-American Development Bank, Washington, D.C.

McRae, Rob, and Don Hubert, eds. 2001. *Human Security and the New Diplomacy: Protecting People, Promoting Peace.* Montreal: McGill-Queen's University Press.

Nafziger, E. Wayne, and Raimo Vayrynen, eds. 2002. *The Prevention of Humanitarian Emergencies.* New York: Palgrave.

Naim, Moises. 2003. "Five Wars We're Losing: Why Governments Can't Stop the Illegal Trade in Drugs, Arms, Ideas, People and Money." *Foreign Policy* January/February: 28–37.

Nef, Jorge. 1999. *Human Security and Mutual Vulnerability. The Global Political Economy of Development and Underdevelopment.* 2nd edition. International Development Research Centre, Ottawa.

Newman, Edward, and Oliver P. Richmond, eds. 2001. *The United Nations and Human Security.* New York: Palgrave.

Norwegian Institute of International Affairs. 2001. "Gendering Human Security: From Marginalization to Integration of Women in Peace Keeping: Recommendations for Policy and Practice." NUPI-Fafo Forum on Gender Relations in Post-Conflict Transitions, Oslo.

Ntegaye, Gloria. 2002. "Being Recognized as Citizens: A Human Security Dilemma in Sub-Saharan Africa." Paper prepared for the Commission on Human Security. [www.humansecurity-chs.org].

Oberleitner, Gerd. 2002. "Human Security and Human Rights." Occasional Paper 8. European Training and Research Centre for Human Rights and Democracy, Graz, Austria.

Ogata. Sadako. 1999. "Human Security: A Refugee Perspective." Keynote speech at the Ministerial Meeting on Human Security Issues of the "Lysoen Process" Group of Governments, Bergen, Norway, May. [www.unhcr.ch/].

———. 2001. "State Security—Human Security." UN Public Lectures, the Fridtjof Nansen Memorial Lecture, UN House, Tokyo, 12 December 2001. [www.humansecurity-chs.org].

———. 2002a. "From State Security to Human Security." The Ogden Lecture. Brown University, Providence, Rhode Island, 26 May.

———. 2002b. "Globalization and Human Security." Weatherhead Policy Forum, School of International and Public Affairs, Columbia University, March. [www.humansecurity-chs.org].

OHCHR (United Nations High Commissioner for Human Rights). 2002. *Draft Guidelines: A Human Rights Approach to Poverty Reduction Strategies.* Geneva: Office of the High Commissioner for Human Rights.

Paris, Roland. 2001. "Human Security: Paradigm Shift or Hot Air?" *International Security* 26(2): 87–102.

Ramcharan, Bertrand G. 2002. *Human Rights and Human Security.* The Hague: Martinus Nijhoff Publishers.

Randel, Judith, and Tony German. 2002. "Trends in the Financing of Humanitarian Assistance." In Joanna Macrae, ed., *The New Humanitarianisms: A Review*

of Trends in Global Humanitarian Action. HPG
    Report 11. London: Overseas Development
    Institute.
Raymond, Susan. 2003. "Foreign Assistance in an Aging
    World." *Foreign Affairs* March/April: 91–105.
Rieff, David. 2002. "Humanitarianism in Crisis."
    Foreign Affairs 81(6): 111–21.
Rubin, Barnett. 2001. "Afghanistan and Threats to
    Human Security." Paper presented at the
    International Symposium on Human Security and
    Terrorism, Tokyo, December.
Rummel, R. J. 1994. *Death by Government: Genocide
    and Mass Murder since 1900.* New Brunswick, N.J.:
    Transactions Publications.
Schmeidl, Susanne, and others. 2002. "The Transition
    from Relief to Development from a Human
    Security Perspective: Afghanistan." Paper prepared
    for the Commission on Human Security.
    [www.humansecurity-chs.org].
Sen, Amartya. 1999. *Development as Freedom.* New York:
    Anchor Books.
———. 2000. "Why Human Security?" Paper presented
    at the International Symposium on Human
    Security, Tokyo, July.
———. 2002. "Basic Education and Human Security."
    Paper presented at the Kolkata Meeting, organized
    by the Commission on Human Security, UNICEF,
    the Pratichi (India) Trust and Harvard University,
    Kokata, India, January.
SIPRI (Stockholm International Peace Research
    Institute). 2002. *SIPRI Yearbook 2002: Armaments,
    Disarmament and International Security.* Oxford:
    Oxford University Press.
The Stanley Foundation. 2002. "Laying a Durable
    Foundation for Post-conflict Societies." Paper
    presented at the 37th United Nations of the Next
    Decade Conference, New York, 15–20 June.

Thouez, Colleen. 2002. "Migration and Human
    Security." Paper prepared by the International
    Migration Policy Programme, for the Commission
    on Human Security. [www.humansecurity-chs.org].
UNDP (United Nations Development Programme).
    Various years. *Human Development Report.* New
    York: Oxford University Press.
United Nations. 2000. "Report of the Panel on United
    Nations Peace Operations." S/2000/809. New York.
———. 2002. "Enhancing the Functioning and
    Utilization of the Central Emergency Revolving
    Fund." A/57/613. New York.
———. 2002. "Report of the Ad Hoc Committee of
    the Whole of the Twenty-Seventh Special Session of
    the General Assembly." Supplement 3, A/S-
    27/19/Rev.1.
United Nations, Economic and Social Council. 2001.
    "Secretary-General Report on Fundamental
    Standards of Humanity, Promotion and Protection
    of Human Rights: Fundamental Standards of
    Humanity." E/CN.4/2001/91.
United Nations, General Assembly. 2001. *Prevention of
    Armed Conflict.* A/55/985. New York.
———. 2002. *Strengthening of the United Nations: An
    Agenda for Further Change: Report of the Secretary-
    General.* A/57/387.
UNHCR (United Nations High Commissioner for
    Refugees), Executive Committee of the High
    Commissioner's Programme. 2000. *The Security,
    Civilian, and Humanitarian Character of Refugee
    Camps and Settlements: Operationalizing the "Ladder
    of Options."* EC/50/sc/inf.4.
United Nations, Office of the Secretary-General. 2000.
    *We the Peoples: The Role of the United Nations in the
    21th Century.* New York.
United Nations, Population Division. 2003. *World
    Population Prospects: The 2002 Revision.*

2

ESA/P/WP.180. New York: Population Division, Department of Economic and Social Affairs, United Nations Secretariat.

United Nations, Security Council. 2001a. *Children and Armed Conflict: Report of the Secretary-General.* A/56/342. New York.

———. 2001b. *Report of the Secretary-General to the Security Council on the Protection of Civilians in Armed Conflict.* S/2001/331. New York.

———. 2002a. *Report of the Secretary-General to the Security Council on the Protection of Civilians in Armed Conflict.* S/2002/1300. New York.

———. 2002b. *Report of the Secretary-General on Small Arms.* S/2002/1053. New York.

———. 2002c. *Report of the Secretary-General on Women, Peace and Security.* S/2002/1154. New York.

USAID (United States Agency for International Development). 2003. *Foreign Aid in the National Interest: Promoting Freedom, Security, and Opportunity.* Washington, D.C.

Varshney, Ashutosh. 2002. *Ethnic Conflict and Civic Life: Hindus and Muslims in India.* New Haven, Conn.: Yale University Press.

WHO (World Health Organization). 2002. *World Report on Violence and Health.* Geneva.

Reports of meetings
Cels, Johan. 2002. "Final Report: 'Rethinking Peace, Coexistence and Human Security in the Great Lakes Region.'" Organized by the Commission on Human Security, Kigali, Rwanda, April.

Conference on "Promoting Human Security in the Democratic Republic of Congo." Institute for Human Security, Fletcher School of Law and Diplomacy; United Nations Development Programme; and the Feinstein International Famine Center School of Nutrition Science and Public Policy, February 2002.

Symposium on "Economic Insecurity in Africa." Organized by the Commission on Human Security, Cotonou, Benin, May 2002.

Workshop on "Relationship Between Human Rights and Human Security." San José, Costa Rica, December 2001.

Tadjbakhsh, Shahrbanou. 2002. "Final Report: 'Transition in Central Asia and Human Security.'" Organized by the Commission on Human Security, Ashgabat, Turkmenistan.

People on the move

3

For many people migration is vital to protect and attain human security

The movement of people across borders reinforces the interdependence of countries and communities and enhances diversity. It facilitates the transfer of skills and knowledge. It stimulates economic growth and development. And for the majority of people, whether they are migrating temporarily or permanently, it creates new opportunities for pleasure or business.

Most people move to improve their livelihood, seek new opportunities or escape poverty.[1] They also leave to rejoin family members elsewhere, the main legal means of migration into Europe and North America since the adoption of more restrictive immigration policies in the 1980s. Another reason for moving is forcible displacement or coercion because of war, violent conflict, human rights abuses, expulsion or discrimination.[2] For many people, therefore, migration is vital to protect and attain human security, although their human security may also be at risk while they are migrating.

At the end of the 20th century, there were an estimated 175 million international migrants, nearly 3% of the world's people and twice the number in 1975.[3] Some 60% of the international migrants, about 104 million, are in developed countries—the rest, 71 million, are in developing countries. (Table 3.1 shows the 10 countries with the largest numbers of international migrants.)

Of the 175 million international migrants in 2000, nearly 16 million were refugees, roughly 9% (figure 3.1).[4] That is down from the peak of nearly 19 million refugees in 1993, with the smaller number of violent conflicts (chapter 2) and the return home of people after peace settlements (chapter 4).[5] The movements within borders are considerably larger than those across them. Internal

Table 3.1 Countries with the largest number of international migrants, 2000

Country	Number of people
United States	34,988,000
Russian Federation	13,259,000
Germany	7,349,000
Ukraine	6,947,000
France	6,277,000
India	6,271,000
Canada	5,826,000
Saudi Arabia	5,255,000
Australia	4,705,000
Pakistan	4,243,000

Source: United Nations, Population Division 2002b.

Figure 3.1 UNHCR data on refugee population and movements, 1992–2001

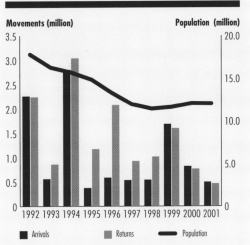

Note: These data do not include Palestinian refugees, who are under the mandate of the United Nations Relief and Works Agency for Palestine Refugees in the Near East.
Source: UNHCR 2002b.

displacement from armed conflict, generalized violence and human rights abuses is estimated to have affected more than 25 million people in 47 countries in 2002, of which 5.3 million are the concern of the UN High Commissioner for Refugees (UNHCR).[6] (Table 3.2 shows the 8 countries with the largest numbers of internally displaced persons.)

The political transformation in the former Soviet Union and the opening of societies previously closed, such as China, have meant that more people can leave their country. The breakup of states has also resulted in massive population movements. Consider the former Soviet Union. Nearly 9 million people were directly affected, as migrants, refugees and displaced persons. People previously deported returned home, and many Russian nationals were expelled from the newly independent states (box 3.1).

In addition to political change, economic developments have also influenced the magnitude and direction of labour migration. Developed countries seek skilled migrants while deterring unskilled labourers. And there is increasing migration of workers between developing countries, particularly in Western Asia, Southeast Asia and Southern Africa.

In 2001, 44% of developed countries had restrictive immigration policies. So did 39% of developing countries.[7] These restrictive policies have contributed to the proliferation of traffickers and smugglers. It is estimated that more than half the 15–30 million illegal migrants in the world have been assisted by smugglers or been forcibly relocated by traffickers.[8] Although comprehensive figures are unavailable, an estimated 700,000 persons, mainly women and children, are trafficked

Table 3.2 Countries with the largest number of internally displaced persons, 2002

Country	Number of people
Sudan	4,000,000
Angola	3,500,000
Colombia	2,100,000
Congo, Dem. Rep.	2,275,000
Indonesia	1,100,000
Turkey	1,000,000
Iraq	1,000,000
Afghanistan	920,000

Source: Norwegian Refugee Council 2002.

every year, the majority from South and Southeast Asia. An estimated 50,000 women and girls a year are trafficked into the United States for sexual exploitation.[9]

Movements of people and state security

Massive population movements affect the security of receiving states, often compelling them to close their borders and forcibly prevent people from reaching safety and protection. Armed elements among civilian refugee populations may spread conflict into neighbouring countries.

Recent efforts to combat terrorism have put state security concerns at the forefront in discussions of international migration, often to the detriment of migrants and refugees. In the name of preserving state security, the detention of illegal migrants without due process is on the rise globally. People are frequently turned back by force at border points, returned to countries where their human rights may be at risk. "Profiling" aliens and imposing stringent visa requirements for certain groups have contributed to a climate of intolerance.

Box 3.1 Managing massive population movements—the break-up of the former Soviet Union

When the Berlin Wall fell in 1989, the euphoria in Western Europe was quickly muted by the fear that large numbers of Central Europeans would come seeking employment. These worries increased when the Soviet Union dissolved in 1991 and conflicts broke out between Armenia and Azerbaijan over the enclave of Nagorno-Karabakh, in the regions of Abkhazia and South Ossetia of Georgia, Moldova, and Tajikistan. Within the newly created Russian Federation, violent conflicts broke out in North Ossetia and Chechnya. But the outbreak of fighting in the former Yugoslavia quickly overshadowed the complex large-scale population movements in the former Soviet Union, whose relatively successful efforts to manage them were largely overlooked. This experience shows that the orderly and predictable management of population movements is feasible, even in very complex and fluid situations.

Between 1989 and 1996, nearly 9 million people were on the move in the Commonwealth of Independent States (CIS)—one in every 30 inhabitants:

- Refugees, internally displaced persons, and involuntary relocating persons   3,632,000
- Repatriates to country of ethnic origin   3,296,000
- Return movements of formerly deported peoples   1,184,000
- Ecological migrants   689,000
- Illegal migrants   580,000
- Asylum-seekers, non-CIS refugees   68,000

In addition, the fear of further massive population displacements loomed large, in particular with respect to the 34 million or so Russians, Ukrainians and Belarussians in the newly independent states. Without even moving, their status changed from citizen of the Soviet Union to aliens in their new home countries. In addition to complex citizenship questions, growing intolerance and resentment over past injustices, identity politics and the prospect of their forcible expulsion to the Russian Federation raised the spectre of future conflict.

Realizing the complexity of the population movements, the Russian Federation launched an initiative to hold the 1996 UN Conference on the "Problems of Refugees, Returnees, Displaced Persons, and Migrants". Before the conference, a study identified 164 ethno-territorial disputes and claims within the former Soviet Union. The objective of the conference was to provide a forum for the countries of the region to discuss population displacement in a humanitarian and non-political way, to identify the different categories of people affected and to adopt a normative and policy framework. The conference adopted a comprehensive plan of action to address population movements and promote preventive strategies.

Among the successes of the process were development of clearer policies, greater coordination of policies, the adoption of a flexible institutional arrangement and a normative framework to protect displaced persons, and the provision of humanitarian assistance. Among the shortcomings: difficulty mobilizing financial resources and inadequate integration of humanitarian and development dimensions of population movements.

Source: UNHCR 2000, pp. 185–209.

Combating the trafficking in and smuggling of people, approached primarily from a state security perspective, has been part of the effort to fight the spread of crime. Criminal networks exploit the absence of multilateral migration policies and cooperation among countries. Traffickers force women and girls into prostitution. According to a recent study, 90% of foreign migrant sex workers in the Balkan countries are victims of trafficking.[10] But only 30% are so recognized, and only 7% receive assistance and support. Rather than being protected, women and girls are prosecuted for having entered the country illegally. Of particular concern is the growing number of unaccompanied minors being trafficked.[11] In Italy, they made up a third of irregular arrivals in 2000. Some 15,000 unaccompanied minors arrived in the United States that year.

The HIV/AIDS crisis also brought to the fore the relationship between movements of people and public health. Migrants are more at risk of contracting and spreading the disease than people who do not move. They also are more vulnerable to sexual violation and physical abuse. And they have greater difficulty getting health services. So policies to prevent the spread of HIV/AIDS and other infectious diseases need to protect migrating people and their families and populations along major migratory routes. This requires the development of programmes across borders and the inclusion of migrating people in national plans.

Movements of people—and development

The movement of people is also a development issue. The growing inequity between and within countries affects displacement patterns.[12] As long as inequity and imbalances between labor demand and supply are growing among countries, people will seek every opportunity to better their livelihoods. The relationships among development, poverty and displacement are complex and poorly understood. Poverty is often cited as one of the main causes of irregular migration. So, from a policy perspective, less poverty should mean less migration pressures. To address the growing number of irregular migrants, the European Union adopted a comprehensive policy at its 1999 Tampere Summit in Finland to "address political, human rights and development issues in countries and regions of origin and transit…. This requires combating poverty, improving living conditions and job opportunities, preventing conflicts and consolidating democratic states and ensuring respect for human rights."

But research also shows that poverty reduction strategies may contribute to increased movements of people in the short and medium terms because

people have access more to the money, information and networks that are essential for moving from one country to another.[13] The largest movements originate from middle-income countries, not from the poorest countries. Only after years of development is a gradual decline in migration noticeable.

For developed countries the ageing population prompts a steady demand for more labour migrants. Since the mid-1990s, several European countries have introduced temporary worker programmes for highly skilled professionals. But this need for additional labour migration has not been translated into public support for such programmes. Instead, there has been public intolerance of migrants, sentiments often exploited by politicians.

Policies to overcome this gap between public perception and economic need will determine whether managed and predictable migration policies will be feasible. The effectiveness of these policies will also be determined by the way the brain drain of skilled professionals from developing countries is addressed.[14] Some 15 percent of college-educated Ghanaians and more than 20 percent of Mexicans with a secondary education have migrated to the United States.[15]

Sudden economic downturns and structural adjustment programs directly affect people's human security and migration aspirations, yet little attention has been paid to this interconnection. Experiences in Southeast Asia and Latin America indicate that the impact is significant. During the Asian financial crisis in the late 1990s, several countries resorted to the forcible expulsion of illegal migrants and refused to renew the work permits and visas of legal workers. In Latin America, too, the economic crisis is pushing people

There is no single institutional arrangement for the orderly management and protection of people moving across borders

to migrate. According to a 2001 survey, nearly 500,000 Argentines have applied for immigration visas to other countries.

Nor does enough attention go to the development needs of people internally displaced by war and conflict or by development projects. A 2002 World Food Programme study on internal displacement in Indonesia shows that food security is significantly lower among internally displaced persons than among host communities.[16] The incidence of poverty is much higher in the initial stages of displacement, especially for female-headed households, and gradually improves over time. The study also noted greater health problems for displaced people. Children's schooling is also disrupted during displacement, and many children stop attending school or cannot attend because they are needed for work.

Filling gaps in the institutional and normative frameworks

From a human security perspective, the movement of people should be looked at comprehensively, taking into account the political, civil, security, economic and social dimensions affecting peoples' decision to move. It cannot be approached solely from the perspectives of the countries of origin, transit or destination. It must also be approached from the perspective of the different stages and motivations for displacement—for many people, migration is the only option. Today's policies, norms and institutions are not doing this, leaving major gaps.

Except in the case of refugees, it is left largely to individual states to regulate the movement of people within and across borders. The absence of an international migration arrangement—ordering and regulating the movement of people between

countries through the adoption of agreed norms, principles and institutions—is remarkable, since it affects the security of people and of states.

Institutional arrangements

There is no single institutional arrangement for the orderly management and protection of people moving across borders. The International Labour Organization has a mandate to protect migrant workers. The International Organization for Migration facilitates the orderly movement of people at the requests of member states.[17] The General Agreement on Tariffs and Trade also had a mandate to promote the freedom of movement of people, but it was not implemented. The UNHCR has a mandate to protect refugees and identify solutions.

Several other institutions also focus on migration, including United Nations Development Programme, the World Bank and the United Nations Population Division, which produces the most comprehensive migration data. For the internal displacement of people, efforts to coordinate the responses by international agencies are also under way through the UN Office for the Coordination of Humanitarian Affairs.

Normative frameworks

The Universal Declaration of Human Rights states that "Everyone has the right to freedom of move-ment and residence within the borders of each state" and that "Everyone has the right to leave any country, including his own, and to return to his country" (article 13). But if the right to leave one's country is to have practical effect, people must be able to enter another country. States have carefully guarded their right to determine who is permitted to enter and reside in their territory. Consequently, there has been little progress in developing a normative framework to regulate the movement of people between states and to protect their rights.

The most significant effort is the 1990 International Convention on the Protection of the Rights of All Migrant Workers and Members of Their Families, which came into force in December 2002. The convention applies to regular and irregular migrants and their family members and provides for the protection of their fundamental human rights and freedoms. But as only 19 migrant-sending countries have ratified the convention so far, its effective implementation by receiving countries remains doubtful. In addition, legal migrants benefit from the 1949 International Labour Organization Migration for Employment Convention and the 1975 Convention on Migrant Workers. But few states have ratified these instruments. There also are regional instruments, such as the 1977 European Convention on the Legal Status of Migrant Workers, but they too have attracted few ratifiers.

The most positive policy developments have been in combating the smuggling and trafficking in people, with the G-8 countries making it a priority. Two protocols in the United Nations Convention against Transnational Organized Crime contain provisions criminalizing the smuggling and trafficking in migrants by emphasizing the obligation to prosecute offenders.

The most developed normative framework is for refugees, under the 1951 Convention Relating to the Status of Refugees and its 1967 Protocol. The convention defines a refugee and prohibits the return of people to situations in which their lives may be in danger for refugee-like reasons. It also includes an extensive list of rights and obligations of refugees. In Africa, instruments have been adopted to broaden the definition of a refugee and recognize the right of asylum.[18] But the effective application of these instruments has come under pressure in recent years. More migrants are applying for refugee status to circumvent the restrictive immigration regulations, undermining the protection under the convention. Governments are interpreting the definition of refugee narrowly and preventing people from applying for refugee status by imposing stringent visa requirements, detentions and returns at the border.

Efforts to strengthen the rights of migrants have also been taken up at various UN international conferences in the past decade. The most significant progress was at the 1993 Vienna World Conference on Human Rights and the 1994 Cairo International Conference on Population and Development, where states agreed to uphold basic standards and implement a program of action. At the 2001 Durban World Conference against Racism, fear and hatred of migrants, refugees and asylum-seekers were recognized as one of the main manifestations of modern racism. (Subsequent efforts to organize an international UN conference to examine the relationship between migration and development failed for lack of international support.[19])

Adopting a human security approach

The UN Secretary-General, in his 2002 report on *Strengthening of the United Nations: An Agenda for Further Change,* argues for a comprehensive examination of the different dimensions of migration, as well as the causes of population movements and their impact on development.[20] Similarly, the Organisation for Economic Co-

Achieving these ambitious goals requires a careful balance between national sovereignty, security and development needs and the human security of people

operation and Development has argued that migration is critical in globalization but that more cooperation is required to manage it.[21] The most successful example of cooperation on migration is the European Union, which will permit the free movement of more than 450 million people between 25 countries by 2007. Regional strategies are also freeing the movement of people between countries in West Africa, Central America and Latin America—and within the North American Free Trade Agreement. In addition, regional discussions are coordinating strategies of sending, transit and receiving countries through the sharing of information and agreements on visa regimes and return policies. Examples include the Puebla Process in Central America, the Asia-Pacific Consultations, the Berne Initiative and the Dakar Consultations.[22]

Common to these initiatives is coordinating restrictive policies at the highest possible level, while agreeing to protect migrants at the lowest possible level.[23] From a human security perspective, managing migration has to go beyond coordinating restrictive policies among states. The importance of migration for protecting human security should be recognized, in particular for people fleeing serious human rights violations, persecution and violent conflict. Also, migration should be seen as a process that empowers people and creates new opportunities for people and states alike. At the same time, the migration of people between countries cannot be seen in isolation from the displacement of people within countries, given the permeability of borders and the ease of travel. Because internally displaced persons seldom benefit from the protection of national and local authorities, meeting the protection and essential

needs at home of internally displaced persons enables them to remain and not seek protection elsewhere.

Achieving these ambitious-goals requires a careful balance between national sovereignty, security and development needs on the one hand and the human security of people on the other. And achieving that balance requires filling the policy and institutional gaps identified earlier.

The Commission on Human Security proposes the development of an international migration framework that, among other issues, would address:[24]

- Taking steps towards the orderly and safe movement of people, including increasing migratory opportunities and burden-sharing among countries.
- Developing international and regional norms for the movement of people between countries and for the rights and obligations of migrants.
- Formulating strategies to combat trafficking and smuggling and implementing the relevant international and regional conventions, while protecting the rights of victims.
- Protecting against racism and intolerance and other human rights violations.
- Developing an institutional framework.

Existing international and regional instruments should be promoted, and new ones developed. The protocols on the trafficking and smuggling of people show that cooperation among states is feasible, often with the close involvement of civil society. Attention should go to adopting national anti-trafficking legislation and protection and referral mechanisms for trafficked persons, who should be treated not as criminals but as victims of human rights violations.

For refugees

More than 50 years since its adoption, the refugee regime is under severe strain, leaving gaps in the protection of people fleeing war, violent conflict, human rights violations and discrimination. To help close these gaps, states have signed on to an Agenda for Protection, developed under the UNHCR through global consultations.[25] Strengthening the protection of refugees requires a better understanding of the causes and actors forcing people to flee. A narrow state-centric understanding of persecution and protection fails to address the needs of people who have fallen victim to rebel groups and criminal triads—and whom the state fails to protect. A broader understanding would include grave threats of generalized violence, internal conflicts, massive violations of human rights and other serious disturbances of public order.[26] Moreover, interpretations of the criteria for refugee status need to be harmonized among countries to avoid people who are rejected in one country moving on to another.

Protecting refugees is the responsibility not only of states and the UNHCR, but also of civil society organizations and refugees themselves. Civil society can work to improve education and training for refugees, provide employment and health care for women and support community development and integration activities. Refugee community groups should take responsibility for identifying their own needs and managing their resources.

From the outset, the emphasis should be on the productive capacities of refugees, not on their vulnerabilities, for this will allow them to regain their livelihoods and dignity. The record of many humanitarian and development agencies in empowering refugees is far from exemplary.[27] Too often, protection and empowerment strategies aimed at women and children are considered "non-core" activities, even though women and children represent more than 75 percent of the refugee population.[28]

With the burden of hosting refugees unequally divided among countries and with most of it borne by low-income countries,[29] developed countries need to increase their financial contributions and provide more technical assistance. Among the priorities: establishing secure livelihoods, protecting people against downside risks, reducing inequalities among communities, strengthening governance and respecting human rights.

Solutions to refugee crises depend primarily on the transition to peace and stability in post-conflict countries (chapter 4). Voluntary repatriation and reintegration of people into their home communities are the best option. If these steps are not feasible, donor countries should help refugees become self-sufficient—and if agreed by the host country, to settle permanently in their new community. Opportunities to resettle in a third country remain limited, despite the importance for protection. Between 1992 and 2001, some 284,000 refugees were resettled, primarily to the United States, Canada and Australia. But such opportunities were choked off by the fight against terrorism. The number of refugees resettled to the United States declined from 70,000 in 2001 to 27,000 in 2002 because of stringent security checks.[30] Expanding resettlement opportunities for qualified and needy refugees, particularly in Europe, will contribute to burden-sharing, facilitate the orderly movement of people and ease the need to attract labour migrants.

Solutions to refugee crises depend primarily on the transition to peace and stability in post-conflict countries

Guaranteeing the security of refugees is another priority.[31] The presence of combatants among civilian refugee populations undermines the humanitarian and non-political character of granting asylum. Security threats take many forms—ranging from sexual violence against women to armed conflict. The military recruitment of refugees, particularly children, should also be prevented by separating armed elements from the civilian refugee population—often very difficult because of the lack of capacity or political will. Failures to ensure the security of refugees may spill conflict into the country of asylum, threatening regional peace and security. To meet these challenges, security packages should strengthen police units in unsafe refugee-hosting areas, and experienced security officers should provide technical assistance (box 3.2).

Such changes can happen only with stronger institutional arrangements. Unilateral restrictive action by individual states merely shifts problems without addressing them. Agreements are needed on issues not covered by the Refugee Convention and requiring a multilateral approach involving states, international actors and civil society organizations. Such "Convention Plus" strategies should clarify responsibilities and ensure that the UNHCR can carry out its mandated responsibilities.[32]

For internally displaced persons

The needs of internally displaced persons are similar to those of refugees in many respects. But whereas refugees benefit from a clear set of internationally recognized rights and principles, as provided under the international refugee system, internally displaced persons do not. In war and conflict, the 1949 Geneva Conventions and their Additional Protocols provide for the protection of civilians, including internally displaced persons.[33] But international legal norms do not cover all situations of internal displacement; nor are the norms universally respected.[34] So the Guiding Principles on Internal Displacement were formulated by the United Nations in 1996, drawing on human rights, norms and humanitarian and refugee law.[35] The Guiding Principles cover the protection of people from and during displacement, access to humanitarian assistance, and the return, resettlement and reintegration of people.

The innovative approach in drafting the Guiding Principles, led by Francis Deng, shows what might be done to develop norms for other human security issues. The Guiding Principles link relevant provisions in human rights and humanitarian and refugee law, giving a unique framework that stipulates how internally displaced persons should be protected.[36] The Guiding Principles also strengthen the application of the (broader) human rights norms by demonstrating their relevance to specific issues and situations.

Although the Guiding Principles do not bind states, they can be an important tool for protection and empowerment if translated into concrete and practical policy guidelines and operationalized. In Sri Lanka, the Guiding Principles contributed to the effective functioning of the open relief centres, which serve as gathering points for protection from armed skirmishes as well as for food distribution. Efforts to incorporate these Guiding Principles into national legal frameworks should be promoted, as in Angola, Colombia and Sri Lanka. And strengthening the capacity of national and local human rights

Box 3.2 Ensuring refugee security

In late 2000 and early 2001, some 300,000 Sierra Leonean and 90,000 Liberian refugees in southern Guinea were victims of cross-border rebel attacks from Sierra Leone. To escape the attacks, the refugees fled deeper into the country, accompanied by more than 100,000 Guineans who feared for their own safety. Fighting interrupted the delivery of humanitarian assistance, and a UNHCR staff member was killed and another was abducted. Many of the Sierra Leonean refugees returned home, considering it safer than their country of asylum.

The impact of the crisis was profound. Of the nearly 400,000 Liberian and Sierra Leoneon refugees before the crisis broke out, only 80,600 remained in the country. Inflammatory statements on radio and television accused the refugees of responsibility for the ills befalling the country and suggested that all refugees be rounded up and pushed across the border, ending decades of generous hospitality toward refugees nearly overnight.

The experience in Guinea is not unique. Other recent examples include Ethiopia, the Democratic Republic of Congo, Côte d'Ivoire, Tanzania, Thailand, the West Bank and Gaza, and Uganda.

Among the most serious protection problems facing refugees is the militarization of settlements. The mixing of armed elements among civilian refugee populations creates the real danger that the conflict will spread across borders, affecting the host country as well as refugees.

Following the Rwandan genocide of 1994, members of the militia and soldiers of the former Rwandan army suspected of having committed genocide joined the refugees fleeing to then-Zaire and Tanzania. They took control of some of the refugee camps, intimidated the civilian population and staged attacks on Rwandan territory. The lack of support by the international community in separating the armed elements from the civilian population contributed to the collapse of Zaire and to the persisting humanitarian crisis in the eastern part of the country. Nearly 10 years after the genocide, the region is still in turmoil. Separation of armed elements from the civilian populace in 1995–96 could have made a dramatic difference in the human security of the whole region.

Several steps can be taken to ensure the safety of refugees, attuned to escalating or diminishing threats:

- Adopting preventive and corrective measures, such as locating camps away from the border and establishing refugee security committees.
- Dispatching international fact-finding missions and observers.
- Strengthening law enforcement mechanisms.
- Supporting national police and military forces.
- Deploying international police forces.
- Deploying military forces under Chapter VI or VII of the UN Charter.

Source: Faubert [www.humansecurity-chs.org].

institutions to act on behalf of internally displaced persons should be a policy objective.

The empowerment of internally displaced persons has not received enough attention, despite the crucial role internally displaced persons play in meeting their own needs and influencing the course of conflict.[37] In many situations, internally displaced persons develop survival and coping strategies. In some, they and host communities develop self-defence units, to ensure that people have time to flee. In others, women have organized to secure livelihoods for themselves and to provide basic health and education to children. But as in refugee settings, humanitarian actors do not adequately draw on or support such community development activities.

More emphasis needs to go to protecting people in their country of origin, so it is critical

that international organizations enhance their capacity to protect internally displaced persons. Progress has been made toward strengthening coordination, planning and monitoring through the UN Office for the Coordination of Humanitarian Affairs, but implementation of effective programmes on behalf of internally displaced persons remains lacking.[38] Further clarification of responsibilities may require designating lead agencies, based on their capacity, comparative advantage and complementarities.

Too often, internally displaced persons have been viewed as solely a humanitarian issue. But their protection and empowerment cannot be considered apart from national development and poverty reduction strategies, both critical for ending internal displacement through return,

Migration issues have to be squarely put on the development and poverty reduction agendas

resettlement or reintegration. The World Bank, for example, has specific guidelines on "involuntary resettlement" that emphasize the need for prevention, compensation and participation of people displaced by development projects.[39] The experience of development actors should inform the policies of humanitarian actors. At the same time, the Guiding Principles on Internal Displacement may provide a normative base for development actors to ensure the protection of people displaced by development projects.

For economic migrants

To protect the human security of migrants, a minimum requirement is a secure legal status that will enable them to access basic services and to benefit from legal protection of their fundamental rights. Various countries have regularized the status of migrants residing illegally. To facilitate the integration of permanent migrants and their families, the granting of citizenship should be eased, particularly for second- or third-generation migrants.[40] If not, a second or third class of people will have their human security at risk, perhaps giving rise to tensions and conflict among communities. Research shows that migrants granted permanent resident status or citizenship are more likely to return to their country of origin and re-establish links—because they have a new secure base.

Migration issues also have to be squarely put on the development and poverty reduction agendas.[41] Only by understanding the links among migration, development and poverty reduction can effective migration policies be developed.

Transnational social networks of people sharing the same identity or nationality (the diaspora), such as Armenian, Chinese, Indian or Irish communities

abroad,[42] offer an important channel to share information and mobilize resources. They also provide a safety net to newly arriving members abroad. But not all expatriate activities are benevolent: in some instances, the networks serve as an informal conduit for illegal activities, such as human trafficking and the financing of violent conflict in the country of origin.

Countries of origin are mobilizing such networks to act as a powerful political pressure group and source of financial resources.[43] Remittances by migrants, much greater than the total amount of official international development assistance, alleviate poverty of the family members remaining in the country of origin. According to International Monetary Fund data, remittances by migrants were estimated to be about $70 billion in 1995 and $100 billion in 2000, nearly twice the official development assistance of some $51 billion in 2001.[44] The 7.3 million overseas Philippine workers are estimated to have sent $8 billion home in 2002.[45] El Salvador is among the countries most dependent on remittances—at least 15 percent of the population depends on them. In Sri Lanka, remittances reached nearly $1 billion in 2000, again twice the official development assistance of $490 million in 1998.[46]

These remittances shed a new light on the ongoing debate on the brain drain of skilled workers from developing countries. The focus could be on benefiting from the "brain gain" rather than on ways to stop the brain drain.[47] By adopting policies for maintaining links with nationals abroad—such as the right to own property, voting in national elections and dual citizenship—countries of origin can attract the return of skilled migrants, either permanently or temporarily. For example, the Philippines adopted legislation allowing Filipinos abroad to vote in elections.[48]

Setting up an effective institutional arrangement for all this requires:

- Collecting and analyzing migration data and research.
- Promoting an international normative framework and ensuring its effective implementation.
- Facilitating the development and coordination of policies at regional and national levels.
- Protecting migrants when their human security is seriously threatened and they cannot seek protection in their country of nationality.

Many of these tasks are now shared among different actors, greatly complicating integrated policies and operations.

Policy conclusions

Multilateral approaches are essential for promoting orderly and predictable movements of people. Needed is an international migration framework of norms, processes and institutional arrangements to ensure such order and predictability. In that framework, the sovereignty and security of states would be balanced by the human security of people.

- A high-level and broad-based commission should explore available options and areas of consensus, including alternative institutional arrangements. Parallel to this process, international, regional and national actors should cooperate more on migration issues. Given its unique mandate, the United Nations should take the lead.
- Concerted efforts to identify and implement solutions to displacement situations are required through voluntary repatriation, resettlement or

integration into host communities. But to achieve this, displacement issues can no longer be seen as solely a humanitarian concern; they should also be placed on the development agenda.

- The security risks arising during large-scale forced population movements need to be acknowledged and better understood. Therefore greater attention should be given to efforts to preserve the humanitarian character of granting asylum by separating armed elements from civilian refugee populations.
- Given the permeability of borders and the ease of travel, efforts to strengthen the refugee regime and establish an international migration framework need to be accompanied by improvements in the protection of internally displaced persons.

Notes

1. Kothari 2002.
2. If such people cross a border and seek international protection, they are considered *refugees;* if they do not cross a border, *internally displaced persons.*
3. A *migrant* is defined as a person who lives abroad for at least one year. Migration data are notoriously weak, and efforts are being made to collect better data. Often large numbers of people are missed. For example, an estimated 8 million undocumented migrants residing in the United States have not been included in the population census (United Nations, Population Division 2002b).
4. Of the 15.7 million refugees, 12 million were the responsibility of the UN High Commissioner for Refugees, and the 3.7 million Palestinians fell under the mandate of the United Nations Relief and Works Agency for Palestine Refugees in the Near East.
5. UNHCR 2002b.

6. These figures do not include people moving because of development projects (such as the 40–80 million people estimated to have been displaced by the building of large dams) or people moving to urban centres (Norwegian Refugee Council 2002; World Commission on Dams 2000; United Nations Populations Division 2002c).

7. UN Population Division 2002b.

8. A person trafficked is someone forced (against free will or without knowledge) to go to another country. A person smuggled is someone who pays a transporter to arrange to go to another country through illegal channels (Clark 2002).

9. US Department of State 2002, p. 2.

10. UNICEF/UNOHCHR/OSCE-ODIHR 2002.

11. UNAIDS 2001.

12. Bach 2002.

13. Massey and others 1998, p. 277.

14. Tevoedjre 2002.

15. Carrington and Detragiache 1998.

16. WFP 2002.

17. The International Labour Organization World Commission on the Social Dimension of Globalization is examining in detail the impact of globalization and labour migration, as well as the development of a policy framework for international labour mobility and migration.

18. 1969 Organization for African Unity Convention Regulating the Specific Aspects of Refugees in Africa.

19. United Nations, General Assembly 2000a.

20. United Nations, General Assembly 2002b.

21. OECD 2001.

22. For an overview, see International Migration Policy Programme 2002.

23. IOM 2001.

24. At the government level, the Berne Initiative was launched by Switzerland in June 2001 as a global consultative process for inter-state cooperation on migration management. Similar discussions have also been taking place within civil society organizations, such as the initiative taken by the Society for International Development/Netherlands Chapter on the Future of Asylum and Migration.

25. Executive Committee of the High Commissioner's Programme, Agenda for Protection, A/AC.96/965/Add.1, 26 June 2002.

26. 1984 Cartagena Declaration, Colombia.

27. UNHCR 2002a.

28. UNHCR 2002a.

29. UNHCR 2002b, p 65.

30. *Migration News*, vol. 9, no. 12, December 2002, p. 4.

31. United Nations, Security Council 2002a.

32. Lubbers 2002.

33. Protocol II of the Geneva Convention includes several articles (4, 13, 14, and 17) relating to the protection of victims in non-international armed conflicts.

34. Among the areas that needed to be strengthened are protection against forcible return to a situation that may threaten a person's life, right to return to the place of habitual residence, the issuance of personal documentation, compensation for lost property, and right of access to humanitarian assistance.

35. Compilation and Analysis of Legal Norms Pertaining to Internally Displaced Persons, U.N. Doc. E/CN.4/1996/52/Add.2.

36. The Brookings–CUNY Project on Internal Displacement 2002; Kalin 2001.

37. Vincent and Refslund Sorensen 2001.

38. In January 2002, a small Internal Displaced Persons Unit was created within the Office for the Coordination of Humanitarian Affairs, with personnel seconded from UN and non-governmental agencies.

39. World Bank, Operational Policies, OP 4.12, December 2001.

40. Aleinikoff and Klusmeyer 2002.

41. Olesen 2002.
42. "A World of Exiles," *The Economist,* 4 January 2003.
43. Bhagwati 2003.
44. Martin 2001.
45. *Migration News,* 2002, vol. 9, no. 12, p. 29.
46. Koser and Van Hear 2002.
47. *Migration News,* 2002, vol. 9, no. 12.
48. *Migration News,* 2002, vol. 9, no. 12, p. 30.

References

Acharya, Amitav. 2001. "Debating Human Security: East versus West." Paper prepared for Security with a Human Face: Expert Workshop on the Feasibility of a Human Security Report, Harvard University, Massachusetts, December.

Bach, Robert L. 2002. "Global Mobility, Inequality and Security: Reflections on a Human Security Agenda." Paper prepared for the Commission on Human Security. [www.humansecurity-chs.org].

Bhagwati, Jagdish. 2003. "Borders Beyond Control." *Foreign Affairs* 82(1).

Carrington, William, and Enrica Detragiache. 1998. "How Big Is the Brain Drain?" IMF Working Paper 98/102. International Monetary Fund, Washington, D.C.

Clark, Michele Anne. 2002. "The Global Status of Trafficking in Persons." Paper prepared for the Commission on Human Security. [www.humansecurity-chs.org].

Faubert, Carol. 2002. "Refugee Security in Africa." Paper prepared for the Commission on Human Security. [www.humansecurity-chs.org].

IOM (International Organization for Migration). 2001. *The Role of Regional Consultative Processes in Managing International Migration.* IOM Migration Research Series 3. Geneva.

International Migration Policy Programme. 2002. "Migration and Human Security." Paper prepared for the Commission on Human Security. [www.humansecurity-chs.org].

Kalin, Walter. 2001. "How Hard Is Soft Law? The Guiding Principles on Internal Displacement and the Need for a Normative Framework." Paper presented at a Roundtable Meeting, Ralph Bunche Institute for International Studies, City University of New York Graduate Center, 19 December.

Koser, Khalid, and Nicholas Van Hear. 2002. "Asylum Migration: Implications for Countries of Origin." Paper prepared for the UNU/Wider Conference on Poverty, International Migration and Asylum, Helsinki, 27–28 September.

Kothari, Uma. 2002. *Migration and Chronic Poverty.* Manchester: Chronic Poverty Research Centre.

Lubbers, Rudd. 2002. "Opening Statement, 53rd Session of the Executive Committee of the High Commissioner's Programme." Geneva, 30 September. [www.unhcr.ch].

Massey, D.S., J. Arango, G. Hugo, A. Kouaouci, A. Pellefrino and J.E. Taylor. 1998. *Worlds in Motion: Understanding International Migration at the End of the Millennium.* Oxford: Oxford University Press.

Norwegian Refugee Council. 2002. *Internally Displaced People: A Global Survey.* London: Earthscan Publications.

OECD (Organisation for Economic Co-operation and Development). 2001. *Trends in International Migration.* Paris.

Olesen, Henrik. 2002. "Migration, Return and Development: An Institutional Perspective." Expert working paper prepared for the Centre for Development Research, Migration-Development Links Project. Copenhagen.

Tevoedjre, Albert. 2002. *Winning the War against Humiliation: Report of the Independent Commission on Africa and the Challenges of the Third Millennium.* Paris: Tunde.

UNAIDS. 2001. *Population Mobility and AIDS.* Geneva.

UNHCR (United Nations High Commissioner for Refugees). 1997. *The State of the Worlds Refugees 1997: A Humanitarian Agenda.*

———. 2000. *The State of the World's Refugees, 2000: Fifty Years of Humanitarian Action.* Oxford: Oxford University Press.

———. 2002. "Meeting the Rights and Protection Needs of Refugee Children." EPAU/2001/02, Evaluation and Policy Analysis Unit, Geneva.

———. 2002. *Statistical Yearbook 2001.* Geneva.

UNICEF (United Nations Children's Fund), OHCHR (UN Office of the High Commissioner for Human Rights) and OSCE-ODIHR (Organization for Security and Co-operation in Europe/Office for Democratic Institutions and Human Rights). 2002. *Trafficking in Human Beings in Southeastern Europe.* Belgrade: Federal Republic of Yugoslavia.

United Nations, General Assembly. 2000a. "International Migration and Development, Including the Question of the Convening of a United Nations Conference on International Migration and Development to Address Migration Issues." A/56/167, 3 July 2001. New York.

———. 2001b. *Prevention of Armed Conflict.* A/55/985, 7 June. New York.

United Nations, Population Division. 2002a. *International Migration from Countries with Economies in Transition: 1980–1999.* ESA/P/WP.176. New York: Population Division, Department of Economic and Social Affairs, United Nations Secretariat.

———. 2002b. *International Migration Report 2002.* ESA/P/WP.178. New York: Population Division, Department of Economic and Social Affairs, United Nations Secretariat.

———. 2002c. *World Urbanization Prospects: The 2001 Revision.* ESA/P/WP.173. New York: Population Division, Department of Economic and Social Affairs, United Nations Secretariat.

———. 2003. *World Population Prospects: The 2002 Revision.* ESA/P/WP.180. New York: Population Division, Department of Economic and Social Affairs, United Nations Secretariat.

United Nations, Security Council. 2001a. *Children and Armed Conflict: Report of the Secretary-General.* A/56/342. New York.

———. 2001b. *Report of the Secretary-General to the Security Council on the Protection of Civilians in Armed Conflict.* S/2001/331. New York.

———. 2002a. *Report of the Secretary-General to the Security Council on the Protection of Civilians in Armed Conflict.* S/2002/1300. New York.

———. 2002b. *Report of the Secretary-General on Small Arms.* S/2002/1053. New York.

———. 2002c. *Report of the Secretary-General on Women, Peace and Security.* S/2002/1154. New York.

United States, Department of State. 2002. *Victims of Trafficking and Violence Protection Act 2000: Trafficking in Persons Report.* Washington, D.C.

Vincent, Mark, and Birgitte Refslund Sorensen, eds. 2001. *Caught between Borders: Response Strategies of the Internally Displaced.* London: Pluto Press.

World Commission on Dams. 2002. "Displacement, Resettlement, Rehabilitation, Reparation, and Development." Working paper. Cape Town.

WFP (World Food Programme). 2002. "Internally Displaced Persons (IDPs) in Indonesia—Livelihood Survey: Synthesis Report, Findings and Strategy Options." Rome.

Recovering from violent conflict

4

Helping countries recovering from conflict lays the groundwork for development to take off as well as for human security

Cease-fire agreements and peace settlements mark the end of violent conflict, but they do not ensure peace and human security. According to the World Bank, there is a 50-50 chance that renewed violent conflict will erupt, and the chance is even higher when control over natural resources is at stake.[1] Violent conflict causes millions of dollars of damage and destroys societies, often erasing years of development. Recovery requires yet more resources. At the beginning of the 21st century, nearly 60 countries are in conflict or have recently emerged from it, the majority among the poorest.[2] In many conflicts, the state and its institutions have collapsed, and lingering conflicts rage over control of contested territories.

Helping countries recovering from conflict, one of the most complex challenges confronting the international community, lays the groundwork for development to take off as well as for human security. Conflicts' aftermath affects hundreds of millions of people in numerous ways, and the financial resources required are enormous. The responsibility of states and the international community to protect people in conflict should be complemented by a responsibility to rebuild— including after an international military intervention.[3] The measure of an intervention's success is not a military victory—it is the quality of the peace that is left behind. And the benefits of peace must be felt quickly if people are to plan for the future.[4]

Since the 1990s, successive cease-fires and peace settlements have followed the outbreak of violent conflicts. The changing international environment permitted the negotiation of agreements ending long-term conflict, as in Cambodia and Mozambique. In other situations, the fighting stopped after a cease-fire, but there was no peace to keep, and the conflict resumed after a lull, as in Burundi and Liberia.

International involvement has varied considerably. In Cambodia and Timor-Leste, the United Nations took on de facto administration of the country until elections could be organized. In countries of the former Yugoslavia, deep international involvement has continued many years after the wars ended. In Angola, Liberia and Somalia the involvement of the international community has been patchy—due to lasting insecurity and lack of political will and interest. In many other post-conflict situations, there has been little or no international effort to rebuild the country, as in Armenia, Azerbaijan and Georgia.

The transition from conflict has been approached as a continuous process—from humanitarian relief to rehabilitation and reconstruction, leading to development. The presumption has been that only short-term relief is feasible immediately after the conflict ends, and that any efforts at that time towards rehabilitation and reconstruction would likely be wasted. Only when the situation is stable and secure and immediate humanitarian needs have been met can rehabilitation and reconstruction take off, and only after that can development be launched in earnest.

In reality, recovering from violent conflict seldom follows a linear process. Latent conflict lingers, and interpersonal violence and crime may actually increase. Power-sharing arrangements, subject to continual confrontation, are difficult to implement. And massive numbers of people, displaced internally and sometimes externally, need to be returned and reintegrated into their communities. Inequalities among communities may sharpen—leading to new grievances. Famine and infectious diseases may spread, causing additional human suffering.[5]

Several initiatives have been launched to overcome the challenges. Closer cooperation is being sought among humanitarian actors, development agencies and financial institutions. Special units have been set up to respond to post-conflict situations, such as the Bureau for Crisis Prevention and Recovery in the United Nations Development Programme and the Conflict Prevention and Reconstruction Unit of the World Bank. The Organisation for Economic Co-operation and Development has developed donor guidelines on the prevention of violent conflict.[6]

In 1997, the UN High Commissioner for Refugees (UNHCR) and the World Bank jointly launched the Brookings Process to involve all partners in coordinating and jointly programming activities in a country.[7] Concentrated on institutional and funding arrangements, its success has been limited. Rather than hand over activities from international relief to international development actors, the goal should be to strengthen the capacities of national and local actors—so that relief, rehabilitation and development assistance can be handed over to them.

Adopting a human security approach
Post-conflict situations provide opportunities to promote change, to fundamentally recast social, political and economic bases of power—opportunities for including the excluded, healing

fragmentation and erasing inequalities. But post-conflict situations can also create new uncertainties and deepen alienation. If human security is to protect and enlarge people's choices by promoting their individual and collective empowerment, their rights to political, social and economic freedoms in post-conflict situations must be reasserted:

- *Political.* The key issue is establishing a new democratic political order, preventing competing social, political and economic forces from causing potentially destabilizing reactions. The institutional capacity and policies of the state are critical to ensuring that grievance is contained and further violence prevented.
- *Social.* Conflict makes poverty and deprivation even worse. Social protection systems and other coping strategies must be built so that people's essential needs and livelihoods are met. The reestablishment of social capital is critical so that divisions can be healed, and trust promoted.
- *Economic.* Recovery from conflict is often related to profound economic adjustments, at the macro- and micro-levels, that create further hardship for some people and communities. Equitable and inclusive economic growth is critical to promoting political and social stability, while enlarging opportunities for people.

Given the linkages, no element of post-conflict transition can be dealt with in isolation. Yet many gaps remain in today's post-crisis strategies (box 4.1). Protecting people and communities requires guaranteeing public safety, providing lifesaving humanitarian relief and essential services and returning and integrating people affected by the conflict. Empowering people

Box 4.1 Gaps in today's post-conflict strategies

From a human security perspective, today's post-conflict strategies have many shortcomings, leaving many gaps:

Security gaps
• Military troops are frequently deployed to separate combatants—troops that are ill-equipped to deal with public security issues, such as civil unrest, crime and the trafficking in people.
• From the outset, emphasis in peacekeeping operations is on pursuing an exit strategy that is not directly related to the security needs of the people.
• Security strategies do not take into account the needs of humanitarian and development actors.

Governance gaps
• Peace-building is seen as a "top-down" process, commonly led and imposed by outside actors—rather than as a process to be owned by national institutions and people.
• Little attention goes to building national and local civil society and communities—or to drawing on their capacities and expertise.
• Organization of national elections receives the most attention (and is often seen as a manoeuvre for handing over international mandates and responsibilities to the newly elected authorities), with little regard for further efforts to support governance and democratization.
• Reconciliation efforts pay too little attention to the coexistence of divided communities and the building of trust.

Gaps in international responses
• The international architecture is segregated along security, humanitarian and development lines, encouraging fragmented and competitive responses.
• International actors tend to focus on mandates—not on presence, comparative advantages and needs of specific situations. Coordination is emphasized, not integration.
• Too little attention goes to building national capacities and institutions, resulting in the absence of national ownership.
• Humanitarian agencies focus on speedy interventions but often fail to consider the impact on reconstruction and development activities. Development actors require long periods to mobilize resources and implement their plans, hampering the conversion of humanitarian activities to longer term development strategies.

Resource gaps
• Assistance tends to peak in the early phases, when the capacity to absorb it is low. It has been difficult to sustain aid over the medium term, just when reconstruction and development take off.
• International actors use many fundraising mechanisms—comprehensive appeals, round-tables, consultative groups and country-specific trust funds—some competing, many raising false expectations about the amounts pledged. Negotiations over debt arrears often delay the full participation of international financial institutions.
• Donors and multilateral agencies separate their budgets into humanitarian and development assistance, making it difficult to transfer funds from one cluster to another.
• Funds are earmarked for specific activities and countries, reflecting the primacy of economic, strategic or political interests over human security needs.

Table 4.1 Key human security clusters following violent conflict

Public safety	Humanitarian relief	Rehabilitation and reconstruction	Reconciliation and coexistence	Governance and empowerment
Control armed elements • Enforce cease-fire • Disarm combatants • Demobilize combatants	Facilitate return of conflict-affected people • Internally displaced persons • Refugees	Integrate conflict-affected people • Internally displaced persons • Refugees • Armed combatants	End impunity • Set up tribunals • Involve traditional justice processes	Establish rule of law framework • Institute constitution, judicial system, legal reform • Adopt legislation • Promote human rights
Protect civilians • Establish law and order, fight criminal violence • Clear landmines • Collect small arms	Assure food security • Meet nutrition standards • Launch food production	Rehabilitate infrastructure • Roads • Housing • Power • Transportation	Establish truth • Set up truth commission • Promote forgiveness • Restore dignity of victims	Initiate political reform • Institutions • Democratic processes
Build national security institutions • Police • Military • Integrate/dissolve non-state armed elements	Ensure health security • Provide access to basic health care • Prevent spread of infectious diseases • Provide trauma and mental health care	Promote social protection • Employment • Food • Health • Education • Shelter	Announce amnesties • Immunity from prosecution for lesser crimes • Reparation for victims	Strengthen civil society • Participation • Accountability • Capacity building
Protect external security • Combat illegal weapons and drugs trade • Combat trafficking in people • Control borders	Establish emergency safety net for people at risk • Women (female- headed households); children (soldiers); elderly; indigenous people; missing people	Dismantle war economy • Fight criminal networks • Re-establish market economy • Provide micro-credit	Promote coexistence • Encourage community-based initiatives (long-term) • Rebuild social capital	Promote access to information • Independent media • Transparency

Each post-conflict recovery requires an integrated human security framework, developed in full partnership with the national and local authorities

and communities requires building social capital, nurturing the reconciliation and coexistence of divided communities, and restoring governance.

Each post-conflict recovery requires an integrated human security framework, developed in full partnership with the national and local authorities to ensure ownership and commitment to the objectives (table 4.1). The framework should incorporate the human security issues and needs identified under each of five clusters, emphasizing their relationships:

* Ensuring public safety.
* Meeting immediate humanitarian needs.
* Launching rehabilitation and reconstruction.
* Emphasizing reconciliation and coexistence.
* Promoting governance and empowerment.

To the extent possible, all relevant tools and instruments—political, military, humanitarian and developmental—should come under unified leadership, with integration close to the delivery points of assistance. The strength of the United Nations is its active involvement in country and field operations, through which it makes many of its biggest contributions. For each of the five clusters, lead actors should be identified—based on presence and comparative advantage, not just mandated responsibilities. Mandated responsibilities should be interpreted flexibly, in line with people's needs and operational necessities. And partnerships should be established for donors, other multilateral organizations (particularly the World Bank), non-governmental agencies and businesses.

Transition processes also have a deep impact on neighbouring countries and their people. Yet too often, little or no attention goes to wider regional and international dimensions. Because

many human security issues are transnational, the regional consultations on Central Asia—organized by the Commission on Human Security and held in Asghabat, Turkmenistan—underscored the need for regional cooperation.[8] In Afghanistan, Kosovo, Rwanda and elsewhere, neighbouring countries have been deeply involved in the conflict and have sought to influence the outcome. That is why it is so important that neighbouring countries be incorporated in the unified strategic framework and support it.

Ensuring public safety

After internal conflict, national authorities are seldom in a position to ensure the security of people. Public safety deteriorates frequently following conflict. While the fighting may have stopped, increased crime rates, revenge killings and reverse ethnic cleansing threaten people's safety in post-conflict situations. And the police and military authorities are often violators of human rights rather than protectors. In addition, inter-personal violence increases, in particular gender-based violence, as families and communities are torn apart and seek to come to terms with the consequences of the violence (see box 2.2 in chapter 2).

The deployment of an international or regional military force contributes significantly towards creating a secure environment (chapter 2). From a human security perspective, such engagement needs to be rethought. Peace settlements focus on the warring parties, not on public safety. The limited deployment of the International Security Assistance Force in Afghanistan to Kabul and its immediate surroundings reveals the shortcomings. A degree of security may have been

The disarmament, demobilization and reintegration into society of former combatants and their dependents are critical steps towards human security

established in the capital, but the rest of the country is largely left to fend for itself. This is detrimental to the security of people, seriously hampering humanitarian and reconstruction projects as well.

The disarmament, demobilization and reintegration into society of former combatants and their dependents are critical steps towards human security. Equally critical is the removal of small arms and light weapons and landmines from conflict areas. Without their removal, people are prevented from returning home, and fertile land is left barren. But the demobilization of armed combatants is much more than a political and military step towards peace. Economic opportunities are also required. For many combatants, soldiering is no more and no less than a lucrative job opportunity, a way to escape debilitating poverty.[9] So demobilization efforts, to be sustainable, should go beyond short-term skills training to include employment opportunities. In addition, emphasis should go to social integration, particularly for child soldiers who have received little or no education. If not, former combatants will turn to crime or join armed groups to earn their livelihood.

But these steps are not adequate for meeting the safety needs of people in post-conflict situations. First, there is a need to gradually shift the focus of international actors from ensuring military security to public safety. Second, the reform of the state security sector must be part of the rehabilitation and governance strategies.

Just after conflict, national and international authorities will focus on military security, separating armed elements, registering and demobilizing combatants, curtailing illicit arms trade, ensuring external security and assisting and protecting humanitarian relief and reconstruction efforts. As the situation stabilizes and military security is maintained, the goals should shift towards upholding public safety through fighting crime (domestic and transnational) and building the capacity of national and local police.

Building on the recommendations in the Brahimi Report, setting up a trained and well-equipped United Nations and other regional civilian standby police forces can be an important step towards enhancing public safety.[10] Crowd control, rather than military deployment or firepower, is more effective for tense situations involving civilians. By emphasizing public safety, police can prevent abuse and corruption among local law and order officials. They can also assist in rebuilding trust and legitimacy in the new national law and order institutions.

The reform, or creation, of the state security sector should be part of the ongoing effort to attain public safety. It is essential not only for wresting control from armed groups and warlords and regaining the monopoly over the legitimate use of armed force, but also for transparency, accountability and democratic control. In Afghanistan, reform of the security sector is foreseen in the Bonn Agreement of 5 December 2001. It provides for integrating all armed groups into official security forces, with the assistance of the international community, building a national army and a national police force and demobilizing civilian militia.[11] In addition to reforming the army, police and intelligence services, reform of the security sector needs to be accompanied by changes in the legal system, setting up an independent judiciary and providing services to manage prisons. Reform of the state security sector also implies

Reform of the state security sector should be seen as an integral part of any strategy to strengthen governance and development

getting the income and expenditures of the military, police and other security institutions under control, as a part of efforts to establish a transparent and accountable government, something that has so far received too little attention from donors.[12]

Effective state security institutions upholding the rule of law and human rights are an essential component for achieving human security, development and governance. They are keys to rebuilding trust and confidence in institutions and creating a climate for reducing poverty and attracting investments. Despite the growing attention to the reform of the state security sector, multilateral actors, such as the World Bank, have been reluctant to engage. They see such efforts as interfering in the internal and political affairs of a country.[13] Far from it, however: reform of the state security sector should be seen as an integral part of any strategy to strengthen governance and development.[14]

Meeting immediate humanitarian needs

When the fighting stops and humanitarian actors gain access to the people affected, the immediate requirement is to provide life-saving humanitarian assistance, in the form of food, basic health services, shelter and water and sanitation. In the 1990s, much effort went into expanding the capacity to meet people's basic needs. All major multilateral organizations and NGOs have developed an emergency capacity and can respond quickly. The closer working relationships between peacekeeping operations and humanitarian actors have contributed much to mobilizing and delivering life-saving supplies.

But assistance is often compartmentalized for different categories of people—refugees, returnees, internally displaced persons, demobilized combatants—reflecting the mandates of agencies providing assistance, not overall needs. So little or no attention goes to some groups of people, mainly internally displaced persons and affected host communities. The massive population movements immediately after the fighting ceases often make the humanitarian situation worse. Communicable diseases, such as the cholera outbreak in Katanga in the Democratic Republic of Congo in 2001, spread to other areas as people return home. New arrivals also put added pressure on food rations.

The trauma and psychosocial impact of suffering also go largely unattended.[15] Without professional assistance and traditional coping strategies, people who have undergone traumatic experiences can come to feel a profound sense of shame, hopelessness and mistrust—which can often lead to increased criminal activity and domestic and gender-based violence. In addition to psychological care and counselling, family members and communities need to be reunited, and the missing identified, located and accounted for. Such interventions can help overcome the shame over the violence, help renegotiate understanding of cultural and religious norms and ethics and contribute to coexistence and reconciliation.

In many post-conflict situations, the targets of war and persecution in turn become the victims of peace. It is the responsibility of states to create the conditions for people to return in safety and dignity. Ideally, returns following a peace settlement are voluntary, and people are able to benefit from national protection and opportunities to earn a living. But this is rarely the case. Returns often are abrupt and under pressure. At the first glimmer of peace, people are forced home against their will. Scores of refugees and internally displaced persons are made to settle elsewhere, rather than return home and start their lives again. Nearly 1 million of the 2 million Afghan returnees from refugee camps in Iran and Pakistan have settled in Kabul and other large urban areas. Such sudden and large-scale population influxes strain meagre humanitarian resources and increase tensions.

In post-conflict situations more attention should also go to children and youth, who tend to be forgotten or ignored. In Sierra Leone and the Occupied Palestinian Territories a whole generation of youths knows only violence. If they are to rebuild their community, society and country, investments need to be made in their education, skills, employment and health. But concerted efforts are also needed at the international level.

Launching rehabilitation and reconstruction
The huge economic cost of violent conflict needs to be factored into the reconstruction agenda. In Africa, there is a 2% loss of annual economic growth across the continent as a consequence of violent conflict.[16] In some countries, as much as 40–75% of fiscal and foreign exchange earnings are diverted to fighting a war.[17] Since September 2002, the number of poor in the Occupied Palestinian Territories has tripled to nearly 2 million, or 60% of the population.[18] Unemployment has soared to 53% of the workforce. Despite the desperate situation, the economy continues to function, in part because key essential services and wages are still provided by the authorities—creating a safety net.

During and immediately after conflict, rehabilitation and reconstruction efforts should

focus on providing key services, rebuilding basic infrastructure, reintegrating displaced people and demobilized combatants and establishing a social safety net as well as a macroeconomic framework. Such steps permit people to become independent of humanitarian relief. There is growing realization that launching rehabilitation and reconstruction as soon as possible, even when conflict is still ongoing, can be a major incentive for peace. Relief and development activities should work in parallel, with relief gradually phasing out. This calls for much quicker mobilization of reconstruction and development resources and implementation of activities than under the long time frames now required.

Among the key issues is the reintegration of people affected by the conflict, particularly returning refugees and internally displaced persons. Their needs are not systematically incorporated in rehabilitation and reconstruction strategies or development planning (chapter 3). So returning refugees and internally displaced persons pose a large burden, especially in urban centres where they tend to overstretch essential services and assistance and may give rise to higher crime rates. But if the return is properly managed, refugees and internally displaced persons can become an asset in the recovery from conflict rather than a burden.

To overcome these shortcomings, multi-actor programmes should be established, integrating repatriation, reintegration, rehabilitation and reconstruction activities.[19] This requires rethinking current working arrangements, such as the compartmentalizing of activities along human-itarian or development lines, and refocusing attention from relief and development actors to national authorities and communities. A people-

Each situation is unique and each society has different ways of achieving justice and reconciling differences

centred strategy views returning refugees and internally displaced persons as resources, not victims. By emphasizing the economic potential of formerly displaced persons and their role in reconstructing, reconciling and governing their country, such an approach makes the reintegration of formerly displaced persons in communities and societies as a whole more feasible.

Land and agricultural reforms are receiving renewed attention in response to pressure from social movements in Colombia, Indonesia, Mexico, the Philippines, South Africa and Zimbabwe.[20] In Rwanda, inheritance and property laws were amended so that women could own the land and property of their husbands killed in the genocide. This has promoted greater gender equality—and prevented countless women and their families from becoming destitute. It has also contributed to food security.

Bringing the conflict economy under control in the immediate post-conflict transition is essential. Conflict expenditures contribute to massive macroeconomic problems. First, there is usually an unsustainable debt burden. Of 49 heavily indebted poor countries, 13 were affected by conflict in 2001.[21] High interest payments siphon off funds that should go to social spending. Second, there is a tendency to put macroeconomic policy reforms above social reforms, especially social protection objectives, to stabilize economies. Third, this trade-off usually results in declines in education, health, social and infrastructure spending just when people can least bear the social and human costs. Stringent fiscal and economic adjustments during transitions create setbacks for the most vulnerable. The situation is often made worse by criminal networks illegally trading in

natural resources and corrupt officials siphoning off aid monies.

Emphasizing reconciliation and coexistence

Conflict erodes trust in people, communities and government institutions, undermining social cohesion. If these effects are ignored, the result can be radicalized identity politics, manipulation and grievances—which in turn can lead to renewed violence, human rights abuses and conflict.

The relationship between justice and peace is thorny and complex. But more "justice" does not necessarily lead to more "peace". Today nearly every peace agreement and post-conflict programme includes references to justice and reconciliation, seen as integral to peace-building and governance. But between vengeance and forgiveness lie a broad range of options for coming to terms with the past and building trust.[22] Each situation is unique, however, and each society has different ways of achieving justice and reconciling differences.

Justice and reconciliation programmes in post-conflict situations centre on two strategies. The first, relating to the events that occurred in the conflict phase, focuses on establishing the truth of what has happened, upholding justice for the victims and punishing the perpetrators. The second focuses on establishing the rule of law, developing a human rights regime and strengthening judicial systems. In most transitions from conflict to peace, a combination of the two strategies is in place.

Truth and reconciliation commissions have been set up in Argentina, Chad, Chile, El Salvador, Guatemala, South Africa, Sierra Leone and Timor-Leste. Amnesty legislation—or immunity from prosecution for all or lesser perpetrators of human rights abuses—has been adopted in Chile, Greece, Rwanda, South Africa and Uruguay. International criminal tribunals have been created for Rwanda and the former Yugoslavia. Reparations and compensation have been paid in Germany, Switzerland and Timor-Leste. Common to these processes is the need to:

- Acknowledge and come to terms with what has happened.
- Promote healing and restoration of the dignity of victims as well as communities.
- Punish perpetrators for their crime through confession of guilt, public shame or prosecution.

These are important steps towards peace-building and reconciliation, with great symbolic value. But to be successful and effective requires:

- *Time and commitment.* Neither justice nor reconciliation can be served within short time frames. They require sustained commitment throughout the process.
- *Strong and effective institutions.* To carry out justice, a strong and independent legal system is essential. And institutions must be able to reach out to all people to foster reconciliation.
- *Participation and an agreed framework.* Ownership and legitimacy necessitate people's participation and consultation in designing the process and the objectives.

In countries emerging from conflict, the requirements for an effective justice and reconciliation strategy are seldom present. Institutions are weak or non-existent. Few mechanisms exist to effectively involve people in public policy debates. No effective legal framework functions to administer justice. And justice and reconciliation efforts are often imposed and led by outsiders.

From a human security perspective, a community-centred approach involving as many people as possible is essential to complement the institution-driven justice and reconciliation processes. The challenge is to make sustainable reintegration of people into their communities a realistic option. But this requires a minimal degree of trust and confidence. A first priority is to recognize the legitimacy and dignity of the victims of the conflict and to enable former enemies to interact, even at a minimal level. Restoring trust requires a space for dialogue among people and communities. Encouraging joint activities among the divided communities, through income generation activities and the provision of essential services, can create that space.

Compared with the justice and reconciliation objectives, the goals of coexistence are modest: they focus on creating a dialogue among communities (box 4.2). By engaging in parallel activities, members of conflicting groups build a greater sense of security and respect for others. Through the gradual recognition of increasing economic opportunity and human security, members of different groups can again come to accept one another as participants in society and as interdependent actors. They can begin to imagine themselves living together in peace. In this sense, coexistence bridges vengeance and reconciliation.

Promoting governance and empowerment

The UN Secretary-General has asserted that "good governance at the local, national and international levels is perhaps the single most important factor in promoting development and advancing the cause of peace".[23] The key issue is how to establish a democratic political order, buttressed by social

Box 4.2 "Imagine Coexistence" projects in Rwanda and Bosnia

"Imagine Coexistence" grew out the efforts to integrate returning refugees and internally displaced persons into their communities. Except for a meagre food ration and some household utensils, little attention had been given to their effective and sustainable reintegration, thought to be the responsibility of national government actors as part of their "protection" function. Incidents of reverse ethnic cleansing and increasing violence and crime brought to the foreground the need to promote community-based reconciliation strategies.

In 2000, recognizing that reconciliation is a distant goal and that people first need to learn to "coexist" with each other again, the UN High Commissioner for Refugees launched pilot projects in Bosnia and Herzegovina and Rwanda, funded through the UN Trust Fund for Human Security. The objective was to assess the factors contributing to coexistence between divided communities and to devise strategies for promoting the coexistence dimension in humanitarian projects.

Bosnia and Herzegovina

The coexistence projects are implemented through Genesis, a local non-governmental agency that focuses on community needs. The projects concentrate on income generating activities, arts and vocational training. The projects reveal links between coexistence and restitution and compensation for property lost. Tensions and distrust increased if the divisions among the communities were ignored or if the perception existed that one group was favoured over another. Some local authorities opposed the introduction of coexistence projects, demonstrating the importance of including local authorities in the design as well as the implementation of coexistence projects. Participants felt that the coexistence framework adds an important qualitative dimension to humanitarian and development assistance: a smooth transition from relief to development, preventing further conflict, requires not only a community-based approach, but also involvement of people from different communities.

Rwanda

The projects are developed at the community level and revolve around an economic activity. The projects are implemented through Oxfam (UK) and the Norwegian People's Aid, which in turn operates with grass-roots associations such as Equipes de Vie, which works with groups of widows and women whose husbands are imprisoned on charges of genocide. Considerable attention is given to creating a local network, which meets regularly with government officials and representatives of multilateral organizations and donor governments. Training in peace education and conflict resolution has been included.

At a regional meeting on coexistence, conflict resolution and human security, participants expressed the belief that projects aimed at promoting coexistence require long-term commitment and need to be integrated into rehabilitation- and development-oriented strategies. Particular attention was drawn to the role of women in bringing communities together, because they tend to be more outspoken and challenge official policies that diminish the human security of the family and community. Finally, participants argued that there was tension between the government's emphasis on reconciliation and national unity and people's need to discuss ethnic issues in order to come to terms with the past.

and economic growth. The process leading to a democratic system is fraught with risks and potential reversals as competing social, political and economic forces vie for control and power. The (short-term) shortfall of policy frameworks, institutional systems and personnel capacity further compound the problems by being unable to contain and prevent grievances.

Among the key governance issues are democratization, participation in decision-making, accountability of decision-makers, respect for the rule of law and human rights, and inclusive, equitable and fair rules and institutions. Governance issues are closely linked to the empowerment of people and communities. Without effective governance, people are not empowered. And unless people and communities are empowered to let their voices be heard or to participate in decision-making, governance is not feasible.

Nearly all peace settlements address governance to varying degrees, but the focus has too often been on short-term stability rather than long-term sustainability. Holding elections and establishing a "legitimate democratic" regime become part of the exit strategy for international actors, rather than a realistic measure of good governance.[24] The organization of elections is often the objective—rather than a tool for accountability, participation and good governance.[25] Numerous internationally negotiated peace settlements have broken down because of ill-designed democratic institutions, processes and power-sharing arrangements in deeply divided communities. Rather than prevent conflict, such arrangements can fuel tensions if they are perceived as solidifying existing imbalances and inequities along identity lines. That is why many post-conflict countries

have had difficulty consolidating gains and furthering the democratic process.

A top priority: establishing institutions that protect people and uphold the rule of law. To meet the responsibility to protect people, a state must have functioning institutions. In turn, institutions require rules and regulations to operate justly and effectively. This requires promoting the rule of law, to ensure basic rights and freedoms, which in turn form the basis for democratic governance. Given the centrality of the rule of law in the recovery from conflict, both for political governance and for social and economic growth, growing attention is being given to developing specific assistance programmes.

For the first time in 2002, the experiences gained in the various peace operations and in developing comprehensive rule-of-law strategies have been pulled together.[26] Establishing the rule of law requires more than drafting a constitution and laws and establishing courts and a judicial system. Most important to include are the norms, principles and practices that establish relations among people and between people and the state. Therefore, establishing or re-establishing the rule of law does not simply imply copying laws and institutions from abroad. Considerable efforts are required to involve people in the process and to be aware of how they understand, use and value law and its institutions.[27]

Few international actors have the capacity to rapidly deploy civilian law experts, to contribute towards national legislation, institutions and procedures for strengthening the rule of law. Capacity in these areas should be strengthened. Ultimately, good governance depends on people and communities, and this may not come

Greater coherence is required in planning, budgeting and resource mobilization for countries emerging from conflict

spontaneously to them, especially if they have no positive experiences with participation in public life. So civic education should increase people's ownership of the norms, processes and institutions that are fundamental to democratic and well-governed communities and states.

A vibrant civil society provides a mechanism for people to participate, express their views and hold decision-makers accountable. Post-conflict strategies should aim at strengthening civil society by encouraging participation and capacity building, particularly for women's groups, because women face limited participation in formal peace processes and implementation of post-conflict transition strategies. This will also help ensure that gender equality is incorporated in legislative reforms. The accountability and transparency of civil society groups also need to be enhanced—through codes of conduct and a legal framework stipulating rights and obligations.

A new resource mobilization strategy

Pledges of aid help to consolidate peace agreements. The legitimacy and credibility of new leaders often depend on their ability to deliver peace dividends. In practice, it takes too long to translate pledges into commitments and actual disbursements that can be spent flexibly. In many instances, the pledges do not mean additional money, just a repackaging or redirecting of existing funds, to the detriment of people in other countries. Some situations attract considerable funding, others little. Compassion fatigue and donor fatigue set in quickly, especially in the face of sudden downturns (see box 2.3 in chapter 2). In 2002, 16 of the 25 consolidated appeals for humanitarian assistance received less than half of

the requirements, often reflecting strategic, political and economic interests of donors.[28]

Greater coherence is required in planning, budgeting and resource mobilization for countries emerging from conflict.[29] As long as the myriad fund mobilization mechanisms continue to operate in parallel—and resist close coordination and information sharing—the gaps in responses will not be overcome (see box 4.2). There are good examples of improving the process, such as the 1994 Johan Jørgen Holst Peace Fund for channelling donor support for the day to day activities of the Palestinian National Authority. But donors are reluctant to relinquish their prerogative to select and fund projects that receive high levels of domestic support. At the bilateral level, gradual steps are being taken towards more flexible funding mechanisms, exemplified by the transitional budget lines adopted by Denmark and Norway, Japan's Peace Building Grant Aid and the European Union's Linking Relief, Rehabilitation and Development.

A transition fund focusing on human security should be set up for each post-conflict situation. The fund would finance the activities agreed to under the integrated human security framework, pooling resources for human security-related activities. That would enable financing a broader range of human security issues than is done today, with more attention to activities that are chronically underfunded, such as education, reconciliation and coexistence, reform of the state security sector and the reintegration of internally displaced persons. To allow flexible disbursement, the funds should not be earmarked.

To maintain the confidence of participating donors and beneficiaries, management of such funds should emphasize transparency and accountability.

Participation by national authorities is essential for setting priorities and gaining ownership of the process. To the extent possible, other parties to conflict should be included, to ensure the equitably sharing of the benefits of peace.

Policy conclusions

Implementing a human security approach in post-conflict transition requires significant changes in the way donors, multilateral agencies, non-governmental organizations and national authorities pursue their goals—at both micro and macro levels. For human security, peace and development to be achieved, the multiple gaps in the present strategies need to be overcome:

- All actors should recognize the responsibility to rebuild in post-conflict situations.
- People's safety should be assured by focusing on public safety.
- Life-saving humanitarian assistance should be provided, safety nets set up for people most at risk and rehabilitation and reconstruction activities launched to rebuild infrastructure and create the conditions for economic activities to take off.
- Conditions for democratic governance need to be created by empowering people, emphasizing reconciliation, coexistence and rule of law.
- The international community should develop a human security framework and set up a human security transition fund for each recovery from post-conflict, in full partnership with national actors.

Notes

1. "World Bank Study Says 50-50 Chance of Failure," *The Washington Post,* 26 November 2002.
2. Chapter 5 discusses the protection of people following an economic downturn and natural disasters.
3. ICISS 2001, pp. 39–46.
4. Ogata 2003.
5. Drèze and Sen 1989.
6. OECD 2001.
7. Ogata and Wolfensohn 1999.
8. www.humansecurity-chs.org
9. Sen 2001.
10. United Nations 2000.
11. In post-conflict Afghanistan, France and the United States are responsible for rebuilding the national army. Germany is training the police. The United Kingdom is overseeing the anti-narcotics trade. Japan is leading the demobilization and registration of former combatants.
12. Bal 2002.
13. Coletta 2002.
14. UNDP 2002, pp. 83–100.
15. Leaning, Arie and Holleufer 2002.
16. DFID, 2001.
17. Green, 1994, p. 48.
18. World Bank 2003.
19. Also known as the 4Rs. UNHCR has launched an initiative, in cooperation with United Nations Development Programme and the World Bank, towards overcoming the gaps between relief and development. Pilot projects are underway in Afghanistan, Eritrea, Sierra Leone and Sri Lanka.
20. FAO 2002.
21. DFID 2001.
22. Minow 1998.
23. United Nations, General Assembly 2002, p. 11.
24. Dennis McNamara, "The UN has been learning how it's done." Op-Ed, *International Herald Tribune,* 29 October 2002.

25. Paddy Ashdown, "What I Learned in Bosnia." Op-Ed, *New York Times,* October 28, 2002.
26. An interdepartmental task force was established in April 2002 by the Committee on Peace and Security following a recommendation of the Department of Peacekeeping Operations.
27. Carothers 2003.
28. United Nations 2002.
29. United Nations, General Assembly 2002.

References

Ball, Nicole. 2002. "Human Security and Human Development: Linkages and Opportunities." Report of a conference organized by the Programme for Strategic and International Studies, Graduate Institute of International Studies, 8–9 March 2001, Geneva.

DFID (Department for International Development, UK). 2001. "The Causes of Conflict in Africa." Consultation document by the Cabinet Sub-Committee on Conflict Prevention in Africa. London.

Minow, Martha. 1998. *Between Vengeance and Forgiveness: Facing History after Genocide and Mass Violence.* Boston: Beacon Press.

Coletta, Nat J. 2002. "Conflict, Human Security and Poverty: Implications for IFI Reform." Paper prepared for the Commission on Human Security. [www.humansecurity-chs.org].

Drèze, Jean, and Amartya Sen. 1989. *Hunger and Public Action.* Oxford: Clarendon Press.

FAO (Food and Agriculture Organization). 2002. *The State of Food Security in the World 2002.* Rome.

ICISS (International Commission on Intervention and State Sovereignty). 2001. *The Responsibility to Protect.* Ottawa: International Development Research Center.

Leaning, Jennifer, Sam Arie and Gilber Holleufer. 2002. "Conflict and Human Security." Paper prepared for the Commission on Human Security. [www.humansecurity-chs.org].

OECD (Organisation for Economic Co-operation and Development). 2001. *Helping Prevent Violent Conflict.* DAC Guidelines. Paris.

Ogata, Sadako. 2003. "Building Peace: The Lessons of Afghanistan." *Global Agenda.* Davos, Switzerland: World Economic Forum [www.globalagendamagazine.com/].

Ogata, Sadako, and James D. Wolfensohn. 1999. "The Transition to Peace in War-Torn Societies: Some Personal Observations." Brookings Institution Round Table on the Gap between Humanitarian Assistance and Long-Term Development, Washington, D.C., 15 January.

Sen Amartya. 2002. "Global Inequality and Persistent Conflicts." Paper presented at the Nobel Awards Conference, Oslo, 6 December, 2001.

UNDP (United Nations Development Programme). 2000. *Human Development Report 2000: Human Rights and Human Development.* New York: Oxford University Press.

United Nations. 2000. *Report of the Panel on United Nations Peace Operations.* S/2000/809. New York.

United Nations, General Assembly. 2002. *Strengthening of the United Nations: An Agenda for Further Change: Report of the Secretary-General.* A/57/387. New York.

World Bank. 2003. *Two Years of Intifada, Closures and Palestinian Economic Crisis.* Washington, D.C.

Economic security—
the power to choose
among opportunities

5

Human security at its core requires a set of vital freedoms for everyone

A fifth of the world's people—1.2 billion—experience severe income poverty and live on less than $1 a day, nearly two-thirds of them in Asia and a quarter in Africa. Another 1.6 billion live on less than $2 a day. Together, 2.8 billion of the world's people live in a chronic state of poverty and daily insecurity, a number that has not changed much since 1990.[1] About 800 million people in the developing world and 24 million in developed and transition economies do not have enough to eat.[2]

Economic and financial crises reduce average wages and consumption, and poor people, especially the very poorest, feel the worst of the impact. Annually throughout the 1990s, natural disasters took the lives of some 80,000 people, affected 200 million people and cost an average of $63 billion.[3] The attacks of 11 September 2001 deepened the global economic downturn, with 10.5 million people in the travel and tourism industry alone losing their jobs.[4]

Poverty and human security

When people's livelihoods are deeply compromised—when people are uncertain where the next meal will come from, when their life savings suddenly plummet in value, when their crops fail and they have no savings—human security contracts. People eat less and some starve. They pull their children out of school. They cannot afford clothing, heating or health care. Repeated crises further increase the vulnerability of people in absolute or extreme poverty (box 5.1).

But vulnerability and insecurity are experienced not only by people who live in extreme poverty. There are also people who have jobs and yet cannot afford essential prescription medicines, or safe living conditions, or school uniforms, lunches and transport costs to send their children to school. And people who have no means to replace earnings when disaster hits.

Thus people's human security is only partly produced by improving individual and household ability to generate and marshal resources.[5] That is why human security at its core requires a set of vital freedoms for everyone, to prevent those who are income-poor or unable to grasp opportunities to develop their capabilities from going to the wall when crises hit. Besides basic income and resources, the freedoms to enjoy basic health, basic education, shelter, physical safety, and access to clean water and clean air are vitally important. Access to these basic resources and opportunities—to what might be called a social minimum—can be provided by negotiated arrangements by the state, political parties, public and private interest groups and many other social actors, operating at community, national and global levels.[6]

Adopting a human security approach

Three situations of economic insecurity regularly impair human security: insufficient economic resources, unstable economic flows and asset losses. An ability to save or invest or access resources is also instrumental to human security. People further their own security by setting aside savings and investing in physical, financial and human assets (a savings account, health insurance or education).

Three kinds of crises—economic (including financial crises, debt crises, terms of trade crises), natural disasters, and conflict—inflict the greatest shocks on society and people's human security.[7] Economic downturns seem inescapable. Disasters are increasing.[8] And conflicts continue.

Box 5.1 The challenge of extreme poverty

At times considered part of the social order, poverty was believed to be an inevitable evil associated with the human condition. Theories for eradicating poverty have abounded, from those of utopian visionaries such as Thomas More to others in more recent times. Society has responded through various institutional measures for alleviating poverty. The Millennium Development Goals, recently adopted by the United Nations, place the fight against poverty among the top priorities of the international community. It is unconscionable to think of human security while ignoring the problem of poverty.

In pre-modern societies, assistance to the poor was provided through local communities—by corporate associations, by religious communities, by the warm responses of human beings towards those who found themselves in distress. These forms of solidarity were effective in stable situations, when the incidence of poverty did not reach dramatic levels. However, during recurrent crises, such community-based activities can do very little to alleviate the suffering of the pauperized masses, defenseless against starvation and epidemics. Modern societies prohibited begging and isolated the poor in forced labour institutions. Faced with the magnitude of poverty, and driven by fear, organized society resorted to repression and exclusion, without being able to resolve the problem.

These social concerns and attendant reflection led to the emergence of modern-day social sciences and social policies. As early as the late 18th century, Jacques Necker, the Swiss-born finance adviser to the French king, developed the idea that assistance to the poor is not only the expression of good intentions, but also a political imperative for maintaining order. Thus, the fight against poverty appeared as a part of security in its national dimension as well as in its global one.

Discrepancies in the material situation of individuals and even differences in development or prosperity levels need not always be considered within the framework of security, however. Economic growth, social solidarity policies and social assistance must also provide answers to these social challenges. But it is extreme poverty that creates the most dramatic threats in today's societies.

Extreme poverty concerns all—individuals, families, groups—who subsist in a state of utter deprivation, without enough to eat and or a roof above their heads. It is not possible to measure extreme poverty only in income terms, since the poverty level also depends on the economic and social context. In Sub-Saharan Africa, death by starvation or malnutrition is at the horizon of everyday life, a threat that erodes the social fabric. In developed countries, continuous unemployment means not only loss of income but also a sense of total failure and exclusion from society. These groups of *laissés pour compte,* called the "Fourth World" in Europe, focus attention on the need for inclusionary social policies, not only for relief and temporary assistance.

It has rightly been said that poverty does not necessarily generate terrorism, since terrorists also come from among the privileged. It is nevertheless true that terrorism takes advantage of misery, knowing that despair creates favourable conditions for terrorist projects and actions.

Human security policies must consider the fight against poverty as a major challenge for the international community. It is imperative to develop global strategies supporting growth and sustainable development while at the same time implementing policies of economic development and social protection at the national level. Among these, the financing of micro-projects among the poor, as in Bangladesh and elsewhere, has proved its worth.

Bronislaw Geremek

Promoting basic economic security, by reducing poverty and raising living standards, can have substantial social impact

Promoting basic economic security, by reducing poverty and raising living standards, can have substantial social impact. Economic security and the development of social capabilities reinforce each other. An extensive body of literature and policy experience already exists on these issues. This chapter identifies four priorities for policy action to promote human security:

- Encouraging growth that reaches the extreme poor.
- Supporting sustainable livelihoods and decent work.
- Preventing and containing the effects of economic crises and natural disasters.
- Providing social protection for all situations.

Encouraging growth that reaches the extreme poor

Economic growth is essential for reducing income poverty. Projections estimate that it might be possible to achieve the Millennium Development Goal of halving the proportion of people who live on less than $1 a day (from 29% in 1990 to 14.5% in 2015) if growth in average per capita income averages 3.6% a year. But this is nearly twice the average growth rate achieved over the past decade—an average that hides the spectacular success of China and the failed growth in 70 countries.[9]

Markets and trade are basic to economic growth and have been a source of unprecedented wealth for some. Market systems can also widen people's ability to choose and act on their own behalf. While some defend market economies and others criticize them, extensive use of markets will be required to generate the kinds of growth and human security measures that an expanding human population needs. The central issue from a human security perspective is not whether to use markets. It is how to support the range of diverse institutions that ensure that markets enhance people's freedom and human security as effectively and equitably as possible—and that complement the market by providing core freedoms that the market cannot directly supply (see box 5.2).

Identifying the balance of institutions, policies and processes necessary for poverty-reducing growth has become somewhat of an international preoccupation. The poverty reduction strategy papers and comprehensive development frameworks of multilateral agencies and the donor community—and the combined effects of the United Nations Development Programme, World Bank, International Monetary Fund (IMF) and other international economic agencies and regional development banks—tend to emphasize these issues. Some advances have been made in understanding what is required, particularly in understanding the dynamic role that poor communities themselves can play in promoting, sustaining and benefiting from growth.

Addressing distributional issues. Human security is improved if the poor benefit from a greater share in the wealth and income generated by economic growth, as in Taiwan and the Republic of Korea. Also, the overall increase in national prosperity can help finance public services, including health care and education. But the fruits of growth certainly do not always expand social services or promote the protection and empowerment of people throughout a society. For example, "based on existing income distribution patterns, Brazil has to grow at three times the rate of Vietnam to achieve

Box 5.2 The market economy, non-market institutions and human security

Globalization has much to offer, but even as we defend it, we must also see the legitimacy of many of the questions that anti-globalization protesters ask. Can the deal that different groups get from globalized economic and social relations be changed? Can this be done without undermining market relations and without destroying the global market economy? There is evidence to argue that the answer is "yes".

It is hard to achieve economic prosperity without making extensive use of the opportunities of exchange and specialization that market relations offer. Although the operation of the market economy can be significantly defective—and that must be taken into account in making public policy—there is no way of dispensing with markets as an engine of economic progress (see, for example, Akerlof 1970; Spence 1973; Stiglitz 1985).

Recognition of the significance of the market economy does not end the discussion about globalized market relations; it only begins it. Market economies can have many different ownership patterns, resource availabilities, social opportunities and rules of operation (patent laws, anti-trust regulation). Depending on these enabling conditions, a market economy would generate different prices, terms of trades, income distributions and overall outcomes. The arrangements for social security, social protection and other public interventions can also alter the outcomes of market processes. All of these enabling conditions depend critically on economic, social and political institutions that operate nationally and globally. As amply established in empirical studies, the nature of market outcomes is strongly influenced by public policies in education, health care, social protection measures, land reform, microcredit facilities and appropriate legal protections. It is the combined use of markets and non-market institutions that offers the best prospects for less global inequality and more human security.

Source: Adapted from Sen 2002.

the same average income increase in the poorest one-fifth of the population. Similarly, Mexico would have to grow at almost twice the rate of Indonesia or Uganda to achieve a similar increase".[10] The initial distribution of resources—including human capital as well as economic resources—matters a great deal. Political processes and decisions need to address distributional issues in order to address persistent levels of inequality. The inequality of distribution across the globe also needs to be addressed (see box 5.3).

Reducing developed country trade barriers. Protectionist barriers in many developed countries block developing country access to markets that could help them generate productive growth and increased employment, exports and other opportunities for poor people (box 5.4). For example, in the agriculture and textile sectors, farmers and garment workers from developing countries face import barriers that are four times as high as those faced by producers in rich countries, making it difficult for their exports to compete. Average tariffs in countries of the Organisation for Economic Co-operation and Development on

agricultural goods and textiles, the predominant exports of developing countries, are higher than those in such sectors as cars and machine tools. Trade restrictions in rich countries are estimated to cost developing countries around $100 billion a year—several times what they receive in official aid.[11] Opening up agricultural and textile markets by removing such protectionism would benefit the poorest countries most.

Developing governance and policies that empower. Distributional and trade issues aside, policy choices also affect how equitable growth will be. For example, the Republic of Korea did much better in channelling resources to education and health care than Brazil did in the 1960s and 1970s, despite Brazil's significant economic growth at the time. This helped Korea achieve more equitable growth. Equitable development outcomes are fostered by the "human capital" that educational systems generate, the initial distribution and redistribution of assets and income, the availability of microcredit and legal protections, the extent of corruption and rule of law and the power of people's movements to engage in social dialogue in support of the poorest.

Box 5.3 The importance of foreign direct investment

The spectacular increase in direct investment in developing countries by companies in high-income countries in recent decades offers one of the most important mechanisms for a fairer distribution of opportunity around the world.

Direct investment offers a lifeline connecting emerging economies to world markets. It is almost impossible to envisage how a poor country lacking the technology, management know-how and access to markets could start from scratch in any industry today. To develop a diverse range of high-value industries and services that will create and spread prosperity, such countries need the catalyst of finance and expertise from outside their borders.

The financial crises of the late 1990s tarnished the appeal of cross-border investment. But direct investment has in fact proven relatively stable, in contrast to portfolio investments in financial markets. Although the total flow of foreign direct investment to developing countries has declined from its peak of about $150 billion a year during the 1990s because of the world economic slowdown, this was much less than the plunge in bank lending and portfolio investment in shares and bonds in recent years (World Bank 2002; IMF 2002).

Private business investment dwarfs the scale of official aid flows to poor countries. It is also, by definition, a productive transfer of funds. Business is about wealth creation, growing capital and paying dividends to shareholders. But this is not the only wealth it creates, nor are the shareholders the only beneficiaries. Multinational investors generate value in producing and distributing higher value products that local businesses and consumers need, as well as generating export earnings by serving markets overseas.

Successful businesses, whoever owns them, create wealth for the immediate community in other ways, through the extra jobs generated, and the salaries and benefits paid to employees. These wages help generate additional purchases and jobs, multiplying the beneficial impact on the local economy. Investment by multinational corporations also tends to improve pay and working conditions and to introduce cleaner and more energy-efficient technologies. It can also transfer technology and build markets for local businesses. And the taxes collected and paid by multinational corporations help fund public services.

Investment by multinational firms has nevertheless sometimes been criticized for a variety of reasons. And there have been some cases of abuse. But emotional attacks on foreign direct investment threaten to damage the prospects for economic prosperity and security for people living in poor countries. Of course, companies must ensure that they have a robust corporate governance framework wherever they operate. But the evidence stacks up decisively in favour of the benefits of foreign direct investment for the host country (Klein, Aaron and Hadjimichael 2003).

These benefits mean that there is a challenge in ensuring that foreign direct investment in future is not concentrated on just a handful of countries, as it has been in the past. Most foreign direct investment still flows between the rich economies. Of the minority share flowing to developing countries, China, along with some East Asian and Latin American nations, has benefited the most. Just 10 countries accounted for more than half of all foreign direct investment inflows to developing countries through the 1990s, and 20 countries for almost three-quarters (UNCTAD). China alone attracted almost half the total in 2002, and about a quarter through the 1990s. The countries that have received the most foreign investment have also enjoyed the fastest growth in trade and GDP and the biggest declines in poverty.

As this contrast suggests, countries that could benefit enormously from foreign investment need to become more attractive places to do business. The reasons some of them fare badly in attracting investors vary, but include over-regulation, corruption, weak legal systems and political instability. In this way, the different sources of human insecurity in such countries reinforce each other, at great cost to their people.

Peter Sutherland

Economic security—the power to choose among opportunities

Box 5.4 Trade and protection

International trade is a crucial tool for development. But the reality facing the poor countries of the world is that rich countries still maintain high barriers against their exports. A poor person in a developing country trying to sell goods and services in global markets faces barriers twice as high as the typical worker in an industrial country. A recent study has estimated that full elimination of agricultural protection and production subsidies in rich countries would increase annual rural income in low- and middle-income countries by about $60 billion, or 6 percent—more than worldwide aid. The recent Farm Bill in the United States and the European Union's decision to postpone reform of the Common Agricultural Policy show an unwillingness to address this injustice.

In a world where more than 2 billion people live on less than $2 a day, European cattle farmers receive an average of $2.50 a day per cow in subsidies. U.S. subsidies to cotton growers will total $3.9 billion this year, three times U.S. foreign aid to Africa. And it is poor farmers in North and West Africa, for whom cotton is the main cash crop, who will be hit hardest. Tariffs and quotas for textile imports to rich countries cost developing countries an estimated 27 million jobs.

Most perversely, it is often the higher value-added goods that face the highest barriers. A Chilean tomato exporter faces a U.S. tariff of 2.2% on exports of fresh tomatoes. But the tariff rises to 8.7% if producers dry and pack the tomatoes and to 11.6% if they process the tomatoes into sauce. This additional tax hampers efforts to move into higher value-added activities that would pay better wages and improve the economic security of workers. Such policies indicate the chasm between rich countries' rhetoric on trade liberalization and their actions, with far-reaching impacts on the livelihoods, incomes and dignity of poor people in the least developed countries.

Source: World Bank 2002a, 2003, Stern 2002.

In sum, crucial to healthy and sustainable growth is the mix of policies that support productivity, employment creation, enterprise and human resource development.

The development process in East and Southeast Asia shows what countries need to do to promote growth with human development:

- First, there has to be an emphasis on basic education as a prime mover of change.
- Second, wide dissemination of basic economic entitlements (through education and training, land reform, credit) broadens access to the opportunities offered by the market economy.
- Third, state action has to be judiciously combined with the use of the market economy.
- Fourth, a wide range of institutional interventions is required to enhance capabilities, promote social opportunities and support market arrangements.[12]

The capacity of states to promote governance that empowers people and to manage processes of economic globalization largely depends on changes to the institutional architecture for legal, educational, health, political, protective and judicial systems. The Bretton Woods institutions and United Nations system set up after World War II have made major progress in strengthening market economies. In the 21st century, corresponding energy must be devoted to cultivating "non-market" institutions to ensure human security within the market economy and to protect people during downturns and other crises. When people experience repeated crises and unpreventable disasters that cause them to fall—whether from extreme poverty, personal injury or bankruptcy, or society-wide shocks or disasters—the human security perspective is that there should be hands to catch them.

Supporting sustainable livelihoods and decent work

Most people build or lose their economic security in the workplace—whether a factory or farm or financial centre or in the public sector or the service sector. In some instances, workers unions empower people to represent their needs to management and thus to protect their human security. In other instances, long-term firm loyalty and relationships provide some security. Changes in the global economy have altered production and

Women have less time to engage in activities that can generate income or enable them to overcome their marginalization

work patterns. Some trends have had a significant impact on the availability of jobs, especially for low-skill level workers, such as a growing informal sector[13] and increasing female participation in the work force. Cutting across these trends are the needs to deal with environmental factors, address gender asymmetries in livelihoods and support microcredit initiatives to enable poor people to participate in economic activity.

Informalization of the labour force. With an estimated 400 million new entrants in the labour market and an existing pool of unemployed and under-employed people, more than a billion jobs need to be created by 2010,[14] 60% of them in Asia. Indeed, given structural conditions, the skill pool and numbers of new job entrants in developing economies, employment in the formal sector may cease to be the norm anywhere—in developed and developing countries.

Recent trends in Latin America also indicate that significant growth in the labour force resulted in more self-employment. Self-employment plays a particularly strong role in Bolivia, where half the work force is self-employed. Substantial growth in self-employment also occurred in Colombia, rising from 32% to 39% of the labour force.

Developing livelihoods outside typical formal arrangements must involve creative ways of securing both income and meaningful work that build on the capacity and ingenuity of poor people themselves. Critical aspects to be addressed include access to land, credit, training and education.

The International Labour Organization's goal to promote "opportunities for women and men to obtain decent and productive work, in conditions of freedom, equity, security and human dignity" is

directed to "all workers", irrespective of their sectors and whether they are waged or unwaged, home workers, or regulated, unregulated or self-regulated.[15] Taking such a comprehensive approach ensures that different parts of the working population "whose fortunes do not always move together" are not neglected in the process of furthering the interests and demands of other groups.[16]

But working conditions and job-related benefits—such as pensions, health insurance and minimum wages—are only part of the problem. The insecurities of many self-employed rural workers are compounded by other conditions, such as environmental degradation and a lack of access to credit. Women's livelihoods merit particular attention.

The environment and livelihood insecurity. Many poor people have to depend on their local environment for their survival. Some 1.3 billion people live on marginal lands. Particularly for those who live in rural areas, economic security is intimately connected to the natural environment. People in rural areas rely on forests for fuel and on agriculture for subsistence. In Sub-Saharan Africa and Asia, 75% of the poor live in rural areas.[17] Most are heavily reliant on common lands for necessities such as wood for fuel and fodder. In some states in India, the poor obtain 66–84% of their fodder from common lands.[18] When these resources are degraded, the effect is direct and immediate: poor families are forced to migrate to ever more marginal lands, household income falls as non-timber forest products become depleted, and human security plunges.

Women suffer the effects of environmental degradation even more acutely since they are forced to walk further and further to collect wood and water. As a result, they have less time to engage in activities that can generate income or enable them to overcome their marginalization. Time taken up in the struggles to survive places further limits on their limited resources and energy to participate in household and community decision-making processes.

Microcredit: supporting the livelihoods of poor people. The *State of the Microcredit Summit Campaign Report 2002* notes that "As of December 31, 2001, 2,186 microcredit institutions reported reaching 54,904,102 clients, 26,806,014 of whom were among the poorest when they took their first loan".[19] This is a significant advance since the campaign started in 1997, when microcredit schemes reached some 7.6 million of the poorest people. The campaign's goal is to reach 100 million of the poorest families, especially the women of these families, with credit for self-employment and other financial and business services by 2005. The campaign is guided by four core themes:

- Reaching the poorest (defined initially as the bottom half of those living below their nation's poverty line but expanded to include all those living under the international $1 a day poverty line).
- Reaching and empowering women through other supportive initiatives (women constitute 21.2 million of the 26.8 million clients reached through microcredit initiatives thus far).
- Building financially self-sufficient institutions.
- Ensuring a positive, measurable impact on the lives of microcredit clients and their families.[20]

Illustrative of the impact of microcredit financing is the experience in Bangladesh, where "as much as 5% of program-participating households should be able to lift their families out of poverty every year from borrowing from a microcredit program".[21] Clearly, enhancing microcredit schemes to sustain poor people's livelihoods under conditions that promote their active participation becomes a viable social protection and empowerment strategy. There is tremendous scope for strategic investment to scale-up initiatives that offer microcredit facilities to the poorest people.

Governments and the international aid community can align their interests to address poverty in a developmental way by creating an enabling environment for institutions owned and governed by the poor themselves, such as the Grameen Bank and the Self Employed Women's Association's Bank (box 5.5), so that they can better mobilize savings as well as lend money to poor people. One way to overcome barriers to such schemes is to set their capitalization requirements low enough that many of the thousands of small microfinance institutions that operate as non-governmental organizations can convert over time to regulated, special-purpose institutions.

Local strategies can also be aligned with effective actions by governments and the aid community to help create independent wholesaler on-lending institutions such as the Palli Karma-Sahayak Foundation in Bangladesh that can provide technical assistance and reliable financing to a large number of microfinance institutions in every country. The establishment of one or more wholesaler on-lending institutions creates a local currency mechanism for dynamic expansion and growth of a competitive microfinance sector. Ideally, this will give greater choices and options to the poorest.

Box 5.5 People's alternatives: the case of SEWA

A family illness or several days of rain can be just as devastating to the security of poor people as an earthquake or drought. The poor confront personal crises daily. Because poor people live in chronic insecurity, they draw on their own resilience under the harshest conditions. Yet poor people's ways of coping with crisis and protecting themselves and their families from future crises are rarely recognized.

Since 1972, the Self Employed Women's Association (SEWA), based in Ahmedabad, India, has been helping female workers in the informal sector to counter and cope with the many risks and vulnerabilities they experience—from the search for employment to dealing with illness to the lack of child-care. In the absence of state-supported basic social protection measures, few of these everyday problems and vulnerabilities are considered "risk worthy" by typical insurance arrangements. SEWA offers its members opportunities to access the kinds of banking and insurance services from which they are normally excluded, to further develop their skills and to organize for their political rights. Emphasizing that poor women's resilience is not a substitute for state and private sector responsibility, SEWA has identified some ways for shoring up poor people's coping strategies to achieve long-term human security:

• International organizations and the poor perceive disaster in different ways. For the poor, it matters little whether the cause of their hunger or loss of livelihood is an earthquake or a broken leg, because their daily insecurity relates to lack of access to opportunities and conditions for their advancement at a structural level. These must be addressed with their participation.

• Especially in times of crisis, protecting poor people's livelihoods is essential. With few possessions left to lose, the loss of livelihood is often the most devastating. In 2001, for instance, flooding in Ahmedabad resulted in the destruction of many slum houses. Yet for the paper pickers who lived there, the most serious challenge was their loss of livelihood.

• Ongoing state-provided social services must be integrated into effective disaster-response strategies. Responding to drought through relief work and food programmes, for example, can help to improve people's security in the short-term. But mitigation and coping strategies—from fodder banks to rainwater harvesting to artisan training for alternative income—can make a long-term impact.

• Women, because of their multiple roles, especially in caring for children and the elderly, respond to disaster differently than men do. Women tend to plan for future downturns and, in the absence of material assets, look to skills-building, savings, insurance and group support to get them through times of vulnerability.

Source: Adapted from Vaux and Lund 2002.

Livelihoods for women. The notable increase in female-headed households, concentrated among the poor in developing countries, has implications not only for household composition but also for the division of labour between production and social reproduction activities. Illustrative of this trend: women head 31% of rural households in Sub-Saharan Africa, 17% in Latin America and the Caribbean and 14% in Asia.[22] Women are experiencing increasing time, space, labour and financial pressures that affect their sense of security. Migration and internal displacement also contribute to changes in household composition as (usually male) workers cope with poverty by searching for jobs elsewhere.

Men and women experience economic insecurity differently and suffer from its consequences differently. Women are often denied access to critical resources such as credit, land and inheritance rights, reflecting the effects of gender inequality in many societies. Gender can have an enormous impact on economic insecurity, especially in societies where women have a much lower status than men. In these situations, women are much more economically dependent on men. Even in agriculture and food production, women have limited access to resources and services to enable them to improve their economic security. While access to resources is generally limited in developing countries, cultural and traditional factors impose further restrictions on women.

The result is that the distribution of many income-generating assets is heavily skewed in favour of men. Women own less than 2% of land globally,[23] even as the proportion of female heads of households continues to grow. Even where land reform programmes have been instituted specifically to address inequality, land rights have often been transferred directly to male heads of households. The break-up of communal land holdings has led to similar results. In these situations, the property rights of female heads of households and those of married women are often dismissed.

A similar problem exists for access to credit. Only 10% of credit funds are extended to women,[24] primarily because national legislation and customary law prevent women from sharing land rights with their husbands or exclude female heads of households from land entitlement schemes, depriving them of the collateral required by lending institutions. As women's survival strategies are eroded within households, they run the risk of engaging in hazardous activities to earn an income.

Women's economic insecurity is often not treated with the same gravity as men's because women's labour takes place primarily in the household or non-market sphere, without formal financial compensation. Women often perform basic but critical activities, primarily in the social sphere, such as child rearing, caring for the elderly and undertaking community work. Although this work improves economic security at the household level, it is not recognized or valued. Depending on the region and the cultural practices, women may even be restricted to home-based activities because they are not permitted full mobility within society, or even the opportunity to interact socially outside of their homes. So empowering women with livelihoods is important for their economic security and that of their families. In addition, employment catalyzes the change in attitudes

towards women that alone can lead to enduring empowerment.

Preventing and containing the effects of economic crises and natural disasters

A market economy can spread risk and reduce volatility. But as the East Asian financial crises demonstrated, when volatility does occur those who are least able to bear the consequences, especially small and micro producers and poor people, are the most vulnerable to its impacts.

Containing economic and financial crises. Economic crises in developing countries often bring immediate threats to human security through shrinking output, declining incomes and rising unemployment, causing sharp increases in income poverty. Financial crises can also have damaging long-term effects on human security. The social dislocation and loss of human capital during crises limit the ability of poor people to participate in economic recovery.

- *Impacts on people.* Many people who previously had secure jobs and livelihoods suddenly lose them. Many others feel vulnerable, threatened by the risk of losing jobs and income. This was evident in Mexico (1994–95), in East Asia (1997–98), in Russia (1998), in Brazil (1999), and in Argentina, Turkey, and Uruguay (today).[25] In the wake of the Asian crisis of 1997, 4–5 million Indonesian workers lost their jobs, and an estimated 40 million people fell into poverty. During the first six months of the peso crisis in Argentina—which for years had the highest GDP per capita in Latin America—the value of the currency fell by 70%, unemployment skyrocketed to over 25% and

Market fluctuations generate insecurity in all states, including prosperous ones, and these fluctuations affect human security

real wages dropped. More than half the population is now impoverished.[26]

Those already poor before a crisis hits are especially vulnerable.[27] First, the self-employed or family workers and unemployed are excluded from social insurance. Even wage earners are not spared since employers often are unable or unwilling to make contributions to employee benefit systems. Second, the poor are unlikely to save enough to self-insure or to rely on informal insurance. Third, credit mechanisms and private insurance are often unavailable because of high transaction costs and asymmetric information. Fourth, often the poor have no voice to demand the changes needed to improve their human security.[28] Fifth, the health, education and assistance programmes that do exist are often cut back during crises.

- *Crises in developing countries—deeper and longer.* Not all markets have the same risks, and the risks affect different population groups differently. The severity, frequency and duration of economic and financial downturns (both crises and recessions) are far greater in developing countries than in industrial countries.[29] As the IMF's *World Economic Outlook 2002* put it, "Economic fluctuations in developing countries are more severe and have more serious consequences than those in industrial countries. The volatility of real GDP growth in developing countries is higher than that in industrial countries, and the volatility of consumption growth is much higher".[30] Some groups are more likely to pay the costs of crises than others. "Labour in the informal economy, by definition that large segment deprived of any form of social protection, is most vulnerable.

The burden of a global financial crisis falls not so much on investors but on the households of workers made unemployed as a result of it— and within them disproportionately on women".[31] The burden also falls on those who are still employed, but who are impoverished by rising prices and diminishing wages.

- *Financial contagion.* Globally integrated markets can promote abundant growth but they can also transmit downturns. The way various crises spread in the late 1990s astonished the world. Not only did Thailand's economic crisis spread through East Asia; reverberations were also felt in Africa, Latin America, Central and Eastern Europe, and Russia. While the incidence of economic and financial crises does not appear to have increased, the crises seemed to have a faster onset and to be "more severe and even less predictable and to come in waves".[32] These interlinkages are important, as demonstrated in the willingness of the G-8 to provide $300 billion in emergency loans to Mexico, East Asia, Brazil, and Russia to stabilize their economies— and thereby everyone else's.

Market fluctuations generate insecurity in all states, including prosperous ones, and these fluctuations affect human security. Such perturbations are a "hardy perennial" in the global economy.[33] During a third of the time since 1990, there has been a financial crisis somewhere in the world.[34] Instead of being surprised again and again, there must be preparations for these perennial uncertainties just as there are for perennial uncertainties of health, accidents and other threats. In the wake of the crises of the late 1990s, a number of institutional reforms, as well as new institutions, have been proposed and are under discussion.[35]

The prevention or rapid mitigation of crises in developing countries would also improve human security in emerging markets and developed countries

With developing countries more prone to economic and financial crises (and in need of financial investment), and with such crises having a greater impact on the consumption of already vulnerable populations, an obvious step towards human security would be to prevent or mitigate crises. How? By developing early warning systems and by ensuring emergency lending. Social protection, discussed later in this chapter, is also essential.

Since the mid-1990s, two forums have been working to prevent and address economic crises. In 1998, the G-7 developed a "financial stability forum", based in the Bank for International Settlements in Basel.[36] While it has conducted regional meetings, and involved developing country representatives in working parties, that forum does not yet represent the interests—and very different financial trends—of developing countries.[37] The other forum—the G-20— consists of a broader, informal grouping of countries, including 11 developing and transition economies, and it has had some success in negotiating more effective World Bank and IMF policies. Yet even this forum does not represent small or low-income countries, nor does its agenda as yet incorporate effective crisis prevention.

Required, then, is that all institutions improve the early warning systems now being developed and apply them to developing as well as developed countries. In an interlinked global economy, financial crises can spread rapidly, so the prevention or rapid mitigation of crises in developing countries would also improve human security in emerging markets and developed countries.

Preparing for natural disasters. The third large cause of shocks is natural disaster—earthquakes, floods, droughts and famine, windstorms. Over the 10 years from 1992, two-thirds of the people affected by disasters were affected by floods, nearly one quarter by drought and famine and 2% by earthquakes. But earthquakes were the leading cause of disaster-related deaths in 2001, mostly because of the terrible quakes in Gujarat, India. In Africa, 82% of the people who faced disasters faced drought and famine. Over the same 10-year period, earthquakes cost $238 billion—34% of the total costs of natural disasters in that decade.

As terrible as these numbers are, they also hide tremendous progress. Disaster-related deaths in the 1990s were 40% of their level in the 1970s, despite the fact that there were more than twice as many reported disasters. Although natural disasters in the 1990s cost $63 billion annually—more than all development assistance combined—and although global warming could push costs to $300 billion, the good news is that preventive measures can be quite successful. On average, 13 times fewer people die in countries with high human development than in those with low.[38] But countries with low or medium human development can also manage recurrent natural forces.

- In Bangladesh, a cyclone-preparedness programme "has successfully warned, evacuated, and sheltered millions of people from cyclones since its inception in the early 1970s". In the 1990s, the program evacuated 2.5 million people into emergency shelters before cyclones hit.[39]
- "When floods struck Vietnam in 1999, only one of 2,450 flood- and typhoon-resistant homes built with Red Cross assistance succumbed".[40]

Measures to ensure that there is adequate social protection for all, including the working poor and those not in paid work, are critical

- "When two years of record floods inundated Mozambique, well-prepared local and national resources saved 34,000 people from drowning".
- "When the most powerful hurricane for half a century hit Cuba…effective disaster planning and preparedness ensured that 700,000 people were evacuated to safety".[41]

A human security approach would improve disaster preparedness, for example, by identifying risk-prone areas and encouraging families to move or develop insurance and coping mechanisms or by teaching earthquake-resistant building techniques and irrigation and planting techniques that acknowledge fragile environments. Direct investment in disaster preparation, and targets for reducing disaster risk, have been called for strongly by those who work in disaster preparedness.

Providing social protection for all situations

International, regional and national recognition of the precarious situation of people in a globalizing world has resulted in the search for new ways to meet people's basic security needs in countries in all regions, including the provision, delivery and financing of social services. The search for responses to new and persistent problems prompted reform of welfare systems in developed countries, a revised social agenda following the collapse of state provision of social services in countries in transition, and a new interest in social "safety nets" and social protection in developing countries suffering economic setbacks engendered by financial volatility (as in East Asia), undergoing fundamental structural change (as in Latin America and elsewhere), or experiencing long periods of stagnation and even economic regress (as in Africa and elsewhere).[42]

Social protection aims to provide a social minimum to ensure that every person is able to develop the capabilities to participate actively in all spheres of life. Measures to ensure that there is adequate social protection for all, including the working poor and those not in paid work, are critical interventions required of governments, business and citizens. Such measures should include employer- and employee-based contributions—to unemployment insurance, pensions, training—as well as government-subsidized social assistance (through public works) and cash and in-kind transfers) to those in need. These measures can provide a minimum economic and social standard, based on dialogue with all social actors, for those in chronic poverty as well as those who suffer temporary economic hardship during economic downturns and other crises. Policies and programmes to address the special needs of children, the elderly and the disabled should also be incorporated into social protection arrangements.

Establishing social protection measures may seem particularly difficult in times of acute economic or social stress, and each situation requires a set of policies that are responsive to specific contexts and history. Still, the lessons of the recent crises have shown the virtues of:

- Putting systems in place to ensure basic economic security before economic or catastrophic crises hit.
- Expanding existing programmes if the crisis has already hit. Scaling up existing programmes is one of the most cost-effective and time-effective ways of responding to a financial crisis or emergency.
- Setting up regular in-depth information-gathering mechanisms.

Negotiating policy priorities and the mix of public, private and community-led initiatives must be expanded to include poor people themselves

Decisions on the mix of policy and programme measures need to emerge from a social dialogue with all actors, not just the government, the private sector and workers organizations. Because the majority of the poorest people are not represented by these groups, or covered by any form of social security or social protection measures that can provide a springboard to propel them out of poverty, policy negotiations on what should be included in social protection programmes need their active engagement. The process of negotiating policy priorities and the mix of public, private and community-led initiatives must be expanded to include representation and voice of poor people themselves. This requires government and private sector support to provide the space and the information needed for the appropriate representation of community members. And it requires resources and aid to build the capacity to negotiate from informed positions. Some of the objectives of such an agenda:

- *Empowering workers to better integrate with the market.* Markets work more effectively in generating wealth and security if built on foundations that include adequate social security and social protection measures. Then, when downturns occur—and they will—people are protected, able to recover and to move ahead. In the absence of social protection, crises will threaten the market system itself, which flourishes only in the presence of productive workers, socio-political stability and sound social policies and investments. Conversely, financing social protection requires growth. Thus it is very important that countries both design and view "social protection interventions

as investments rather than costs. For example, helping poor people to maintain their access to basic social services during shocks fosters their future productive capacity".[43]

- *Sustaining poverty reduction.* Social protection measures should include active labour market initiatives, such as training and retraining the unemployed, the underemployed and new job entrants. Governments and other actors need to review private sector and public incentive measures, such as direct and indirect subsidies for job creation and enterprise development of micro initiatives at the community level. Also essential is redirecting resources into effective and sustained social expenditures, with better targeting towards the poorest and most vulnerable.

- *Fulfilling ethical and basic socio-economic obligations.* Governments, working with all stakeholders, have often committed themselves to promote, respect and protect people's right to core capabilities and minimum economic security alongside their commitments to civil and political rights. These include the 145 governments that have ratified the International Covenant on Economic, Social and Cultural Rights. The obligation to end transient and chronic poverty by honouring the fundamental rights of people means that the state must take appropriate legislative, administrative, judicial and budgetary action to achieve this. The policies and institutional arrangements—including macroeconomic strategies and service delivery programmes that protect people's rights to basic education, health care, food, shelter, water and income—must be made accessible and available to the most vulnerable and at-risk as a first priority.

Mechanisms must be in place to ensure multi-level and multi-stakeholder monitoring of social policy objectives

Many countries, including developed countries, in parallel with implementing social protection are actively incorporating social protection policies into the core business of the state. In that way, these policies anchor a human security approach of safeguarding people who are vulnerable and suffer the worst impacts of political and economic downturns and crises. What is needed is not large amounts of additional financial capacity within the state but more efficient integration of social policy objectives into macroeconomic and trade-related policy processes. Moreover, mechanisms must be in place to ensure multi-level and multi-stakeholder monitoring of these policy objectives. That requires leadership from within state and private sector-led processes and civil society initiatives. The emphasis would be on creating a broad participatory process to arrive at a focused agenda for social protection and to create the institutional and policy space to work towards achieving such an agenda in a systematic and phased way.

Governments cannot provide social protection alone (see box 5.6). Significant engagement by civil society also generates pressure and undergirds political will and policy choices—as India, Thailand and Latin America have shown.[44] To communicate concerns and develop an advocacy agenda to deal with insecurities, people need support from the range of institutions around them, as well as an umbrella of resources above them.

Supporting community organizations: the "first frontier". At the community level, the capacity of grass-roots organizations and other intermediaries between the state and people is important. If properly supported, people's creative responses and resilience can provide the bulk of protection for human security. Grass-roots efforts to build people's resilience through community-based savings schemes, credit facilities and insurance systems are important to enable people to survive low-intensity crises. For example, a local community-based organization might set up a revolving credit fund, from which community members can borrow to purchase a sewing machine or goat or table saw or other productive tool. Insurance costs are built into the repayment schedule. As loans are repaid, money becomes available for additional loans to other community members.

Such initiatives should be supported as the first frontier in building up productive assets and saving habits, thus helping to mitigate the impacts of some downturns. Grass-roots work can be strengthened from the outside. International NGOs such as Oxfam provide seed capital and technical assistance for revolving credit schemes run by community-based organizations. Community-driven development projects of international donors, such as the World Bank's district poverty initiatives in four states in India or the Kecamatan Development Project in Indonesia, have granted large loans ($100–200 million or more) to be disbursed to small self-formed groups at the village level for productive purposes. And then there are the microcredit institutions such as the Bangladesh Rural Advancement Committee and the Grameen Bank.

Promoting this first frontier of institutions requires assistance well beyond seed capital, assistance that builds up the institutional fabric itself. For small community-based organizations to support human security, they must mature into

Box 5.6 Civil society and human security

With more than 30,000 international non-governmental organizations (NGOs) and many more local and national NGOs, they are emerging as a visible, credible and accountable force in advancing human security. Cutbacks in state-run services and social expenditures have left many core health, education, livelihood and social security needs unmet, especially among poor people. NGOs and community-based organizations have moved in to fill some of the gap, developing creative responses to address poor people's needs. Less rigid in their operations than governments, they are able to find closer connecting points to people in need more quickly. Some NGOs have also become important advocates for policy change responsive to poverty and inequality.

Programmes in education, microfinance, insurance schemes and health care help to reduce and prevent livelihood insecurity, economic deprivation and the potential for household and community-based violence. Just as threats to people's security are now transnational (disease, crime syndicates, cross-border trafficking in women and children), so too are NGO systems of response. NGOs are linked to subregional, regional and international structures. Oxfam, for instance, has offices in more than 80 countries, while Development Alternatives with Women for a New Era (DAWN) has networks in Africa, Asia, Latin America, the Caribbean and Pacific Island states. Such initiatives, linked more closely to the poorest and most insecure people, are able to combine service and care with social movement activism on policy concerns in ways that can enhance human security across national boundaries.

Some civil society initiatives are also finding new ways of working with states to complement and support state-led action on problems faced by poor communities. In South Africa, a broad-based coalition of civil society organizations under the umbrella of the Treatment Action Campaign (TAC) joined the government in its court action against pharmaceutical companies to make anti-retroviral drugs for the treatment of HIV/AIDS affordable and available in South Africa. Civil society organizations help to amplify the voice of the economically and politically disempowered. On issue-specific campaigns related to fair trade, violence against women, human rights and environmental violations, to name a few, international civil society has brought to the world's attention threats to human security. Pointing to problems of unaccountable, unrepresentative systems of political and economic governance at all levels, they highlight the need for better regulatory frameworks and institutional measures in support of poor people.

Civil society representatives ensure that human security is as much about building effective political, economic and social institutions as it is about challenging bad government policy and budget allocations or preparing for downside risks arising from natural disasters and financial crises. NGOs can empower and mobilize a range of civil society organizations within their countries through rights-based education to strengthen citizen participation in economic and political processes and to ensure that institutional arrangements are responsive to people's needs.

Promoting human security within a framework of protection and empowerment requires an enhanced role for civil society supported by more resources. A global initiative for human security is dependent on how well the international community mobilizes and harnesses the energy, commitment and creativity of the NGO sector and other social actors.

Source: Adapted from Michael 2002; Anheier, Glasius and Kaldor 2001.

Much of the motivation and leadership for social protection must come from within

organizations that can work with local govern-ments and strengthen governance by building leadership that ensures the equitable delivery of services. Central is the need to develop the technical and policy capacity of such leadership to promote transparent, accountable, well-managed and financially sustainable processes. Participation in governance processes must ensure representation of previously excluded and marginalized groups and communities so that their interests, needs and concerns become part of a common social agenda.

For many communities, resilience against daily insecurities and risks depends on social networks and informal care arrangements, which provide support during times of crisis and stress. These informal networks are built on patterns of social solidarity that have evolved over time at the grass-roots level. Their effectiveness can be enhanced by giving communities access to basic social infrastructure and income. In numerous examples of household and community survival and coping strategies, orphans, the elderly and disabled, among others, have been able to provide mutual assistance, especially when they themselves have had a social minimum to help them anticipate and respond to risks within their own households.

But there are limits to people's resilience. The enormous and long-term impacts of HIV/AIDS and other infectious diseases, extended deprivation, unemployment, conflict and violence wipe out these coping mechanisms. And people's resilience and survival strategies cannot be a substitute for government responsibility for promoting and protecting human well-being.

Financing social protection internationally. Adequate financing for social protection is largely a matter of

political priority. The national insurance systems in Japan and Western Europe are struggling, and while the US economy was booming in the 1990s well over 40 million US citizens still lacked health insurance.[45] In contrast, Costa Rica, Sri Lanka and the Indian state of Kerala have managed very effective social protection systems on the same budget as other regions that offered no such protections.[46]

The experience of the countries of the Commonwealth of Independent States shows the challenge of providing social protection during deep transitions. In 2000, their GDP stood at 63% of its 1990 level. Income poverty had increased fivefold.[47] How is the state to respond? Sudden economic and financial crises have also shown that even growth with equity, as in the Republic of Korea, was no guarantee that some people would not become poor or be pushed deeper into poverty. The absence of a proper system of social safety nets and a rapid system of compensatory protection led to new pockets of inequality and destitution in Korea, despite the country's remarkable growth and new social protection programmes during the crisis.[48]

Again, much of the motivation and leadership for social protection must come from within—as it did in Korea, which responded to the crisis by instituting unemployment insurance, public works and pensions. Maintaining social protection during times of war or civil unrest, post-conflict reconstruction or economic liberalization is yet more difficult. But it is not impossible to protect at least some primary expenditures. In a study of patterns of government expenditure during 25 internal conflicts, only three countries reduced social and economic expenditures across the board in favour of military expenditures. In Mozambique, Nicaragua and Sudan, social expenditure per capita actually increased by more than 20% during the conflict period.[49]

Moreover, when crises compound or states collapse, the ability to finance social protection evaporates. In many of the transition economies, unemployment was already high. But when the Russian economic crisis struck, social safety nets were incapable of dealing with more unemployment and falling real incomes. As a result, poverty generally worsened. In Moldova, for example, the poverty rate increased from 35% in mid-1997 to 46% at the end of 1998 and to 56% in mid-1999.[50]

If human security is to be realized, then, external resources must be available to national governments or their people for occasional crises, and in a form that does not bind future generations to an intolerable burden of debt. Whether this assistance comes from governments or private sector institutions or a new self-standing funding mechanism, it is and will be integral to human security.

Policy conclusions

Along with the emphasis on "growth with equity", we need a new commitment to "downturn with security". We need to plan realistically how to protect people in adverse (but inevitable) situations of danger, inflation, unemployment and fiscal crises—when the constraints seem overwhelming and the freedom to undertake positive action seems frail.

- One of the keys to meeting the first Millennium Development Goal—to eradicate poverty and hunger—is for governments, the World Trade Organization and other actors together to foster markets that will generate equitable growth. The strategies and policies are more or less known. The challenge: to act on them.
- Given the increased informalization of labour, new ways need to be found to empower workers to maintain a stable and sufficient income stream. Improving female labour markets is particularly important.
- Mitigating the effects of economic downturns and crises requires development and better understanding of early warning systems. It also requires that social protection systems be in place ahead of time. Similarly, preventive work can make an astonishing difference in limiting the human security cost of natural disasters.
- Support for social protection should be infused with the same professionalism, resource base and political will that has characterized support for market policies.

Notes

1. World Bank 1990.
2. FAO 1999 and United Nations Department of Economic and Social Affairs 2001b.
3. Walter 2002, pp. 9–10.
4. World Travel and Tourism Council 2002.
5. The household is a common unit of analysis for studies of income and consumption. The household generally consists of a group of people living together (though it can consist of only one person) and making common provisions for food and other essentials of living. Household members may pool their income to a greater or lesser extent; they may be related or unrelated persons or a combination of both.
6. Sen 1999b.

7. World Bank 2001b.

8. Walter 2002 reports 1,110 natural disasters in the 1970s, 1,987 in the 1980s, and 2,742 in the 1990s.

9. World Bank 2002c, p. 6.

10. Watkins 1998, p. 134.

11. Watkins 2002, pp. 10–11.

12. See, for instance, Sen 1999a.

13. See, for instance, United Nations, Department of Economic and Social Affairs, 2001. In many developing countries there has been a significant increase in the numbers of people working in the informal, unregulated sector of the economy, either as self employed workers at a survivalist level or as unregistered subcontracted workers for micro and small business enterprises.

14. ILO 2003.

15. Sen 2000, p. 120.

16. Sen 2000, p. 120.

17. Pinstrup-Andersen and Padya-Lorch 2001, p. 109.

18. Jodha 1986.

19. Daley-Harris 2002b, p. 3.

20. See Daley-Harris 2002a for research and thinking on these themes.

21. As concluded in Shahidur Khandker's research in the World Bank (1998). He studied Bangladesh: Grameen Bank with 2.3 million members, the Bangladesh Rural Advancement Committee (BRAC) with 3 million, and RD-12 (a government run program).

22. FAO 2002.

23. FAO 2003. [www.fao.org/sd/fsdirect/fbdirect/FSP001.htm].

24. FAO 2003. [www.fao.org/sd/fsdirect/fbdirect/FSP001.htm].

25. This section draws on the research paper by Griffith-Jones and Kimmis 2002.

26. ILO 2003, p. 19.

27. Lustig 2000.

28. Lustig 2000.

29. IMF 2002, box 3.4, p. 125.

30. IMF 2002, box 3.4, p. 125.

31. IMF 2002, p. 14.

32. IMF 1999, chap. 3, p. 68.

33. Kindelberger 2000.

34. Griffith-Jones and Kimmis 2002, p. 3.

35. Grunberg and Khan 2000.

36. Taylor 2002.

37. See IMF 2002, chap. 3, and Griffith-Jones and Kimmis 2002.

38. Walters 2002, p. 172.

39. Walters 2002, p. 174.

40. Walters 2002, p. 15.

41. Walters 2002, p. 6.

42. As discussed in United Nations, Department of Economic and Social Affairs 2001 and Commission on Human Security 2002.

43. World Bank 2001a, p. 9.

44. Gooptu 2001, Archer and Costello 1990, and Anheier, Clasus and Kaldor 2001.

45. Marshall and Butzback 2002.

46. Drèze and Sen 2002. See also Deneulin 2002.

47. World Bank 2002b.

48. World Bank 2002b.

49. Stewart, Huang and Wang 2001, p. 88.

50. World Bank 2002b, p. 13.

References

Akerlof, George. 1970. "The Market for 'Lemons': Quality Uncertainty and the Market Mechanism." *Quarterly Journal of Economics*.

Anheier, Helmut, Marlies Glasius and Mary Kaldor. 2001. *Global Civil Society 2001*. Oxford: Oxford University Press.

Archer, D., and P. Costello. 1990. *Literacy and Power: The Latin American Battleground*. London: Earthscan.

Commission on Human Security. 2002. "Reports on Regional Consultation." [www.humansecurity-chs.org].

Daley-Harris, Sam, ed. 2002a. *Pathways Out of Poverty: Innovations in Microfinance for the Poorest Families.* Bloomfield, Conn.: Kumarian Press.

———. 2002b. *State of the Microcredit Summit Campaign Report 2002.* Washington, D.C.: The Microcredit Summit Campaign. [www.microcreditsummit.org].

Deneulin, Severine. 2002. "Responding to the Values of the Poor through Participation (Part Two): The Case of Costa Rica." Draft. Queen Elizabeth House, Oxford.

Drèze, Jean, and Amartya Sen. 2002. *India: Development and Participation.* New Delhi: Oxford University Press.

FAO (Food and Agriculture Organization). 1999. *The State of Food Security in the World 1999.* Rome.

———. 2002. "Food and Agricultural Organization: Report, 2002." Rome.

———. 2003. "Women in Development Service." Women and Population Division, Women and Sustainable Food Security. [www.fao.org/sd/fsdirect/fbdirect/FSP001.htm].

Gooptu, Nandini. 2001. *The Politics of the Urban Poor in Early Twentieth-Century India.* Cambridge University Press.

Griffith-Jones, Stephanie, and Jenny Kimmis. 2002. "International Financial Volatility." Paper prepared for the Commission on Human Security. [www.humansecurity-chs.org].

Grunberg, Isabelle, and Sarbuland Khan. 2000. *Globalization: The United Nations Development Dialogue—Finance, Trade, Poverty, Peace-building.* UNU Policy Perspectives 4. New York: United Nations University Press.

IMF (International Monetary Fund). Various issues. *Global Financial Stability Report.* Washington, D.C.

———. 1999. *World Economic Outlook 1999.* Washington, D.C.

ILO (International Labour Organization). 2003. *Global Employment Trends 2003.* Geneva: International Labour Office.

Jodha, N.S. 1986. "Common Property Resources and Rural Poor in Dry Regions of India." *Economic and Political Weekly* 21(27): 1169-81.

Kindelberger, Charles P. 2000. *Manias, Panics, and Crashes.* Fourth Edition. New York: John Wiley & Sons.

Klein, Michael, Carl Aaron and Bita Hadjimichael. 2003. "Foreign Direct Investment and Poverty Reduction." World Bank, Washington, D.C.

Lustig, Nora. 2000. *Crises and the Poor: Socially Responsible Macroeconomics.* Washington, D.C.: Inter-American Development Bank.

Marshall, Katherine, and Olivier Butzback, eds. 2002. *New Social Policy Agendas for Europe and Asia: Challenges, Experiences, and Lessons.* Washington, D.C.: World Bank.

Michael, Sarah. 2002. "The Role of NGOs in Human Security." Paper prepared for the Commission on Human Security. [www.humansecurity-chs.org].

Pinstrup-Andersen, Per, and Rajul Padya-Lorch, eds. 2001. *The Unfinished Agenda: Perspectives on Overcoming Hunger, Poverty and Environmental Degradation.* Washington, D.C.: International Food Policy Research Institute.

Sen, Amartya. 1999a. "Beyond the Crisis: Development Strategies in Asia." Institute of South East Asian Studies, Singapore.

———. 1999b. *Development as Freedom.* New York: Anchor Press.

———. 2000. "Work and Rights." *International Labour Review* 139 (2).

———. 2002. "Global Inequality and Human Security." Ishizaka Lecture Series, Tokyo, February.

Spence, Michael. 1973. "Job Market Signalling." *Quarterly Journal of Economics* 87.

Standing, Guy. 2002. *Beyond the New Parernalism: Basic Security as Equality.* London: Verso.

Stern, Nicholas. 2002. "Dynamic Development: Innovation and Inclusion." Munich Lectures in Economics. [http://econ.worldbank.org/files/ 22048_CES_Munich_Lecture_Nov_19.pdf].

Stewart, Frances, Cindy Huang and Michael Wang. 2001. "Internal Wars: An Empirical Overview of the Economic and Social Consequences." In Frances Stewart and Valpy Fitzgerald, eds., *The Economic and Social Consequences of Conflict (War and Underdevelopment).* Vol 1. Oxford: Oxford University Press.

Stiglitz, Joseph E. 1985. "Information and Economic Analysis: A Perspective." *Economic Journal* 95.

Taylor, Lance. 2002. "Global Macroeconomic Management." In Deepak Nayyar, ed., *Governing Globalization.* WIDER Studies in Development Economics. Oxford: Oxford University Press.

UNCTAD (United Nations Conference on Trade and Development). Various years. *World Investment Report.* Geneva.

United Nations, Department of Economic and Social Affairs. 2001. *Report on the World Social Situation 2001.* New York.

Vaux, Tony, and Frances Lund. 2002. "Overcoming Crisis: Working Women and Security." Paper prepared for the Commission on Human Security. [www.humansecurity-chs.org].

Walter, Jonathan, ed. 2002. *World Disasters Report 2002: Focus on Reducing Risk.* Bloomfield, Conn.: Kumarian Press.

Watkins, Kevin. 1998. *Economic Growth with Equity.* Oxford: Oxfam.

———. 2002. *Rigged Rules and Double Standards: Trade, Globalisation and the Fight against Poverty.* Oxford: Oxfam International.

World Bank. 1990. *World Development Report 1990: Poverty.* New York: Oxford University Press.

———. 2001a. *Social Protection Sector Strategy: From Safety Net to Springboard.* Washington, D.C.

———. 2001b. *World Development Report 2000/2001: Attacking Poverty.* New York: Oxford University Press.

———. 2002a. *Global Economic Prospects and the Developing Countries 2002.* Washington, D.C.

———. 2002b. *Transition—The First 10 Years: Analysis and Lessons for Eastern Europe and the Former Soviet Union.* Washington, D.C.

———. 2002c. *World Development Indicators 2002.* Washington, D.C.

———. 2003. *Global Economic Prospects and the Developing Countries 2003.* Washington, D.C.

World Travel and Tourism Council. 2002. [www.wttc.org].

Better health for human security

One of the most significant human achievements of the 20th century is the spectacular progress in health. About a billion people today have average life expectancies of nearly 80 years, twice the average of a century before. These gains were made possible by material advances in the provision of food, education and clean water; medical developments in scientific knowledge; and political and social advances that harnessed new knowledge for human betterment.[1]

But good health, like so many things, is inequitably distributed. Entering the 21st century, about half the world's people had been left behind, unable to achieve their full health potential. World health today spotlights the paradox of unprecedented achievement among the privileged and a vast burden of preventable diseases among those less privileged, the majority of humankind (figure 6.1).

Differing risks and vulnerabilities to avoidable health insults are found among people of different ages, sexes, communities, classes, races and nations. No surprise then that the poor, marginalized and excluded have a higher risk of dying than other groups. Especially vulnerable are children and women across all groups. These disparities are found not only among countries—but within countries, rich and poor.

The World Health Organization (WHO) recently estimated that more than 40% of the 56 million deaths each year are avoidable, given the world's existing knowledge, technologies and resources.[2] Social, behavioural, economic and environmental conditions shape these outcomes. Many of the unnecessary deaths can be prevented by better health behaviour—stopping smoking,

eating more healthful foods, getting more exercise, practicing safe sex. But many avoidable deaths—especially those due to infectious diseases, nutritional deprivations of children and maternity-related risks of unsafe childbearing and childrearing—can be prevented only by reaching people trapped in poverty or conflict. This gap in avoidable deaths is due to differences in risks and vulnerabilities and in access to modern health knowledge and care. Disease and poverty go hand in hand. So, too, do disease and conflict.

Simple comparisons illuminate these tragic health failings. The average lifespan in Sierra Leone and Ethiopia is only about half that in Japan and Sweden.[3] Fewer than half the newborns in Guinea-

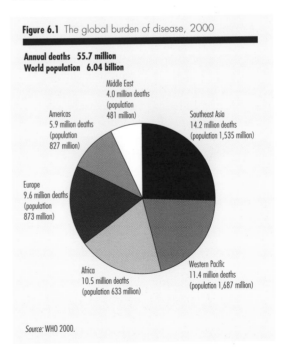

Figure 6.1 The global burden of disease, 2000

Annual deaths 55.7 million
World population 6.04 billion

Middle East
4.0 million deaths
(population 481 million)

Americas
5.9 million deaths
(population 827 million)

Southeast Asia
14.2 million deaths
(population 1,535 million)

Europe
9.6 million deaths
(population 873 million)

Africa
10.5 million deaths
(population 633 million)

Western Pacific
11.4 million deaths
(population 1,687 million)

Source: WHO 2000.

Good health is both essential
and instrumental to achieving
human security

Bissau survive to their fifth birthday. Inequities in health are marked among and within countries. In the United States, children in poverty are far more likely to become sick and die than their better-off counterparts. Disturbing inequities are compounded by "hot spots" of health emergencies around the world. Health crises threaten the interdependence and solidarity of global health efforts.

In just two decades, HIV/AIDS has become the world's fourth ranking cause of death. Life expectancy averages only 47 years in Sub-Saharan Africa, 15 years less than it would without AIDS. With 22 million cumulative deaths and more than 40 million HIV-infected people, HIV/AIDS will soon become the greatest health catastrophe in human history—exacting a death toll greater than two world wars in the 20th century, the influenza epidemic of 1918 or the Black Death of the 14th century. The devastation is being superimposed on other crises, such as the ongoing drought and famine in Southern Africa. Among the few poor populations with reliable health statistics, the worst health condition documented, due to both HIV/AIDS and underdevelopment, is in Bandim, Guinea-Bissau, where life expectancy today is a meagre 36 years.[4]

Health crises also plague the countries in transition to democracy and a market economy. Russia and several Eastern European countries have experienced rising mortality. In Russia, higher mortality rates are particularly marked among less educated adult men, unable to cope with changing circumstances.[5] In Latin America, the transition to democracy and open markets has not yielded the social benefits hoped for, instead perpetuating or exacerbating some of the world's severest income and social inequalities.

Other societies trapped in prolonged conflict (Sudan) or recovering from war (Afghanistan) have "slow-burn" health crises characterized by very high or stagnant death rates. Sixteen of the 20 countries with the worst human development indexes are either in the midst of conflict or recently emerging from it.[6] Worldwide, war and poverty are the gravest threats to health and human security.

The links between health and human security
Good health is both essential and instrumental to achieving human security. It is essential because the very heart of security is protecting human lives. Health security is at the vital core of human security—and illness, disability and avoidable death are "critical pervasive threats" to human security. Health is defined here as not just the absence of disease, but as "a state of complete physical, mental and social well-being". Health is both objective physical wellness and subjective psychosocial well-being and confidence about the future.

In this view, good health is instrumental to human dignity and human security. It enables people to exercise choice, pursue social opportunities and plan for their future. A healthy child can learn, grow and develop. An adult cured of tuberculosis can resume work to support the livelihood of her family. Saving a child's life can secure the future generations of a family. The absence of good health can result in enormous grief (the loss of a newborn or young child) and can precipitate an economic catastrophe for the family (the sudden death of a working adult).

Health's instrumental role is collective as well as personal. Good health is a precondition for social stability. Sudden outbreaks of a contagious disease or other health crisis can destabilize an

Three health challenges stand out as closely linked to human security: global infectious diseases, poverty-related threats, and violence and crisis

entire society. In times of crisis, visible and demonstrable capacity for effective health action is essential to calm public fears. Even during conflict, combatants have agreed on ceasefires to enable immunizations of children, recognizing the shared importance of good health.

Health and human security are inextricably linked, but good health is not synonymous with security. Nor does security encompass all aspects of human health. So, which health challenges are linked particularly to human security?

Health security and military security are directly related. Indeed, from a historical perspective, the legitimacy of rulers has depended on their capacity to protect the health of the public, through military and other means. In recent decades, especially during the Cold War, health and military security fields went separate ways, each developing its distinctive technical aspects, political constituencies and institutional networks.[7]

But throughout human history, military security has had strong health dimensions.[8] Battles have been won by disease rather than arms. Maintaining the health of combatants has been an important element of military preparedness and has motivated research into the control of tropical diseases and the health impacts of military action. Troop movements have spread contagious diseases. Recently, those concerned with military security have redoubled their focus on the health aspects of defence—on germs as weapons, on epidemics weakening fragile states, on health risks among military troops, on the humanitarian impact of military action. The possibility that biological weapons of mass destruction would be used has caused an upsurge of public attention and put health matters squarely on the security agenda.

The health field is also reconnecting to concerns about security. Links extend beyond military security to more comprehensive health security (figure 6.2).

Four criteria influence the strength of links between health and human security:

- The scale of the disease burden now and into the future.
- The urgency for action.
- The depth and extent of the impact on society.
- The interdependencies or "externalities" that can exert ripple effects beyond particular diseases, persons or locations.

Applying these criteria, three health challenges stand out as closely linked to human security: global infectious diseases, poverty-related threats, and violence and crisis. The connection between infectious diseases and human security has been forcefully validated by recent developments—the HIV/AIDS epidemic, the accelerating spread of

Figure 6.2 Health and human security linkages

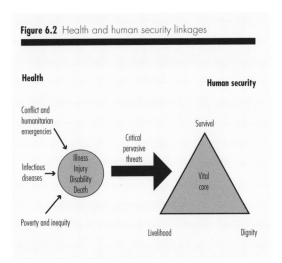

Box 6.1 Controlling infectious disease

Although few infectious diseases have been eradicated throughout the century, the criteria for eradication are clear. Clinical diagnosis of the disease must be possible. There must a low degree of transmissibility and a relatively slow rate of spread. There can be no non-human carrier, such as mosquitoes in the case of malaria. Finally, eradication requires practical and effective interventions that are safe, inexpensive, long lasting and easily deployed and that provide strong immunity to secondary infection.

Attempts to eradicate disease have typically relied on vaccines, as for smallpox, or curative prophylactic methodologies, as for yaws and guinea worm. In some cases, such as tuberculosis, there has been controversy over the best method of disease control or eradication. The BCG vaccine is administered to 85% of the world's children, but its effectiveness is currently unknown. Because of this ambiguity, most countries have turned to a combination of treatment (directly observed treatment, short course) and quarantine.

However, these control methods have been largely ineffective for eradication because of the difficulty of identifying infected individuals, assuring patient compliance with treatment, and combating the disease's resistance to treatment and its ease of transmission.

In an increasingly globalized world, most methods of control and eradication will remain ineffective without coordinated control between poor and rich countries. As global populations move at unprecedented rates, difficulties in the identification of infected individuals, the long incubation periods of diseases like HIV/AIDS and the uncoordinated monitoring procedures of exit and entry countries make control of disease more challenging. The HIV/AIDS epidemic alone has made it clear that there is no place in the world from which a country is disconnected. Increased international cooperation will be required for effective monitoring, control and eradication of infectious diseases, to prevent further outbreaks and decrease transmission both within and between countries.

Source: Heyman 2002.

---

contagious diseases, the looming threat of bioterrorism, epidemics that weaken already fragile states and the creation of new international funds and organizations. Poverty-related health threats are perhaps the greatest burden of human insecurity. Most preventable infectious diseases, nutritional deprivation and maternity-related risks are concentrated among the world's poor. Poverty and disease set up a vicious spiral with negative economic and human consequences. And all forms of violence—collective, interpersonal and self-directed—are public health problems. Indeed, the growing social crises of violence all have strong health dimensions.

Global infectious diseases

Many recent developments explain the emergence of infectious diseases on the global agenda—the discovery of more than two dozen new disease agents, the spread of antibiotic resistance and the devastating impact of recent epidemics—cholera in Latin America, plague in India, the ebola virus in Africa, dengue fever in Southeast Asia and mad

cow disease in Europe. Public fears are aroused. The economic costs are staggering. And government credibility is questioned (box 6.1).[9]

Start with HIV/AIDS. Within a few years of its discovery, this equal-opportunity pathogen has spread to every continent, every country. It kills productive adults, impoverishes families, creates orphans, destroys communities and weakens fragile governments. Even the elderly are affected because of the deterioration of their adult working children. In some heavily-infected countries, HIV/AIDS is depleting skilled workers (teachers, nurses, police officers, civil servants), with health staff losses as high as 40% in some countries.[10]

The burden of HIV/AIDS is overwhelmingly concentrated among the poorest people in the poorest regions, especially in Sub-Saharan Africa. The US National Intelligence Council recently released projections of the "next wave" of the HIV/AIDS epidemic in five populous countries—China, Ethiopia, India, Nigeria and Russia (figure 6.3). The council estimated that the number of

6

The burden of HIV/AIDS is overwhelmingly concentrated among the poorest people in the poorest regions

people infected with HIV/AIDS in these countries is likely to soar from 14–23 million today to 50–75 million in 2010.[11] Even in rich countries, HIV/AIDS threatens to resurge, concentrated among the poor and excluded.

In 2000, the UN Security Council declared HIV/AIDS a national security threat, followed by similar announcements by the G-8 at meetings in Okinawa and Genoa. Underscoring the political imperatives for global action, the UN General Assembly devoted a special session to HIV/AIDS in 2001, and a Global Fund to Fight AIDS, Tuberculosis, and Malaria was launched in 2002.

Poverty-related threats

Poverty and infectious diseases are fellow travellers—each feeding on the other. The poor are at higher risk of infectious disease, and sickness can deepen poverty, creating a vicious cycle of illness and poverty. Especially prevalent among the poor are the first-generation diseases—common infections and maternity-related diseases, mainly affecting children and women (box 6.2). The risk and vulnerability to these poverty-related health threats are compounded by hunger, malnutrition and environmental threats, especially the lack of clean drinking water and sanitation. A significant share of the world's avoidable deaths and human insecurities is linked to poverty.

When poor people have voice, they consistently express fears about the multiple insecurities of everyday life.[12] They worry about economic insecurity from loss of jobs. They fear local violence. They want to immunize their children. And not surprisingly, they rank preventable sickness and premature death high among their priorities, not only to avoid pain and

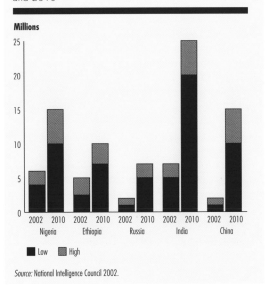

Figure 6.3 High and low estimates of current and future HIV/AIDS-infected adults in next-wave countries, 2002 and 2010

Millions

Low ■ High ▧

Source: National Intelligence Council 2002.

suffering but also to prevent family bankruptcy. For the poor with fragile asset bases, catastrophic sickness deprives the family of daily wages, and compulsory health expenditures put enormous pressures on limited resources.

HIV/AIDS, for instance, decreases the ability of affected individuals to work and increases their health care costs, resulting in greater financial strain on their households. To cope financially, families initially respond by depleting any savings and by selling their non-productive assets. Children are removed from school, to lower family expenses and to care for the sick. The number and quality of meals are reduced to stretch resources, weakening the ability of the sick to fight off

Box 6.2 Ensuring human security for women: reproductive health

Complications from childbirth are the leading cause of death among women in many developing countries. Over 515,000 women die yearly in pregnancy or childbirth, and 99% of these deaths occur in developing countries. The risk of dying from childbirth is 1 in 1,800 in developed countries but 1 in 48 in developing countries. This gap implies that countless pregnancy-related deaths in developing countries could be prevented with adequate resources and services.

For every woman who dies in childbirth, 10–15 more women become incapacitated or disabled due to complications from childbirth. Over a quarter of women in the developing world, approximately 300 million women, suffer from short- or long-term complications of childbirth. Each time a woman gives birth, she is at significant risk of death or disability. She is also exposed to these risks more often since she will be likely to bear more children than a woman in a developed country. High rates of maternal mortality leave over a million children around the world motherless each year. A study in Bangladesh showed that such children are 3 to 10 times more likely to die within two years than children who live with both parents (Strong 1992).

There are many reasons for the high risk of death and disability during pregnancy and childbirth for women in developing countries. First, they lack access to family planning or safe abortion services. The UN Population Fund estimates that meeting family planning needs in developing countries alone would reduce maternal deaths and injuries by 20%. Unsafe abortions account for nearly 15% of all deaths related to pregnancy. Second, many women do not receive any type of antenatal care. Over half of births in developing countries are not assisted by a trained birth attendant. And after birth, as few as 5% of women in poor countries receive postpartum care. Factors impeding woman's access to many of these reproductive health services include the accessibility of clinics, the cost of services, control over resources within households, decision-making power within family units, social isolation and time constraints.

While many other health indicators have improved in recent decades, little progress has been made in decreasing maternal mortality rates. Provision of primary health service is complicated by the social, political, cultural and economic environments of poor countries, which can marginalize women's roles and participation. Women are often discriminated against in access to education, food, employment, financial resources and primary health care services. Addressing issues of women's status and integrating them into mainstream social and political systems will be essential for improving reproductive health and allowing women wider participation within society. In addition, inexpensive and technologically simple methods are needed to promote women's reproductive health. Improving the quality of reproductive health care and women's access to it will not only improve the security of billions of women around the world, but also that of their children and families.

Source: UN Population Fund [www.unfpa.org/mothers/facts.htm; www.safemotherhood.org/facts_and_figures/maternal_mortality.htm; www.unfpa.org/mothers/statsbycountry.htm; www.unfpa.org/mothers/skilled_att.htm] and Strong 1992.

secondary infections. Later, families are forced to sell their land, tools and other productive assets, to borrow money from relatives and friends and to go into debt to money-lenders. These strains continue even after death. Funeral celebrations can be very costly, and traditions of ownership prevent women and children from inheriting productive assets.

Health emergencies like this can precipitate a vicious downward spiral of sickness, compulsory spending, asset depletion and impoverishment. And not just in poorer countries. In the United States, high health care costs account for an estimated half of personal bankruptcies.[13]

Violence and crisis
Today's conflicts are both within and among countries, often driven by inter-group hostilities and fuelled by the proliferation of small arms (chapters 2 and 3).The health dimensions of conflicts are multifaceted, entailing both emergency medical demands as well as long-term health challenges. To protect people, health

All forms of violence—collective, interpersonal and self-directed—are public health problems

responses to complex humanitarian emergencies must navigate through unsafe and unstable political, military and ecological contexts. The tradition of "medical neutrality", sanctioned by humanitarian law and human rights covenants, may be difficult, if not impossible, to uphold. Humanitarianism is often overwhelmed by political and military imperatives.[14] Medical workers must work with the military, the United Nations and non-governmental organizations—each with its own mandate.

Sickness and death can expand beyond the zone and time of conflict. The scale of deaths due to conflict escalate dramatically through ripple effects, extended in time to neighbouring regions. The impact of violence also impairs health, retarding economic recovery, increasing security costs and eroding the trust that underpins the functioning of all social institutions.

The direct casualties of war are modest in comparison with the toll from other forms of violence—physical, sexual, psychological, interpersonal, domestic and self-directed (table 6.1).[15]

Although the underlying causes are not well understood, the overwhelming proportion of interpersonal violence takes place among low-income people and in low-income countries. There is also a growing body of evidence that economic, social and political inequality and alienation provide fertile breeding grounds for all forms of violence.

Natural disasters are also a major threat to health and human security worldwide (chapter 5). The multidimensional devastation of natural disasters can wreak havoc on people's lives. Ecological and climatic disasters—hurricanes, tornadoes, draught, flooding, landslides—are

Table 6.1 Estimated global violence-related deaths, 2000

Type of violence	Number[a]	Rate per 100,000 population[b]	Proportion of total (%)
Homicide	520,000	8.8	31.3
Suicide	815,000	14.5	49.1
War-related	310,000	5.2	18.6
Total[c]	1,659,000	28.8	100.00
Low- to middle-income countries	1,510,000	32.1	91.9
High-income countries	149,000	14.4	8.9

a. Rounded to the nearest 1,000.
b. Age-standardized.
c. Includes 14,000 intential injury dealths resulting for legal intervention.
Source: WHO 2002.

becoming more frequent. These unexpected catastrophes can devastate families and communities, especially the poor living in precarious environments.

Historically well-documented and always feared, the use of germs as a biological weapon became a reality in the United States with the anthrax attacks of 2001. Although the attacks resulted in only five deaths, they generated unprecedented public fears, nearly paralysing the postal service and the Congress. As many as a third of the workers at the US Centers for Disease Control were assigned to combat anthrax.

Public concerns over biological weapons were so aroused that the US government was compelled to rebuild its stockpile of nearly discarded smallpox vaccine. Pre-emptive vaccination against smallpox is now being implemented in North America and Europe. The resulting scrutiny of health institutions exposed the long-standing underinvestment in public health infrastructures, underscoring the centrality of public health for the protection of people.

Adopting a human security approach

Windows of opportunity are opening to tackle the last century's unfinished health agenda, to confront this century's new threats and to build a unified and secure health future. The world's poor are threatened by global infectious diseases, poverty-related threats and violence. But in this globalizing world, no community can be entirely impervious to these contagious threats. Immunizing a child, for example, protects not only that child but also other children, the family and the entire neighborhood. Control of infectious epidemics thus has positive externalities where protecting an individual has wider benefits for others. Poverty and its related health threats are not only morally unacceptable—they also generate conditions for new pathogens, disease transmission and social and political pathologies. Reducing violence protects victims—and also reduces the "culture of violence" that perpetuates it.

Ensuring the health security of the public is, like police and fire protection, an indivisible good, with strong multiplier effects. Improvements in health anywhere benefit everyone everywhere. Protecting the health of the public—locally, nationally, globally—is thus a core public good.[16] Gross health disparities and selective approaches are neither sustainable nor morally acceptable. Reducing health threats to human security will require unprecedented cooperation among diverse actors and nation states.

Recognition of global interdependencies in health is growing among the public and political leaders. Public financing for global health has begun to increase from the low levels at which it has stagnated. After the Monterrey Conference on Financing Development and stimulated by the UN Millennium Development Goals, resource pledges of foreign assistance for health have increased significantly—for the first time in decades. New actors—civil society, business and the media—are joining the field. Non-governmental organizations are proliferating, and media coverage of health and security has increased markedly. New institutional arrangements are being established, such as the Global Fund to Fight AIDS, Tuberculosis, and Malaria. And global health security is increasingly recognized as a political priority. If appropriately harnessed, this new awareness and responsiveness could help energize global health as a human security priority.

A people-centred approach to global health would focus on empowerment and protection. Empowerment strategies would enhance the capacity of individuals and communities to assume responsibility for their own health. These strategies would thus generate the conditions, such as community-based insurance for health care, to enable families and local groups to pursue self-help strategies. While governments and businesses are important, it is people, both directly and through government, who have the authority and responsibility for health and human security.

Protective strategies would promote the three institutional pillars of society: to prevent, monitor and anticipate health threats. Protection aims to prevent avoidable disease by reducing risks and vulnerabilities to the root causes of unnecessary sickness and death. Protection also entails developing early warning systems and building

Good health and human security for all depend on peace and development

standby preparedness capacity. Protection would focus on mitigating and ameliorating the impact of unavoidable crises, such as natural disasters. A key dimension of protection is the recognition that health security is imbedded in allied social, political and environmental conditions.

Fostering peace and equitable development

Good health and human security for all depend on peace and development—to ensure universal access to the basic requirements of food, nutrition, clean drinking water, hygiene and sanitation, and housing. Peace reduces the threat of violent conflict and illegal trafficking in people and drugs, thereby also reducing the threat of HIV/AIDS transmission through sexual violence, exploitation and intravenous drug use. Development is especially important for good health by promoting basic education, especially of women, and secure economic livelihoods. When basic conditions of peace and development are achieved, good health can be attained as part of human security. This does not require great wealth; it is achievable even at very low incomes, as has been well demonstrated in Costa Rica, Vietnam and the Kerala state in India.

Health and human security are knowledge-based and socially driven. The knowledge base generates medical technologies, such as vaccines and drugs. It also educates the public to adopt healthful behaviour, seek health services and participate in democratic decision-making to protect their own health. So, knowledge systems—such as health-based information, data and analyses on disease risks and spread—should be promoted and made openly accessible to achieve health and human security.

Health is also advanced by social arrangements, such as health care systems, local health groups and civic engagement. The role of the information media is growing in educating and engaging the public. Most important, the state's assumption of responsibility and authority for the health of its citizens is a critical social arrangement for producing health and human security.

Creating and using knowledge

With people as the ultimate producers of good health, and with health security dependent on knowledge, achieving universal basic education is one of the most important steps to health and human security. Knowledge also empowers health workers, professional associations and civil society to contribute to public health. And knowledge is the basic building block for improving the tools and technologies for health, such as new vaccines, drugs and diagnostics.

Intellectual property for health security. Knowledge builds on the wisdom of the past and the ingenuity of the present for future generations. Traditional knowledge has given the world such essential drugs as aspirin, quinine and taxol—improving the quality of life of millions of people around the world. The recent acceleration of global trade has sparked international debate over the ownership and application of knowledge for human health and security. The debate is twofold. Although there are many barriers to poor people's access to essential drugs, recently promulgated international rules governing intellectual property could lessen the capacity of the world's poorest people to afford vaccines and drugs essential to their health security. Consider life-saving antiretroviral drugs for HIV-positive people in poor countries. Private markets alone do not provide sufficient incentives for investment in knowledge-creation for the many diseases of the poor. Only 10% of global investment in health research, for example, is aimed at the illnesses responsible for 90% of the global disease burden (box 6.3).[17]

At the centre of the debate is the World Trade Organization's (WTO) agreement on Trade-Related Aspects of Intellectual Property Rights (TRIPS). Ratified by member countries of the WTO in 1994, TRIPS affords 20 years of patent protection on a worldwide basis to technological inventions, including vaccines and medicines. Through patenting, a pharmaceutical company that develops a new drug is granted a temporary global monopoly on all production, pricing and marketing of the patented entity.

In November 2001, the Doha Ministerial Declaration of the WTO recognized the special challenges faced by developing countries. It affirmed that "under WTO rules no country should be prevented from taking measures for the protection of human, animal or plant life or health, or of the environment at the levels it considers appropriate". It also reaffirmed the right of governments to use "compulsory licensing" and "parallel imports" to obtain access to key vaccines and drugs to combat national public health emergencies. Compulsory licensing and parallel imports by many of the poorest countries without domestic manufacturing capacity would, however, have little practical meaning because under the restrictive TRIPS clause, developing countries such as Brazil and India, which now export generic medicines, must cease exports by 2005.

WTO negotiations remain divided over the definition of "insufficient manufacturing capacity", the potential for companies in developed countries to export generic drugs still under patent and the measures necessary to prevent the re-export back to the developed world of drugs manufactured under compulsory licenses. Among participating countries, only the United States insisted on a limited, inflexible list of key diseases that would qualify for compulsory licensing, such as HIV/AIDS, tuberculosis and malaria. All other countries, recognizing that health emergencies are by definition unpredictable—witness the urgent need for the antibiotic Cipro during the anthrax crisis and the emergency production of smallpox vaccine—wanted a more flexible approach that did not restrict "public health emergencies" to a few diseases.

Addressing these issues and meeting the challenge to health security posed by the current intellectual property rights regime will require new approaches and new thinking about the ownership of knowledge, health as a human right, and market and institutional structures to both offer incentives and protect lives.

Information to control priority threats. Health empowerment and protection depend on reliable and up-to-date data and analysis and a capacity to act in response to information. Central to health and human security, therefore, are systems to collect and deploy information for detecting disease threats, monitoring their changes and guiding control efforts. All surveillance and control activities ultimately depend on people and local communities, but national and international systems are needed to empower people and

Box 6.3 What role can antiretroviral drugs play in combating the HIV/AIDS threat?

Over the last decade, the HIV/AIDS epidemic has reached daunting proportions, particularly in Africa and Asia. With a vaccine still years away, and prevention efforts having limited success, large-scale use of antiretroviral therapy could help tip the scale of the epidemic back to controllable levels. Antiretroviral therapies reduce the amount the AIDS virus in affected individuals, improving their clinical condition, quality of life and life expectancy. When provided to pregnant women, antiretroviral therapy decreases the risk of transmission to newborns to less than 10%.

Until recently, there was widespread concern that antiretroviral therapy was too complex and resource intensive for use in developing countries. The programme requires adequate pharmaceuticals and diagnostics, human resources, information management systems and physical infrastructure. Recent work in Botswana, Brazil, Haiti and Thailand, however, indicates that with proper support and financing antiretroviral therapy can play an important role in combination with prevention. Each of these countries developed unique programmes suited to their situation and were able to achieve outcomes comparable to those in developed countries. In addition, because of the relative ease of implementation, programmes to prevent mother to child transmission are now being implemented throughout Africa and Asia.

With new funding sources such as the Global Fund to Fight AIDS, Tuberculosis and Malaria, the wider use of antiretroviral therapy in Africa and Asia is increasingly plausible. There are risks as well as benefits to the use of antiretroviral therapy that must be managed. Major risks include taking attention away from prevention efforts, overburdening weak health systems, creating resistance to drugs and improperly communicating the limitations of therapy. The benefits, however, are substantial and include bolstering prevention efforts by reducing the stigma of the disease and increasing testing, maintaining the integrity of communities by increasing life expectancy of affected adults, improving economic performance by sustaining work forces, and increasing hope. Many African nations have now committed to providing therapy for their people and are working to consolidate the support needed to make this promise a reality.

Making large-scale use of antiretrovirals a reality will require increased access to low-cost pharmaceuticals and diagnostics, innovative approaches to bolstering human resources for health, better integration of therapy programmes, and prevention programmes to keep the focus on control of the epidemic. If developed and developing countries commit to these changes, among others, antiretroviral therapy can be a critical measure for improving human security until a vaccine for HIV/AIDS is found.

Source: Shisana, Zungu-Dirwayi, and Shisana 2002.

communities. The transnational spread of contagious diseases and the ripple effect of health problems call for a global surveillance and control system for health and human security. National disease surveillance and control systems, in variouse stages of maturity, should be strengthened and then networked into a global system (box 6.4).

That global system would allow for the rapid sharing of information and responses. It should be plural in participation—including non-governmental organizations, the media and others. But the state and the intergovernmental system must play a key role. The central mission would be to protect the world public from infectious and other contagious threats, irrespective of national boundaries. These national and global systems

should not be dependent on "foreign aid". They are central to health and human survival for all and should thus be supported by the global public through all member governments.

Surveillance systems would naturally focus on the greatest health threats. In many regions of the world, HIV/AIDS, tuberculosis and malaria demand high priority action. Diverse priorities, however, would be expected among different communities and countries. There is sufficient commonality of shared disease threats to link these local systems into a coherent global system—a win-win situation for all participants.

Among these major killers, HIV/AIDS is a global security emergency. But assisted by information, intelligence and monitoring, some

Box 6.4 Minimizing threats to human security through global health surveillance

The challenge of infectious diseases has changed remarkably over the last 30 years. Today the world is more mobile and interconnected as transportation has become more rapid, communication more instantaneous and borders more permeable. The epidemiology of many infectious diseases is rapidly changing, as are the geographical patterns of disease distribution and drug resistance. To respond to infectious disease threats to human security, communities must be able to identify infectious outbreaks and respond rapidly with international support. Improving global surveillance systems represents the best chance for reducing such threats.

Global health surveillance began in 1896 when the International Sanitary Conference agreed on the need for international health surveillance. In 1907 the Organisation Internationale d'Hygiene Publique was established in Paris to gather information on disease outbreaks for eventual distribution to participating countries. Despite these efforts, international health legislation proved ineffective because treaties did not keep pace with scientific advances, and poorer countries were reluctant to participate, for fear of possible repercussions.

After World War II the Organisation Internationale d'Hygiene Publique was replaced by the World Health Organization (WHO). In 1951, WHO issued the International Sanitary Regulations, renamed the International Health Regulations in 1969 and later revised in 1981. The aim was to achieve the greatest possible security against the spread of disease and minimal disruption of international trade and travel. These regulations required member states to notify WHO within 24 hours of outbreaks of cholera, yellow fever and plague. WHO possessed no enforcement powers, working only through persuasion and recommendation. Again, not all countries complied, fearing the costly repercussions on trade and tourism that other reporting countries had faced in the past. The present International Health Regulations cover only three diseases (cholera, plague, and yellow fever) and fail to address other infectious diseases with the potential for international spread.

Today, as globalization has accelerated the spread of disease through trade and travel, the global community must invest anew in every aspect of infectious disease surveillance systems, from basic laboratory and clinical capacity to international agreements on lines of communication and appropriate responses to epidemics. One of the most successful recent initiatives for global surveillance has been the collaborative development of a highly sensitive global infectious disease surveillance and response system, the Global Outbreak Alert and Response Network, initiated by the WHO and maintained by Health Canada. Under development since 1997, it has created a network of over 100 laboratory and disease reporting systems, providing up-to-the-minute reports of infectious disease outbreaks by systematically scanning electronic resources, including web sites, news wires, public health email services and electronic discussion groups. These sources are collaboratively linked to information networks from government centres, academic institutions, UN agencies, overseas military laboratories and prominent non-governmental organizations, including Médecins sans Frontières and the International Federation of Red Cross and Red Crescent Societies.

For outbreaks of international concern, electronic communications are initiated immediately with the affected country to provide rapid, confidential assistance. The Global Outbreak Alert and Response Network also maintains a global database of health professionals who can advise on infectious disease control strategies. The WHO's network of collaborating centres of national laboratories and institutes similarly helps affected countries make efficient use of scarce public health expertise and resources.

From July 1998 to August 2001 the network identified 578 outbreaks in 132 countries, from cholera, meningitis, haemorrhagic fever, and viral encephalitis to anthrax. The network has also undertaken numerous containment activities in developing countries. The network has coordinated large-scale monitoring and international assistance by establishing standardized procedures for verifying infectious disease outbreaks and by coordinating responses with the help of international experts. This approach has helped to minimize the infectious disease-related threats to human security. As the world continues to shrink, efforts like this will remain crucial to protecting the poor from the ravages of infectious outbreaks and protecting the global community from the rapid international spread of infectious diseases.

Source: Heymann 2002; Fidler 1997; WHO 1983; Zacher 1999; Heymann and Rodier 1998.

Promoting community-based health care through insurance can protect people from the devastating downside of catastrophic illness

heavily-infected countries—such as Thailand, Senegal and Uganda—show that HIV/AIDS can be contained. Other countries, where the disease is less widespread—such as Brazil, Mexico, and in Western Europe—show that it is possible to contain an incipient epidemic. Many others—China, India and Russia—face the possibility of explosive growth in the epidemic. Until an efficacious vaccine is developed, the only effective approach to HIV/AIDS is changing human behaviour. The health yield of "safe sex", as estimated by WHO, is enormous. Urgent priority should be accorded to health education, peer support and changes in the conditions that can accelerate modifications in human behaviour for health and human security.

Mobilizing social action

Knowledge that sits on the shelf does little to advance people's health. Social arrangements and institutions, appropriately motivated, are essential to health protection and empowerment. The health advances in the 20th century can be attributed in part to the revolutionary development that governments increasingly assumed responsibility and authority for the health of their citizens. Social action by civil society organizations, business, mass media and other organizations also contributed to these health advances.

Community-based health. Perhaps because poor people are so vulnerable to health risks, they are attempting to mobilize and deploy their health security assets. When poor women gain rudimentary health education, they can become agents of change for their families. When poor communities train local health workers or set up

health insurance schemes, they can manage many health risks at a local level. In strong civil societies, non-governmental initiatives can complement public sector health activities and also advocate for socially progressive changes in public health. But where individual and institutional advocates of health security are only weakly present, or even discouraged, the health security of a population rests on a fragile public sector or imbalanced private market.

Health emergencies arising from epidemics demanding urgent action are the small visible tip of a large iceberg. More significant and longer in term are the silent crises of poverty-linked illnesses and violence, especially gender-based domestic violence. Too often neglected, these silent crises of human insecurity deserve similar priority. A human security approach would recognize these people-centred priorities.

A central part of the peace and development agenda should be a core public health system shaped to national priorities. Because health threats vary among people and countries, these systems naturally would focus on the health and human security priorities of diverse communities and countries. But the core functions of public health are similar—primary prevention and care for major health threats.

"Health for All", promulgated at the Primary Health Care Conference at Alma Ata in 1978, has not been realized. The reasons for this failure range from weak political will to economic incapacity. Public systems have not been adequately developed, and private markets in health care have catered only to those with the money to pay for care. The revitalizing of Health for All will require renewed political commitment translated into sustained investments in the people and infrastructure for universal prevention and care. As long as people are deprived of primary prevention and care, health and human security for all are unachievable.

Promoting community-based health care through insurance can protect people from the devastating downside of catastrophic illness. Although not all sickness can be prevented or treated, all people should have access to core primary health care services. And all should be protected from the downside risks of devastating illness and catastrophic economic loss. Risk-sharing arrangements based on pooled membership funds and community income generation projects have proven successful, as demonstrated by pioneering innovation of non-governmental organizations such as the Self Employed Women's Association and the Bangladesh Rural Advancement Committee. With health risks more global, risk-sharing requires vastly expanded pools of members. National and global resources should back community-based insurance systems, financially and organizationally (box 6.5).

Global health security. In this globalizing era, a new balance must be established among individual, state and global responsibilities for health and human security. Responsibility for health security is shifting down from the national level to individuals, communities and civil society organizations—and upwards to international institutions and networks. As health security responsibilities shift, a stronger system of global health governance is required. Such a system should support and coordinate local and national initiatives—and establish global ground-rules for health security. How? By modernizing international health rules and regulations, fostering partnerships between public and private sectors and building the architecture for global health.

Formal cooperation in international health began in 1851, when the first international health conference sought to contain disease without impeding international trade. The International Health Regulations, last adopted in 1969, were built on a series of agreements over the previous century and a half. As the first formal recognition of global health interdependence, they maximize security against infectious diseases while minimizing the impact on trade and travel. In this globalizing era, the regulations should be updated and expanded to include many emerging transnational health risks, such as environmental threats, tobacco control and criminal violence.

Given the complexities of these tasks, no single institution can perform them all. Many actors are necessary. Recently, innovative partnership arrangements between public and private actors have filled gaps and exploited new opportunities. Mission-driven partnerships have expanded immunization coverage, developed vaccines and drugs against neglected diseases and accelerated health action against priority diseases. Experimental partnership arrangements should be encouraged along with revitalization of formal organizations.

Any global system must grapple with the different threats confronted by people living in diverse contexts. Privileged people in richer countries, having mostly controlled the common infectious diseases, worry about bioterrorism and new or re-emerging infectious diseases that threaten their health and economy, such as the

Box 6.5 Community-based health insurance

The Declaration of the International Conference on Primary Health Care in Alma Ata in 1978 stated that "Primary health care requires and promotes maximum community and individual self-reliance and participation in the planning, organization, operation and control of primary health care, making fullest use of local, national and other available resources". But the question of how poor communities can contribute to the provision of health care persists.

Disease or illness can cause an individual or household to enter a downward spiral in which poor health results in the depletion of assets, and low levels of assets lead to worsening health and the inability to cope with future illness. Government provision of health care should meet the health needs the poor, but in practice often does not.

Community-based health insurance offers the poor an alternative for coping with health crises. It provides a much-needed level of health security to the poor and allows them to pool their resources to access otherwise inaccessible health services. Individuals or households

pay a premium in exchange for compensation for future medical expenses. The community determines the criteria for eligibility, the level of premiums, the method for their collection and the level of payouts. This may allow developing country health sectors, which are starved for funds, to mobilize resources that would otherwise be unavailable.

Vimo SEWA is one example of a community-based health insurance plan, organized by informal economy workers in India. It has been running for more than 10 years and today has 93,000 insured members. From its experience with community-based health insurance in India, Vimo SEWA has concluded that health insurance is not only a growing need and demand of the working poor, but it is also a significant economic support for them. Its members regularly acknowledge that it is Vimo SEWA's health insurance that protects them from slipping back into the poverty from which they had struggled to emerge. Vimo SEWA's experience has also proven that investing in the poor, and women in particular, through community-based health insurance is viable.

Source: Chatterjee and Ranson 2002.

anthrax threat in the United States and mad cow disease in Europe. People in poorer contexts, no less fearful of terror or economic setbacks, must grapple with the more common infections already controlled among the rich. Measles, respiratory infections, cholera and other common infectious diseases are the greatest threats to the world's poor.

These differences in disease risk underscore the importance of encouraging local and national priorities, while seeking mutual health security through international cooperation. Public health infrastructure can provide "dual-use" capacity for managing natural epidemics and defending against bioterrorism. Early warning and response against bioterrorism require public health capacity to identify, validate and control infectious agents. Developing this core public health infrastructure in every country benefits not only individuals but also the global community.

Policy conclusions

Health and human security are central matters of human survival in the 21st century. Knowledge

and technology can make a difference. The challenges are to make tools and knowledge accessible while promoting incentives and structures for the production of new knowledge. And social action is needed to deploy that knowledge for health and human security.

Health and security have long been distinct fields, to the detriment of both. Health has been seen as a "medical problem", and security, as a matter of military defence. The state was responsible for the health and defence of the public, but it assigned these responsibilities to unconnected ministries. People in all countries want good health and human security. And maintaining artificial distinctions between "health" and "security" distorts the priorities of what the public wants in most democratic societies. The main requirements:

- Urgent action is needed to combat HIV/AIDS and other human security-threatening diseases.
- Intellectual property rights should build in incentives for advancing human security.
- National disease surveillance and control systems should be formally linked into a global

system. Such a system would allow for the rapid sharing of knowledge and quick response to infectious disease-related threats, including those resulting from emerging and re-emerging communicable diseases, drug-resistant strains of disease and incidents of bioterrorism.

- Every country should build a core public and primary health care system, shaped to national priorities.
- Community-based health-insurance should protect otherwise-vulnerable people from the devastating downside of catastrophic illness.

Notes

1. World Bank 1993.
2. WHO 2003.
3. UNDP 2002.
4. INDEPTH Network 2002.
5. Chen, Wittgenstein and McKeon 1996.
6. Petter Gleditsch and others 2001, UNDP 2002.
7. Rothschild 1995.
8. Cash and Narasimhan 2000.
9. McNeill 1998.
10. Cohen 2002.
11. National Intelligence Council 2002.
12. Narayan 2000.
13. Jacoby and others 2001.
14. Leaning, Briggs and Chen 1999.
15. WHO 2002.
16. Chen, Evans and Cash 1999.
17. UNDP 2002.

References

Alkire, S. 2002. "Conceptual Framework for Human Security."

Cash, R., and V. Narasimhan. 2000. "Impediments to Global Surveillance of Infectious Diseases: Consequences of Open Reporting in a Global Economy." *Bulletin of the World Health Organization* 78(11): 1358–67.

Chatterjee, Mirai, and M. Kent Ranson. 2002. "Exploring the Quality and Coverage of Community-Base Health Insurance among the Poor: The Vimo SEWA Experience." Paper prepared for the Commission on Human Security. [www.humansecurity-chs.org].

Chen, Lincoln C., and G. Berlinguer. 2001. "Health Equity in a Globalizing World." In T.G. Evans, M. Whitehead, F. Diderichsen, A. Bhuiya and M. Wirth, eds., *Challenging Inequities in Health: From Ethics to Action.* Oxford and New York: Oxford University Press.

Chen, Lincoln C., and Aafje Rietveld. 1994. "Human Security During Complex Humanitarian Emergencies: Rapid Assessment and Institutional Capabilities." *Medicine and Global Survival* 1(3): 156–63.

Chen, Lincoln C., T.G. Evans and R.A. Cash. 1999. "Health as a Global Public Good." In Inge Kaul, Isabelle Grunberg and Marc Stern, eds., *Global Public Goods: International Cooperation in the 21st Century.* New York: Oxford University Press.

Chen, Lincoln C., F. Wittgenstein and E. McKeon. 1996. "The Upsurge of Mortality in Russia: Causes and Policy Implications." *Population and Development Review* 22(3): 517–30.

Cohen, Desmond. 2002. *Human Capital and the HIV Epidemic in Sub-Saharan Africa.* Working Paper 2. ILO Programme on HIV/AIDS and the World of Work.

Fidler, D. 1997. "Return of the Fourth Horseman: Emerging Infectious Disease and International Law." *Minnesota Law Review* 81: 771–868.

Hampson, F. O., and J. Hay. 2002. "Human Security: A Review of the Scholarly Literature." *Human Security Bulletin* 1(2).

Heymann, David. 2002. "The Evolving Infectious Disease Threat: Implications for National and Global Security." Paper prepared for the Commission on Human Security. [www.humansecurity-chs.org].

Heymann, David, and G. Rodier. 1998. "Global Surveillance of Communicable Diseases." *Emerging Infectious Diseases* 4: 362–65.

INDEPTH Network. 2002. *Population and Health in Developing Countries.* Volume 1. Ottawa: International Development Research Centre.

ICISS (International Commission on Intervention and State Sovereignty). 2001. *The Responsibility to Protect: Report of the International Commission on Intervention and State Sovereignty.* Ottawa: International Development Research Centre.

Jacoby, M.B., T.A. Sullivan and E.Warren. 2001. "Rethinking the Debates over Health Care Financing: Evidence from the Bankruptcy Courts." *NYU Law Review* 76(2): 375–418.

Kaul, Inge, Isabelle Grunberg and Marc Stern, eds. 1999. *Global Public Goods: International Cooperation in the 21st Century.* New York: Oxford University Press.

King, Gary, and Christopher J. L. Murray. 2002. "Rethinking Human Security." *Political Science Quarterly* (Winter).

Lammers, E. 1999. *Refugees, Gender and Human Security: A Theoretical Introduction and Annotated Bibliography.* Utrecht: International Books.

Leaning, Jennifer, Susan M. Briggs, and Lincoln C. Chen. 1999. *Humanitarian Crises: The Medical and Public Health Response.* Cambridge, Mass.: Harvard University Press.

Matsumae, T., and L. C. Chen, eds. 1995. *Common Security in Asia—New Concepts in Human Security.* Tokyo: Tokai University Press.

McNeill, W. 1998. *Plagues and People.* New York: Anchor Books.

Murray, Christopher J. L., Gary King, Alan D. Lopez, Niels Tomijima and Etienne Krug. 2002. "Armed Conflict as a Public Health Problem." *BMJ* 324(7333): 346-49.

Narayan, Deepa, Robert Chambers, Meera K. Shah and Patti Petesch. 2000. *Crying Out for Change: Voices of the Poor.* Oxford and New York: Oxford University Press.

National Intelligence Council, U.S. Central Intelligence Agency. 2002. "The Next Wave of HIV/AIDS: Nigeria, Ethiopia, Russia, India, and China." Washington, D.C.

Palme Commission on Disarmament and Security. 1989. *A World at Peace: Common Security in the Twenty-first Century.* Stockholm.

Petter Gleditsch, N., P. Wallensteen and others. 2001. *Armed Conflict 1946–2000: A New Dataset.* Joint report from the Conflict Data Project in the Department of Peace and Conflict Research at Uppsala University and the Conditions of War and Peace Program at the International Peace Research Institute, Oslo.

Rothschild, Emma. 1995. "What is Security?" *Daedalus* 124(3): 53–98.

Shisana, Olive, Nompumelelo Zungu-Dirwayi and William Shisana. 2002. "AIDS: A Threat to Human Security." Human security background paper. Global Equity Initiative, Harvard University, Cambridge, Mass.

Strong, M.A. 1992. "The Health of Adults in the Developing World: The View from Bangladesh." *Health Transition Review* 2(2): 215–24.

UNDP (United Nations Development Programme). 1994. *Human Development Report 1994: New Dimensions of Human Security.* New York: Oxford University Press.

———. 2002. *Human Development Report 2002: Deepening Democracy in a Fragmented World.* New York and Oxford: Oxford University Press.

WHO (World Health Organization). 1983. *International Health Regulations.* Third annotated edition. Geneva.

———. 2002. *World Report on Violence and Health.* Geneva.

———. 2003. *World Health Report.* Geneva.

World Bank. 1993. *World Development Report 1993: Investing in Health.* New York: Oxford University Press.

Zacher, Mark. 1999. "Global Epidemiological Surveillance: International Cooperation to Monitor Infectious Disease." In Inge Kaul, Isabelle Grunberg and Marc Stern, eds., *Global Public Goods: International Cooperation in the 21st Century.* New York: Oxford University Press.

Knowledge, skills and values for human security

7

The human security perspective underscores the importance of basic education, particularly for girls

In the 1990s, the percentage of children enrolled in primary education increased in all regions of the world, despite the difficulties of conflict or macroeconomic instability or poor growth. Yet the barriers to schooling are sturdy enough to block reaching the goal of universal primary education by 2015. Adult literacy in least developed countries was 53% in 2000, and literacy among youths ages 15–24 was only 66%.[1] Gender parity for youth literacy has been achieved in Central and Eastern Europe and Latin America and is close to being achieved in East Asia and the Pacific. The other regions lag behind: for South Asia, 8 girls achieve literacy for every 10 boys ages 15–24; for the Arab States, it is 8.5 girls and for Sub Saharan Africa, it is 9 girls. These numbers hide huge variations within countries.[2]

Of the word's population of 6.2 billion, about 862 million people—or one in seven—are illiterate.[3] The highest percentage of illiterate people live in Africa, where more than half the women were illiterate in 1997. South and West Asia together house about three-quarters of the world's illiterate populace, although percentages vary greatly within countries (figure 7.1). Other pockets of illiteracy may be identified in displaced populations and refugees, illegal immigrants, nomads and disabled children, but the educational data for these groups are weak.

What about children and youths? Of the world's 775 million primary school-age children, more than 115 million were not in school in 1999.[4] Nearly all of these out-of-school children (97%) lived in developing countries, and 60% of them were girls.[5] So one shortfall is straight-forward: there is not schooling for everyone—no "universal primary education". Most of the children out of school live in Asia and Africa.

Connecting basic education to human security

The human security perspective, distinctive in its emphasis on empowerment and mutal respect, underscores the importance of basic education, particularly for girls. Basic education has been the objective of generations of teachers, parents and government leaders. It is a fundamental human right, both in the International Convention on

Figure 7.1 Estimated world illiteracy rates, by region and gender, 2000

Percent

[Bar chart showing illiteracy rates by region. Y-axis: Percent, from 0 to 60. X-axis regions left to right: Developed countries, Latin America and the Caribbean, East Asia and Oceania[a], Sub-Saharan Africa, Arab states, South Asia. Each region has two bars: Male (black) and Female (gray).]

■ Male ■ Female

a. Excluding Australia, Japa and New Zealand.
Source: UNESCO Institute for Statistics.

Education can give people freedom to promote their human security and that of others

Economic, Cultural and Social Rights and in the Convention on the Rights of the Child. In 1872, Japan's educational code promised that there would be "no community with an illiterate family, nor a family with an illiterate person".[6] In the late 1940s, a newly independent India promised universal primary education for its populace by 1960. Similar campaigns of education for self-reliance were advanced by Ghana's Kwame Nkrumah, Tanzania's Julius Nyerere, Kenya's Jomo Kenyatta and others in post-independence Africa.

Basic education has intrinsic value. The capability to read and write improves the quality of life and directly affects people's security, because illiteracy and innumeracy are themselves insecurities. Illiterate people cannot read public notices or bus signs, utility bills or newspapers, letters or street signs, wills or loan applications. They must find someone to read for them—and hope that the reader is trustworthy and accurate. The most immediate contribution of literacy: to reduce this core insecurity.

Basic education, especially girls' education, is also fundamental for health. It works through many channels. Women, often the primary caregivers, can put their knowledge of health, sanitation, immunization, nutrition, HIV/AIDS prevention and oral rehydration therapy into practice in the family—if they have that knowledge and if the home environment permits. In Ghana, "children of educated mothers are twice as likely to survive to their fifth birthday as children of uneducated mothers".[7] Women's education and women's employment are the two signal influences in reducing fertility rates.[8] The impact of an educated woman on her family's well-being is consistently strong worldwide.

Basic education usually boosts the prospects for gainful employment, increasing returns to land or other assets. It is far more critical today than a generation ago, when the manufacturing and agricultural sectors absorbed more of the workforce. So expanding the reach of education improves economic prospects for individuals, for communities, for countries.[9] The economic benefits from education are pervasive—whether in the informal sector, at the cutting edge of high-technology industries or on a family farm. A woman's earning capacity is particularly important, because it often affects her status and her ability to make other decisions in the family.

In addition to the human security benefits stemming from education, schools can act as delivery points for other human security interventions, such as school feeding, immunization, landmine awareness and cholera prevention programmes. Free school meals or rations increase parents' incentive to send children—especially girls—to school. Better nourishment improves a child's ability to concentrate and thus to learn. Studies in Benin, Burkina Faso and Togo, among others, found that when school meals were provided, children's test scores improved.[10] Thus schooling may enable students to address direct threats to their survival, livelihood and dignity now and in the future.

Education can also give people freedom—through knowledge, public expression and democratic debate—to promote their human security and that of others. Free, independent and pluralistic information media are an integral part of such freedom, as is an education that opens the mind. This was emphasized in the Universal Declaration on Human Rights, which articulates the right to an education that supports "human rights and fundamental freedoms" and promotes "understanding, tolerance and friendship among all nations, racial or religious groups". Without such freedom, when people's ability to communicate with one another and to speak out is suppressed, lives are impoverished. That is why a further set of relationships between education and human security focuses on empowerment.

When people are undereducated, their ability to understand and invoke their rights can be very limited. Basic education, adult literacy classes and informational radio programming offering instruction on specific matters of daily concern—such as HIV/AIDS prevention, human rights, child nutrition, market prices or agricultural techniques—can equip people to deal with the insecurities that loom largest in their lives.

When education enables people to express their needs, the connection to human security becomes powerful. The works of artists, poets, scholars, activists and journalists show the intrinsic value of this freedom. Beyond this intrinsic value, education can foster democratic resilience. When women and men can speak freely and explore ideas without fear of recrimination, the better facets of democracy—including the ability of the group to improve on the initial suggestions of individuals—become visible. Conversely, a lack of knowledge or an inability to communicate can muffle the political voice of the downtrodden and add to their insecurity.

So education and knowledge can enable people to be assertive in society—to speak out on their own behalf. This is particularly important for women, whose empowerment affects their lives, those of other women and those of their family.

Education and knowledge may also enable groups to identify common problems and act in solidarity with others.[11] By making people more effectively vocal, education and information can play a significant protective role and can thus further human security.

Adopting a human security approach
What are the main leverage points for investments in education to further human security? Supporting basic education, eliminating gender disparity and achieving universal primary education are fundamental. Basic education can have a long reach as a tool for achieving human security. This reach is deeply compromised when schooling itself threatens children's security. But it can be considerably extended if students, once in school, are empowered to promote their own security and taught to appreciate and value human diversity. Four priorities for action:
- Promoting a global commitment to basic education.
- Protecting students' human security at and through school.
- Equipping people for action and democratic engagement.
- Teaching mutual respect.

Promoting a global commitment to basic education
One might expect a human security commission to come up with a more novel recommendation than basic education for all. Some issues may no longer startle policy-makers by their originality or cause a storm of newspaper headlines. But, simply put, they are undeniable keys to a more secure future. Basic education is one of these issues.

Box 7.1. Private sector partnerships for education in South Africa

South Africa is the leading economic force in Sub-Saharan Africa, but its educational system, still recovering from its apartheid past, is in crisis. An estimated 10% of South African students in grades 1 through 7 are repeaters. Yet the government invests a great deal in education (over 7% of GNP and 22% of government expenditure during 1995–97).

In 1994, recently elected President Nelson Mandela called on the private sector to help repair the damage done by apartheid to both the education system and the social fabric of the country. Corporations recognized the wisdom of helping to ensure a stable, productive society in which long-term investment could flourish and long-term returns could be realized. Businesses also saw a financial advantage in helping provide a basic education for future employees, rather than continuing to provide

costly on-the-job training for an undereducated workforce.

One example of private sector initiative is the Business Trust, a group of 145 South African companies that invest 2% of after-tax profits over and above their existing corporate social responsibility programmes in education, job creation and crime reduction programmes. The Business Trust has committed 153 million rand (over $15 million) to improving learning at the primary level through programmes such as the Primary School Repeater Reduction Programme. This initiative aims to halve the repeater rate in schools over five years. Thus far 12,000 teachers have completed 21 of the 35 training modules so that they can implement the programme. This undertaking is projected to reach 15,500 teachers and principals and 1 million primary school pupils by its completion.

Source: UNESCO Institute for Statistics 2002; UNDP 2002b, p. 180; Business Trust 2003.

International support and local partnerships. Internationally, the commitment to basic education appears stronger than ever before. There is widespread political acceptance of the importance of education as a means to poverty reduction, economic growth and human development—for all states, including those in or emerging from conflict. At the first global conference on education—in Jomtien, Thailand, in 1990—150 governments pledged to achieve universal primary education by 2000 and to halve adult illiteracy.

In Dakar, Senegal, in 2000, thousands of children marched in the streets, holding up yellow umpire cards as a "last warning" to policy-makers. The Dakar conference occurred 10 years after Jomtien, with the policy-makers' broken promises in plain view. Their promise to provide universal primary education by 2000 "had been comprehensively broken".[12] The UN Secretary-General launched a global Girls' Education Initiative in Dakar. And those supporting the Education for All campaign renewed their efforts. Universal primary education is one of the Millennium Development Goals announced in 2000, and the Literacy Decade began in 2003.

These are tremendously positive initiatives—to be strengthened and sustained.

Equally crucial for successful schooling as international support are local partnerships of parents and community leaders that support local schools and hold teachers accountable for the quality of primary education (box 7.1).

One notable absence from this consensus for basic education: it barely appears on security agendas. If security strategies mention education at all, they tend to promote education of their own personnel or support high-level research that generates military or strategic advantage. The power of an educated woman to look after her own family, to raise and educate healthy children, to speak in the public space, to be vigilant in mediating conflicts before they erupt into violence—that has been overlooked entirely. Yet she, too, is a security asset. Similarly, war-affected boys and girls who learn conflict mediation in refugee schools are security assets that can foster coexistence. Educating girls and boys, women and men, is a cost-efficient investment in human security for a country and beyond.

The World Bank and the United Nations estimate that if four days' worth of the annual military expenditure worldwide were diverted to education every year, that would provide the funding needed to achieve worldwide primary education by 2015.[13] The security advantages of a basic education must be disseminated more widely.

Barriers to education for all. If education is so valuable, to individuals and to societies, why has it been so difficult to achieve universal primary education? The opportunities for education—and the barriers to it—vary by country and locality. But there are three common barriers: poor quality, insufficient funding and the lack of schooling for displaced children.

Cultural factors and gender roles can reduce the demand for education. But as the *Arab Human Development Report 2002* argued, cultural barriers are not impermeable (UNDP 2000a). The quality and affordability of schooling—and the safety and availability of schools—are also powerful drivers of parents' decisions of whether to send children to school. Spending on education will lead to universal enrolment only if education systems address these issues.

Teachers are the crux of any educational system and its quality. A study of schools in India found that in half the schools investigated, there was no teaching going on at the time that the study team visited. The reason for parents'—and students'—disillusionment with schooling arose not from their economic or gender biases but from the dismal quality of schooling. The study also cited a loss of interest in school as the most common reason boys drop out.[14]

To realize universal primary schooling, parents and communities need to be empowered to hold

teachers accountable. And immediate and sustained attention to systems of teacher training, support and supervision is essential at many levels. Otherwise countries may meet the letter but not the spirit of the Millennium Development Goals by subjecting children to sub-standard schooling.

Costs also matter. Providing schools, especially good quality schools, requires political will, financial resources and a solid institutional structure, whether public, private or non-governmental. Countries that have achieved good progress in education have generally devoted 5–7% of their GDP to education.[15] But the actual public investment in education—by national governments as well as bilateral and international agencies—is often inconsistent with the high regard for universal primary education. Indian political parties have professed an ambition to invest 6% of GDP in education. But public expenditure on education declined from 4.4% of GDP in 1989 to 3.6% in 1997.[16] When governments invest too little in education, an astonishing proportion of household expenditure must go to meet the costs of primary school. "In Sub-Saharan Africa, the costs of getting a child through primary school can represent more than a quarter of the annual income of a poor household".[17] While parental involvement is critical, costs of this magnitude clearly subvert the right of every child to primary education.

In emergencies, children are often denied the normalcy of education precisely when they need it most. Many children—displaced by conflict, or development projects, or disasters—live in temporary communities without access to schooling. They are very difficult to reach in wartime—and yet the Millennium Development Goals and human rights apply to them too.

School feeding programmes help reduce immediate and chronic hunger and improve children's learning capacities

Preliminary estimates by the UN High Commissioner for Refugees suggest that enrolment rates among refugee populations are dishearteningly low—about 50%, and less for girls.[18]

This is cause for alarm because displaced and refugee children can benefit greatly from the stable social environment that school can provide. They need schooling to address the economic, health and social insecurities that press in on their lives.[19] They also need an environment that supports positive values to counter the negative and divisive messages that would draw them into the conflict and perpetuate violence. That is why the Dakar Framework and UN Literacy Decade, among other initiatives, specifically identify refugees, internally displaced persons and disaster-affected persons as requiring special support.[20]

These are but three of the issues that need to be addressed for a global commitment to schooling. The barriers to universal basic education vary in different places. But they are not mysterious. And they are surmountable.

Protecting students' human security at and through school

Schooling can give great impetus to protecting many dimensions of human security. But it fails when going to school threatens students' security. The *Voices of the Poor* study found this many times.[21] In Kimarayag, Philippines, children said, "we have to cross three creeks to reach our schools. These creeks swell up to four feet during rainy periods. When the rains come, our mothers fear for our lives".

Many parents are concerned not just about the value of an education, but about their children's safety and well-being. So the protection of human security in the school and its environs should be an integral part of educational quality. Schools should promote physical and mental well-being. They should ensure safety and security for both boys and girls. And they should provide adequate infrastructure, including hygiene and sanitation. They should not be recruiting grounds for militia and armed groups.

Parents' concerns for the security of adolescent girls are particularly high—justifiably. In Malawi, the high drop-out rate among pre-adolescent girls has been linked to concerns about safety in the classroom. Sexual abuse of pre-adolescent girls by teachers is increasing in countries as diverse as Japan and Peru. Studies in South African schools document that male teachers routinely sought sexual favours from their students. In one Ugandan district, 31% of girls and 15% of boys reported being sexually abused, mainly by teachers.[22]

On the positive side, school feeding programmes help reduce immediate and chronic hunger and improve children's learning capacities. Nutritious school meals also provide incentives to keep children in school. The World Food Programme has launched a Global School Feeding Initiative because its research and experience show that "when food is provided at school, hunger is immediately alleviated and attendance often doubles within one year. Within two years, academic performance can improve by as much as 40% and students remain in school longer and more graduate".[23]

Equipping people for action and democratic engagement

Access to information and skills—whether in school or through other communication—allows people to learn how to address concerns that directly affect their security. This can be information about vaccination, oral rehydration therapies, problem-solving, teamwork, agricultural products or legal rights. Armed with such skills, people can address their insecurities.

Take basic education as an imperative to prevent HIV/AIDS. A 2002 World Bank study, *Education and HIV/AIDS,* found that "a general basic education—and not merely instruction on prevention—is among the strongest weapons against the HIV/AIDS epidemic".[24] This is especially important for girls, who tend to take care of ill relatives and are more vulnerable to infection because they are more likely to have older partners and are more easily infected than boys. The Joint United Nations Programme on HIV/AIDS (UNAIDS) found that "in 11 population-based studies, the average infection rates in teenage African girls were over five times higher than those in teenage boys. Among young people in their early 20s, the rates were three times higher in women".[25] Transmitting knowledge, self-confidence and support to girls in their pre-teen years is a matter of survival—not to transmit is unconscionable.

Informational programming—on the radio and television or in the newspaper—can complement schools in combating human security threats. For example, Radio Ada, a not-for-profit community radio station in Ghana, serves about 600,000 people, 60% of them illiterate. All farm-related programming is created directly by the farmers—women and men. Radio programmes discuss agricultural practices, weather, farming calendars, the marketing and prices of farm produce, conservation and government policy.

Radio Ada is highly valued—farmers often take their radios into the fields with them.

Free and diverse information media can also chronicle events and policies—and can air a countervailing opinion to state-run or otherwise controlled press. This information dissemination function of the media allows people to learn of concerns that directly affect their security, including downturns such as macroeconomic shocks and famine, the HIV/AIDS pandemic and government corruption. By providing information the media can promote democratic governance by fostering civic debate, mobilizing democratic engagement and checking abuses of power, as the next section suggests.[26]

Knowledge, education and democratic engagement are inseparable—and essential. Well before the economic value of education and "human capital" became a driving force behind the international support for education, many argued that an educated populace was essential for a stable democracy—among them Aristotle, Nyerere, Nehru and Freire. Of course, much depends on the content of education and on the structure of governance. Yet many have argued that education does create an impetus, however incrementally and imperfectly, for local groups and individuals to hold others accountable—whether these others be international institutions or local schools, government leaders or family members.

Free and diverse information media can provide individuals with the knowledge required to exercise their rights and to influence—or challenge—the policies of the state and other actors. A free and independent press is one of the hallmarks of an open society, where the public is able to debate issues of national interest and

Teachers who aim to empower can raise awareness of the social environment

scrutinize government policies. The information media, therefore, fulfil the very important social need of providing a forum for public discussion and engagement.

As seen repeatedly, there has been no major famine in a country with a genuinely free press (box 7.2). The Chinese famine of 1958–61 killed 15–30 million people; it occurred in the absence of an uncensored press or other means of open communication. Not only were citizens denied information to insist on a change in government policy, but the government did not know the full extent of the catastrophe. Cambodia, the Democratic People's Republic of Korea, the Soviet Union, Sudan, Somalia and Zimbabwe have all suffered severe hunger in a vacuum of information. Elsewhere, with famine threatened or reported, as in India after partition, people tend to mobilize assistance and political pressure to address the insecurity of famine in its early stages.

The information media also play a direct role in holding the political leadership accountable. A recent example was the 2000 Peru cable television broadcast of bribes being paid in exchange for votes. The exchange had been secretly videotaped. The Peruvian press released the tape together with disclosures about military corruption, death squad activities and ties between the illegal drug trade and the government. President Fujimori resigned immediately following the videotape's broadcast.

But the press is substantially free in only about 40% of countries.[27] Members of the press and other information media are vulnerable to harassment, injury and imprisonment in a number of countries—especially in situations of conflict and under totalitarian regimes. In 2001, 118 journalists were imprisoned for pursuing their stories, more than 600 were intimidated or physically attacked and 37 were killed.[28] A restricted press can neither effectively distribute information nor relay people's wishes and human security concerns to policy-makers.

Freedom of the press and of the people who provide accurate information—journalists, human rights activists—sometimes at risk of their lives, deserves deliberate protection. In a world committed to ensuring human security, there is an urgent need to acknowledge that repression of critical opinion and scrutiny in the name of "security" is unacceptable. Human security, with its dual notions of protection and empowerment of people, can materialize only when journalists are free to report on corruption and other potentially dangerous situations without risk to their lives.

Teaching also affects how education and information contribute to popular engagement—for adults and for children. A curriculum that encourages learning by rote can breed a passive populace reluctant to question ideas. Teachers who aim to empower can raise awareness of the social environment and provide the tools to address problems. They can also teach students to reason, to consider ethical claims, to understand and work with such fundamental ideas as human rights, human diversity and interdependence. Chapter 1 argues the need to grasp the reality of human interdependence more directly and more widely. This chapter argues the need to instil in the content of education a new emphasis on ethical values—and on public debate and democracy. A key work force to communicate these ideas: the 59 million people employed as teachers throughout the world, two-thirds of them in developing regions.[29]

Box 7.2 Famines, wars and information media

The worst famines in history have been associated with wars and authoritarian regimes. War-torn countries like Cambodia, Ethiopia and Somalia have faced famine; the Bengal famine of 1943 (which killed 2–3 million people), occurred soon after the Japanese army moved into northeastern India. Famines have occurred under colonialism (as in British India and Ireland), in one-party states (as in Cambodia, China and the Soviet Union), and under military dictatorships (as in Ethiopia and Somalia). Today, the countries with famine or near-famine conditions are authoritarian ones, like the People's Republic of Korea and Sudan (Drèze and Sen 1989).

No famine has occurred in a functioning democracy. Public policies aimed at protecting the vulnerable can prevent famines, and governments in multiparty democracies try to do so, as it is difficult to win elections after a famine. The information media play a central role either by reporting the crisis or by failing to comment on it. For instance, the British government ignored the Bengal famine until an Indian national daily, The Statesman, started running photographs of the dead and the dying and condemning official apathy in its editorials. In the People's Republic of Korea, the state-sponsored television ran advertisements extolling the virtues of dieting while people perished of starvation. An independent media can draw attention to the direst threats facing a country, and thereby prod its government into timely action.

Wars can lead to famine by destroying crops, damaging roads and disrupting the movement of essential commodities. The destruction of medical networks adds to famine mortality through disease. Long-run agricultural and trade-related investments suffer during war, so the general economic stagnation goes well beyond the destruction of existing capital goods to a devastation of productive abilities. Military activities can also accentuate economic and political divisions within a country and make it possible for one group to command an unfair share of resources, thereby depriving others. Ironically, wars also furnish authoritarian regimes with excuses to suppress alternative political views and any media scrutiny, and thus enable the rulers to ignore a national crisis like famine.

Ultimately, much of the protective power of a democracy comes from its free press. Indeed, Zimbabwe, which successfully prevented famines by timely public action in the 1980s, when its multiparty democracy worked and the press was free to scrutinize policy, is now threatened by famine as its political governance has turned much more authoritarian.

Source: Nicholas Kristoff, *The New York Times,* January 14, 2003, p. A2; Sen 2001, 1981, 1987.

An example of teaching that empowers is the well-known approach to popular education championed by Paolo Freire. The REFLECT (Regenerated Freirean Literacy through Empowering Community Techniques) approach, developed by ActionAid in 1993 to engage adults in an active learning process, is used by more than 2,500 groups in more than 30 countries. The focus is to enable people to "recognize the different forces that are at work and how they are changing; address those forces that determine their access to power; see their own centrality to any process of change; and make the orbits spin in their favour".[30] Other forms of adult education, such as public information campaigns and targeted training programmes on human rights and social mobilization, are also central. Whatever the manner of teaching, the aim is to produce citizens who embrace their rights and responsibilities, who become "empowered" agents to promote human security.

Other key work forces for human security include the police, the armed forces, private security forces and others with access to the means of coercive force. Programmes including human rights education, gender awareness and civic engagement should be made available to these groups, for they have the most direct power to violate physical security. Or to protect it.

Teaching mutual respect

Schools and their teachers, whether in developed or developing countries, in primary schools or adult literacy classes, can teach mutual respect and solidarity. They can also perpetuate prejudice.

Education influences a child's sense of identity. In religious schools, children may learn to think of

Schools and their teachers can teach mutual respect and solidarity. They can also perpetuate prejudice

themselves "first" as Buddhists, Christians, Hindus or Muslims. In public schools, children may be taught loyalty to their country's identity and ideals. This can be valuable in giving children self-esteem and in forming strong value systems. But school-children may also learn to construct negative stereotypes. For example, textbooks often present distorted accounts of national history that vilify traditional "enemy" groups. School lessons can immediately influence the actions of children displaced in conflict—especially if schools indoctrinate and recruit child soldiers. Prejudices are not born in a vacuum (box 7.3).

Giving overwhelming prominence to only one identity creates a population that can be mobilized to "fight" for that identity in many ways. Conversely, teaching students to think of themselves and other students as having multiple identities (as a female, Cuban, Catholic, Spanish-speaking football enthusiast) may create a stabilizing force because students can often find some common ground. A human security consultation among 120 partners in Kigali recommended that the concept of ethnicity be demystified so that students could learn to welcome and respect diversity, without focusing on differences that divide society. Participants in a public hearing on human security in Johannesburg recommended that the curriculum challenge destructive gender stereotypes.

Many schools serving refugee populations or conflict sites—such as in Burundi, Liberia and Somalia—have incorporated peace-building, mediation or human rights modules into their curricula.[31] The messages that war-affected children and child soldiers receive in school are tremendously important. As Martha Minow put it, "After mass violence, after terror, the challenge is

not to 'return to normal' after the conflict, for normal is what produced the conflict".[32] In addition to conflict-resolution courses, Minow identifies four constructive kinds of "education for coexistence". *Intergroup education* has students from parties in tension learn together. *Human rights* training introduces students to the basic ideals and concepts of dignity and respect. Instruction in *moral reasoning* includes case studies. By *rewriting history* students learn not to see themselves as victimized.[33] A wisely constructed curriculum can broaden a child's perspective and reinforce positive attitudes.

Just as a curriculum can support respect for diversity or create prejudice, so too can teachers' attitudes shape students' perspectives and feelings of self-worth. Teachers may regularly favour boys over girls, or children from superior castes or influential ethnic groups. They may have much less patience with first generation schoolchildren who do not have the support at home for homework— or with children from stereotypically "inferior" backgrounds. This perpetuates the vicious cycle of discrimination by signalling to young children that it is acceptable to disparage others for their gender, race or academic performance. These attitudes were documented in a survey in West Bengal that found a much higher rate of teacher absenteeism in schools with the majority of children from scheduled castes and tribes (75%, or more than twice the 33% at other schools).[34] That three out of four teachers of the poorest and lowest castes fail even to show up for work demonstrates their disdain for students and absence of concern about censure.

It may seem a luxury to focus on these matters when so many children are outside the school

123

Box 7.3 Inflammatory education

Inflammatory educational material has existed for decades, if not centuries, and is a part of educational systems throughout the world, even today. Recent claims are made, for example, that textbooks used by Palestinian students incite them to become suicide bombers. Other claims are made that Israeli textbooks incite anti-Palestinian sentiments in readers. Without deciding on the validity of these claims, it is possible to draw some lessons from a review of examples of inflammatory content and of the motivations and processes that produce such books.

Begin with some inescapable observations. First, all curricula have to simplify. No book or set of books can cover everything. Textbook writers cannot know everything, and students cannot and should not be expected to learn everything. There must be a process of highlighting and discounting, of including and excluding. In short, there must be a process of decision-making. Consequently, the biases, motivations and attitudes of the decision-makers are involved in the process. Whether these influences are political, economic, ethical, religious, personal or some combination, they are subsequently reflected, to greater or lesser degrees, in the resulting textbooks, which then influence the students who study them.

Of course, textbooks alone do not a student or a person make. Other influences have strong effects. Teachers, for example, guide and motivate, discipline and reward, inspire or disillusion. Other students influence in positive or negative ways, and family and the larger social context all contribute to the education of the student.

Still, textbooks are a critical component of the educational process. They communicate values, and these values are not always consistent with the principles of human security. Quite the contrary, their messages can be destructive of the objectives of human security and, in some instances, actually support the infliction of insecurities, violent or otherwise, on others.

Inflammatory content tends to fall into two basic categories: overly complimentary of one's own group or overly critical of another group. In the first, students are taught to identify themselves with one race, religion or other group. The goal should instead be to teach students that they are part of many groups and can decide how to live out these identities. In the second category, students are taught malice towards "enemies". The goal should instead be to cultivate mutual respect among diverse groups. While teaching materials, especially about national and group histories, are inevitably inflicted by interests and politics, it is nonetheless possible to identify a real difference between those that emphasize superiority of one group or negative stereotypes of others and those that pursue complexity, balance, tolerance and peace.

Source: Adapted from Minow 2002.

---

system. But 660 million children, more than a tenth of the world's population, do go to school. And they are the ones who will inherit the decision-making responsibilities in a few short decades. Their minds are the nerve-centre of future human security. It is important to train them in the ways of mutual respect (box 7.4).

Policy conclusions

Education and information—whether for leaders or for the poorest children—must do more than convey information. It must also kindle compassion, cultivate mutual respect, host open-mindedness, advance clarity of thought, foster determination and develop resolve. Three agendas for action—one familiar and two equally central—

can accelerate progress towards this aim: to empower all people with education and knowledge, to equip all people to exercise their rights and responsibilities and to teach mutual respect.

Empowering all people with education and knowledge. The Commission on Human Security endorses the UN Literacy Decade and the Millennium Development Goals of achieving universal primary education and eliminating gender disparity in education. To these the Commission would add four additional priorities:

- Expanding the "emergency education" programmes of non-governmental organizations and international organizations so that all displaced and crisis-affected children have a basic education.

Box 7.4 The power of the information media for tolerance or terror

In the absence of information, the world is like a darkened room where monsters are created out of shadows. Indeed, autocrats and warlords often seek to preserve and expand their power by creating a darkness through censorship and propaganda that obscures the truth and engenders a fearful ignorance that can easily be transformed into hatred of another ethnic group, political party or religion. Not only education but also a free press can shed light in the corners and expose the true authors of the nightmare. While the information media can be a voice for mutual respect and a forceful advocate for principled behaviour, misused the media can worsen human insecurity.

In 1994 Rwanda, in an organized campaign of violence, the Tutsi were referred to as "cockroaches" and "the enemy" in the media. Rwandan radio broadcasters on Radio Mille Collines declared that it was the duty of every Hutu to kill a Tutsi and noted that "the graves are still only half full". The station broadcast the names and addresses of Tutsis and moderate Hutu along with their vehicle license plates. In less than four months, between 500,000 and a million people were killed. Owners and broadcasters of Radio Mille Collines were later indicted by the International Criminal Tribunal for Rwanda for their role in the genocide.

But the information media can also be a power for coexistence and respect for human rights. In 1993, a series of hate crimes targeting African Americans, Jews and Native Americans shook a small community in Billings, Montana, in the United States. Racist and anti-Semitic fliers were posted, a Jewish cemetery was desecrated and threatening phone calls were made. When a cinderblock was thrown through the window of a Jewish family displaying a menorah for Hanukkah, Billings human rights activists asked that the local newspaper make this incident front-page news. The *Billings Gazette* printed a full page picture of a menorah and urged citizens to put the pictures up in their homes and businesses.

Hundreds of townspeople responded, and printed menorahs appeared in windows throughout the town. Bricks were thrown again, through the windows of a school and two churches that had put up the menorahs, and residents of several homes displaying menorahs had their cars vandalized. The citizens of Billings countered the attacks by displaying more of the printed menorahs. By the end of December, an estimated 10,000 people in Billings had menorahs in their windows. The city did not declare victory, as threats and vandalism continued sporadically. But the violence did not escalate. And the need for a culture of committed tolerance in the Western frontier town was openly discussed both in the information media and in civil society.

Source: Marlise Simons, 2002, "Trial Centers on Role of Press during Rwanda Massacre," *New York Times,* 3 March, p. 3; Human Rights Watch [www.hrw.org/WR2K3/africa9.html].

- Empowering parents, community committees and social movements to hold schools accountable for providing a good quality education, and urging the information media to fulfil their role as public advocates by focusing attention on improving education systems.
- Encouraging states and school authorities to ensure a safe and secure learning environment for all children, free of violence, discrimination and exploitation.
- Advancing innovative uses of curricula, the information media and communications technology (including radio, television, the arts, newspapers and the Internet) to make the knowledge and skills needed to improve human security widely accessible.

Equipping all people to exercise their rights and responsibilities. Students and citizens who learn to value the power of information, spirited inquiry and non-violent argument are better equipped to exercise their rights and responsibilities.

- Increasing partnerships to create and disseminate curricula and teacher training programmes that consistently develop student abilities to form and articulate views and take action on behalf of these views.
- Establishing and enforcing laws safeguarding freedom of information and of the press, and eliminating laws that may be used to arbitrarily restrict such freedoms.
- Insisting that states and other controlling authorities protect the rights of journalists,

human rights activists and other conduits of public information so that they may continue to report on human security concerns without being intimidated or attacked.

Teaching mutual respect. The information media and educational systems should inculcate tolerance and affirm interlocking identities.

- Ensuring that curricula in all schools cultivate mutual respect and emphasize the multiplicity of identities—including gender, ethnic, religious and national—so that students learn to recognize the bonds they share with others.
- Ensuring that teachers counter rather than perpetuate discrimination—among groups and genders within the classroom and among national, religious and ethnic groups. This may require adjustment to teacher training and better supervision and incentive systems.
- Training those with access to coercive force (especially police and peacekeeping forces) to support coexistence and respect for human rights for all people.

Notes

1. UNDP 2002b, p. 233.
2. UNDP 2002b, p. 233.
3. UNESCO 2002a.
4. UNESCO 2002a.
5. UNESCO 2002a.
6. Amartya Sen, "To Build a Country, Build a Schoolhouse," *New York Times,* 27 May 2002.
7. Watkins 2000, p. 3.
8. Drèze and Murthi 2001.
9. On this and related issues, see Drèze and Sen 1995 and Drèze and Sen 2002.
10. Del Rosso 1992, as cited in Watkins 2000, p. 41.

11. The categories of assertion and solidarity are developed in Drèze and Sen 2002, sections 1.7 and chapter 10.
12. Watkins 2000, p. 1.
13. Cited in Watkins 2000, p. 8.
14. Probe Team 1999.
15. Mehrotra 1997, as cited in Watkins 2000, p.210.
16. Drèze and Sen 2002, p. 166.
17. Watkins 2000, p. 172.
18. UNHCR 2001.
19. Sommers 2002.
20. Dakar Framework for Action, paragraph 8. See also Sommers 2002 and Bensalah 2002.
21. Narayan and others 2000a and 2000b.
22. UNAIDS 2000.
23. WFP 2001, p. 1.
24. World Bank 2002, p. 10. See also UNICEF, UNAIDS and WHO 2002.
25. UNAIDS 2000.
26. These are discussed in UNDP 2002b, chapter 3.
27. Sussman and Karlekar 2002, p. 5.
28. UNDP 2002b, p. 77.
29. UNESCO 2002b.
30. Archer 2001.
31. UNESCO Culture of Peace Programme (supported by UN Resolution 57/6 27 November 2002) engages more than 2,000 actors to promote such education widely. See also Aguilar and Retamal 1999, pp. 41–43.
32. Minow 2002, p 5.
33. Minow 2002.
34. Pratichi Trusts 2001.

References

Aguilar, Pilar, and Gonzalo Retamal. 1999. *Rapid Educational Response in Complex Emergencies.* Geneva: International Bureau for Education.

Archer, David. 2001. "The Evolving Concept of Literacy in REFLECT." PLA Notes. *Education Action* 9.

Bennett, Jane. 2001. "Peace-building through Communication in Burundi." *Education Action* 15.

Bensalah, Kasem, ed. 2002. "Guidelines for Education in Situations of Emergency and Crisis: EFA Strategic Planning." UNESCO, Paris.

Business Trust. 2003. "Learning for Living." [www.btrust.org.za/education/primary_schooling/].

Del Rosso, J. 1992. "School Feeding Programmes: Improving Effectiveness and Increasing the Benefit to Education." Partnership for Child Development, Oxford.

Drèze, Jean, and Mamta Murthi. 2001. "Fertility, Education, and Development: Evidence from India." *Population and Development Review* 27.

Drèze, Jean, and Amartya Sen. 1989. *Hunger and Public Action.* Oxford: Clarendon Press.

———. 1995. *India: Economic Development and Social Opportunity.* Oxford: Oxford University Press.

———. 2002. *India: Development and Participation.* New Delhi: Oxford University Press.

Foster, A., and M. Rosenszweig. 1995. "Learning by Doing from Others: Human Capital and Technological Change in Agriculture." *Journal of Political Economy* 103(6).

Funkhouser, E. 1996. "The Urban Informal Sector in Central America: Household Survey Evidence." *World Development* 24(11): 1737–51.

Government of Pakistan. 1996. *Pakistan Integrated Household Survey Round 1: 1995–1996.* Islamabad: Federal Bureau of Statistics.

Grantham McGregor, Sally, Susan Chang and Susan Walker. 1998. "Evaluation of School Feeding Programs: Some Jamaican Examples." *American Journal of Clinical Nutrition* 67: 785S–789S.

Kreuger, Alan, and Jitka Maleckova. 2002. "Does Poverty Cause Terrorism? The Economics and the Education of Suicide Bombers." *The New Republic* 24 June.

Kumar, Krishna. 2001. *Prejudice and Pride.* New Delhi: Viking.

Larweh, Kofi. 2001. "The Community Radio Station as a Resource for Farmers: The Case of Radio Ada." *Voices,* Developing Countries Farm Radio Network. October.

Levinger, Beryl. 1986. "School Feeding Programs in Developing Countries: An Analysis of Actual and Potential Impact." USAID Evaluation Special Study 30. Washington, D.C.

Levinger, Beryl, Cornelia Janke and Kristin Hicks. 1996. "CRS School Feeding/Education Companion Guidebook." Catholic Relief Services, Baltimore.

Mehrotra, S. 1997. "Social Development in High-achieving Countries: Common Elements and Diversities." In R. Jolly and S. Mehrotra, eds., *Development with a Human Face: Experiences in Social Achievement and Economic Growth.* Oxford: Clarendon Press.

Minow, Martha. 2002. "Education for Coexistence." Draft.

Narayan, Deepa, Raj Patel, Kai Schafft, Anne Rademacher and Sara Koch-Schulte. 2000. *Voices of the Poor: Can Anyone Hear Us?* Oxford and New York: Oxford University Press.

Narayan, Deepa, Robert Chambers, Meera K. Shah and Patti Petesch. 2000. *Crying Out for Change: Voices of the Poor.* Oxford and New York: Oxford University Press.

Pratichi Trusts. 2001. "Pratichi Education Report." [www.amartyasen.net/pratichi.htm].

Probe Team. 1999. *Public Report on Basic Education in India.* New Delhi: Oxford University Press.

Sen, Amartya. 1981. *Poverty and Famines. An Essay on Entitlement and Deprivation.* Oxford: Clarendon Press.

———. 1987. Food and Freedom. Washington D.C.: Consultative Group on International Agricultural Research.

———. 2001. "The Delivery of Primary Education."

———. 2002a. "Basic Education and Human Security." Paper presented at the Kolkata Meeting, organized by the Commission on Human Security, UNICEF, the Pratichi (India) Trust and Harvard University, Kolkata, India, January.

———.2002b. "Global Inequality and Persistent Conflicts." Paper presented at the Nobel Awards Conference, Oslo.

———. 2002c. "Human Security: Notes for the Commission." March.

———. 2002d. "Keynote Address." Chulalongkorn University, Bangkok, 11 December.

Sommers, Marc. 2002. "Children, War and Education: Reaching the Education for All Objectives in Countries Affected by War." Conflict Prevention and Reconstruction Working Paper 1. World Bank, Washington, D.C.

Sussman, Leonard, and Karen Deutsch Karlekar. 2002. Annual Survey of Press Freedom 2002. Washington, D.C.: Freedom House.

United Nations, General Assembly. 2001. Report of the Secretary-General. Road Map towards the Implementation of the United Nations Millennium Declaration. A/56/236. New York.

UNAIDS (Joint United Nations Programme on HIV/AIDS). 2000. Report on the Global HIV/AIDS Epidemic. New York.

UNDP (United Nations Development Programme). 2002a. Arab Human Development Report 2002. New York: Oxford University Press.

———. 2002b. Human Development Report 2002. New York: Oxford University Press.

UNESCO (United Nations Educational, Scientific and Cultural Organization). 2002a. Education for All:Global Monitoring Report. Paris.

———. 2002b. "More Children: Fewer Teachers: New UNESCO-ILO Study Sees Global Teacher Shortage Causing Decline in Quality Education." Press release, 5 October.

UNESCO Institute for Statistics. 2002. "Percentage of Repeaters by Grade at Primary by Country and By Gender for the School Years 1998/1999 and 1999/2000" September.

UNICEF (United Nations Children's Fund), UNAIDS (Joint United Nations Programme on HIV/AIDS) and WHO (World Health Organization). 2002. Young People and HIV/AIDS 2002. Geneva.

UNHCR (United Nations High Commissioner for Refugees). 2001. Education 2001 Report. Geneva.

Van Stuijvenberg, Elizabeth, Jane D. Kvalsvig, Marita Kruger, Diane Kenoyer and A.J. Spinnler Benade. 1999. "Effect of Iron, Iodine and B Carotene-fortified Biscuits on the Micronutrient Status of Primary School Children: A Randomized Controlled Trial." American Journal of Clinical Nutrition 69: 497–503.

Watkins, Kevin. 2000. The Oxfam Education Report. Oxford: Oxfam GB.

World Bank. 2002. Education and HIV/AIDS: A Window of Hope. Washington, D.C.

WFP (World Food Programme). 2001. "WFP Brief: School Feeding." July. Rome.

———. 2002. "News Release May 2, 2002." Rome.

Ways to advance
the security of people

8

With human security as the
goal, there can be a stronger
integrated response

This report proposes a new framework—a human security framework—to address the conditions and threats people face at the start of the 21st century. Human security is "people-centred", focusing the attention of institutions on human beings and communities everywhere. By placing people at the centre, the human security approach calls for enhancing and redirecting policies and institutions. Human rights and human development have reoriented legal, economic and social actions to consider their objectives from the perspective of their effect on people. Recognizing the inter-dependence and interlinkages among the world's people, the human security approach builds on these efforts, seeking to forge alliances that can wield much greater force together than alone.

People want peace, human rights, democracy and social equity. But the institutions, policies and priorities of today do not yet match this ardent expectation. Within the United Nations, the economic and security agendas are fragmented, with the Security Council charged with issues of peace and security, and the General Assembly covering a wide range of economic, social and cultural issues, among many others. The major resources and operational strength on development matters are housed in the international financial institutions. So responsibility for the various (inseparable) parts of human security is lodged in separate parts of the United Nations and related bodies.

With human security as the goal, there can be a stronger integrated response—a response that fosters both global and local identities and that encourages people, as citizens of the world, to support each other when so many are in need. The human security approach thus joins, in one integrated perspective, efforts to solve the problems generated by violent conflict and by economic and social deprivation. Recent international efforts to reduce poverty and build more comprehensive development frameworks have attempted to advance integrated responses to common problems. They should now be informed by systematic links to people in conflict and transition.

The Millennium Development Goals also represent a unified response to poverty. Specifying a set of targets and the resource requirements to achieve them, the goals are renewing the momentum to reduce poverty. But the goals are only one of seven priorities in the Millennium Declaration of the United Nations, released in September 2000. Other aspects address "peace, security and disarmament". The declaration also includes strengthening the rule of law, taking action against transnational crime, replacing the culture of reaction with one of prevention, advancing disarmament, and reforming UN sanctions, peacekeeping and peace-building operations. Still other sections address "our common environment", "human rights, democracy and good governance", "protecting the vulnerable" and "meeting the special needs of Africa". Significantly, the Millennium Declaration directs the world's attention to the conditions of billions of people and to the threats to survival and well-being.

Just as the Millennium Development Goals have brought national and international actors together in a focused struggle against poverty, so too must there be a consensus on concrete and feasible policy targets to address other aspects of

Human security should be mainstreamed in the work of global, regional and national security organizations

human security. The targets must go well beyond the Millennium Development Goals to respond to the full range of critical and pervasive threats, as contained in the Millennium Declaration.

A global initiative for human security

The Commission on Human Security proposes that a global initiative be mobilized to place human security at the top of local, national, regional and global agendas. The goals: To prevent conflict and advance human rights and development. To protect and empower people and their communities. To deepen democratic principles and practices. All to promote a human security culture and framework.

Putting human security at the top of the agenda

Human security should be mainstreamed in the work of global, regional and national security organizations. The UN Security Council has gradually broadened its understanding of threats to global peace and stability to include massive refugee movements, HIV/AIDS and serious human rights violations. But that understanding has to be broadened further to include an array of other human security issues, so that mechanisms can be developed to respond to them. That requires emphasizing the security of people along with military security. It also requires normative frameworks and new programmes to address the specific insecurities of different communities and groups.

Putting human security at the top of the agenda will change the way local, national and global actors pursue their missions. It calls for:

- Integrating development concerns with the activities of human rights and humanitarian agencies.

- Complementing the Millennium Development Goals by addressing conflict and violations of human rights.
- Enhancing official development and humanitarian assistance to accommodate these new directions, paying special attention to countries falling behind and to failed and abandoned states.

Preventing conflict and promoting human rights and development

Preventing conflict is now high on the agenda of the United Nations and the G-8. Available tools include early warning mechanisms, targeted sanctions, fact-finding and diplomatic missions, and preventive deployments of peacekeeping operations. And more emphasis is being placed on education, poverty reduction and equity.

Recognizing that protecting people is a common responsibility is an important step forward. The challenge now is to translate this common responsibility into concrete policies and actions. A strong civil society—and strong communities—can prevent conflict by articulating group goals, monitoring abuses of power and proposing effective solutions to the many grievances (box 8.1).

Development advances freedom when it enhances people's capabilities and choices so that they can participate actively in all spheres of life. The freedoms that people enjoy also depend on social and economic arrangements, on political and civil rights (the state, the market, the legal system, political parties, public interest groups). Promoting basic economic security, by reducing poverty and raising living standards, can thus have a substantial positive social impact—especially by making

Box. 8.1 Global inequality and persistent conflicts

It is not surprising that possible connections between the two great afflictions of the contemporary world—violent and persistent conflicts, and massive economic inequality and poverty—should attract attention. Even though definitive empirical work on the causal linkages between political turmoil and economic deprivations may be rare, the basic presumption that the two phenomena have firm causal links is widespread.

Many countries have simultaneously experienced—and continue to experience—economic destitution and inequality and political turbulence and strife. From Afghanistan and Sudan to Ethiopia and Somalia, there are numerous examples around the world of people facing these dual adversities. It is thus not unnatural to ask whether destitution kills twice—first through economic privation and second through political carnage. If the quality of mercy is "twice blessed", the quality of destitution may well be "twice cursed".

This possibility is not in doubt. And its underlying logic is not hard to understand. Penury and deprivation can make people desperate and reckless. It is also not unreasonable to think that people reduced to stark poverty will have reason to fight for tiny rewards, and this could make conflicts and warfare much more likely. The possibility of such linkages must be adequately acknowledged. And yet there are several reasons for caution before jumping to explain hostility and carnage through poverty and privation.

The first concerns empirical evidence. There is no dearth of evidence of conflicts and confrontations in economies with a good deal of poverty and much inequality. But there are also economies with no less poverty or inequality that seem to stay sunk just in economic hardship, without generating serious political turbulence. Indeed, many famines have occurred without much political rebellion, civil strife or inter-group warfare.

The second reason concerns the need to go beyond empirical observations into causal analysis, and the importance of scrutinizing presumed causal linkages. Surely destitution can give reason enough to defy established rules, but it need not give people the courage and the ability to do anything violent. Destitution can be accompanied not only by economic debility, but also by political helplessness. A starving wretch can be too frail and too dejected to fight or even to protest. It is thus not surprising that intense suffering and inequity have often enough been accompanied by peace and quiet. However, the memory of destitution and devastation may well linger—and later contribute to generating rebellion and violence.

The third reason for caution is the difficulty of establishing the direction of causation in cases where economic poverty and violent strife coexist. Do these empirical observations provide evidence for the causation of strife (starting from poverty), or for the causation of destitution (connected with violent disorder)? Indeed, there is at least as strong a causal link from war and violence to famines and destitution, as from the latter to the former.

Of course, avoidance of war and eradication of destitution are both important ends, and it is quite plausible that each feeds the other. The political and military antecedents of destitution seem to deserve more serious attention than they tend to get. In particular, it is worth recollecting how famines and severe impoverishment have often been associated with antecedent military activities and violent encounters.

Source: Adapted from Sen 2002.

---

people more resilient to political, economic and financial downturns.

Protecting and empowering people and communities—to promote a culture of human security

Few societies protect human security with the force and effect of their responses to the many threats to state security. But the aim of human security is to do precisely that—to build a protective infrastructure that shields all people's lives from critical and pervasive threats. That infrastructure includes working institutions at every level of society: police systems, environmental regulations, health care networks, education systems, safety nets and workfare programmes, vaccination campaigns, diplomatic engagements and early warning systems for crises or conflict.

People's ability to act on their own behalf or on behalf of others is one key to human security.

The Commission recommends that the tasks of advancing human security on all fronts start by addressing some of the basics and then building on early successes

Empowered people can demand respect for their dignity when it is violated. They can also create new opportunities for work and address many problems locally. And they can mobilize action and resources for the security of others.

Deepening democratic principles and practices

A democratic political order, buttressed by physical safety and economic growth, helps to protect and empower people. Respecting democratic principles is a step towards attaining human security and development. It enables people to participate in governance and make their voices heard. Deepening democratic principles and practices at all levels mitigates the many threats to human security. It requires building strong institutions, establishing the rule of law and empowering people.

Citizenship, a person's membership in a particular state, is at the centre of democratic governance. It determines whether a person has the right to take part in decisions, voice opinions and benefit from the protection and rights granted by a state. But the outright exclusion and discriminatory practices against people and communities—often on racial, religious, gender or political grounds—makes citizenship ineffective. Without it, people cannot attain human security. So, deepening democratic principles and policies requires inclusive citizenship practices.

Addressing the basics

The Commission recommends that the tasks of advancing human security on all fronts start by addressing some of the basics and then building on early successes:

- Protecting people in violent conflict.
- Protecting people from the proliferation of arms.

- Supporting the human security of people on the move.
- Establishing human security transition funds for post-conflict situations.
- Encouraging fair trade and markets to benefit the extreme poor.
- Providing minimum living standards everywhere.
- According high priority to universal access to basic health care.
- Developing an efficient and equitable global system for patent rights.
- Empowering all people with universal basic education, through much stronger global and national efforts.
- Clarifying the need for a global human identity while respecting the freedom of individuals to have diverse identities and affiliations.

1. Protecting people in violent conflict

Upholding people's rights and freedoms is a serious challenge in violent conflicts, especially for people who face extreme economic and social deprivation. Civilians, not combatants, are the main casualties in conflicts, and civilians are by far the most common targets in ethnic, racial or religious conflicts. There has been considerable progress in strengthening and expanding the normative framework—such as human rights and humanitarian law—for civilians caught up in conflict as well as the institutions, such as UN agencies, the International Committee of the Red Cross, and other non-governmental actors. But few effective mechanisms can be invoked to protect people in violent conflict and immediately afterwards.

To help overcome these gaps, comprehensive and integrated strategies are essential, linking

Comprehensive and integrated strategies are essential, linking political, military, humanitarian and development aspects, all mutually reinforcing and dependent

political, military, humanitarian and development aspects, all mutually reinforcing and dependent. With a focus on protecting people rather than adhering to institutional mandates, the current compartmentalization among the numerous uncoordinated actors should be overcome.

Upholding fundamental human rights and humanitarian law in conflict situations is another gap to be closed—by strengthening human rights organizations at all levels and by reconciling divided communities. The International Criminal Court should prosecute perpetrators of serious human rights violations. And countries should set up tribunals and truth and reconciliation commissions. These institutional and rights-based efforts should be complemented by community-based strategies to promote coexistence and trust among people.

Equally urgent is meeting the life-saving needs of people through humanitarian assistance—in effect, an emergency safety net. Particular attention should go to collapsed states, for reasons not only of life-saving needs, but also of security threats such as terrorism and illegal trafficking in people and weapons. In addition to attending to women and children, protection strategies need to be developed for the elderly, the disabled, the indigenous and the missing.

To establish and maintain the safety of people and communities in conflict situations, responses should give primacy to public safety. After conflict, processes such as national security reforms and the demobilization, disarmament and re-integration of combatants should promote social stability and productivity and prevent a surge in crime and corruption. Civilian police should be strengthened immediately so that they can keep the peace and

protect women, children and other groups from further dangers. Enabling the police to fulfil their role requires deliberate investments in legal and judicial institutions, so that the police are able to promote respect for human rights and the rule of law.

2. Protecting people from the proliferation of arms

There is also a great need to stop the proliferation of weapons that threatens the security of people. Four permanent members of the UN Security Council—France, the Russian Federation, the United Kingdom and the United States—are responsible for 78% of global exports of conventional weapons. Germany, the remaining major contributor, is responsible for an additional 5%.[1] About two-thirds of these exports go to developing countries.[2] This trade in arms foments violent conflicts. It also tends to have terrible indirect effects on society, the polity and the economy.

Small arms. The world holds an estimated 640 million durable and relatively inexpensive small arms. Although the data are very poor, rough estimates indicate that these weapons kill some 500,000 people each year, making them de facto weapons of mass destruction. And they are used to displace, intimidate or coerce millions more. Reducing the spread of illicit small arms requires urgent and concerted attention. The work of more than 500 groups in almost 100 countries that have brought the dangers of small arms to the attention of the states and the United Nations deserves support. Quicker implementation by governments of the findings of the *Report of the United Nations*

The feasibility of a humane international migration framework should be explored

Conference on the Illicit Trade in Small Arms and Light Weapons is also needed.[3]

Proliferation of weapons of mass destruction. The current move towards developing weapons of mass destruction—nuclear, chemical and biological—endangers people in both developing and developed countries. Efforts must be redoubled to strengthen the nuclear non-proliferation regime and to supervise and promote implementation of other treaties and agreements. Efforts to halt proliferation must enter the mainstream public policy debate.

Military spending. Citizens need to be empowered to scrutinize state security priorities—to consider, among other things, military spending in relation to spending on other human security priorities. States should increase the transparency of their reporting, especially on military spending and weapons systems. An internationally accepted common reporting framework would make these reports comparable and enable civil society to influence the changing structures of military security.

3. Supporting the human security of people on the move

The movement of people across borders and continents reflects the growing interdependence among countries and people. For the majority of people, migration represents an opportunity to improve their livelihoods. For others, such as people forced to flee because their lives and property are threatened by war, conflict or serious human rights violations, migrating is vital to protecting their human security. Others may also be forced to leave their homes to escape extreme poverty, chronic deprivation or sudden downturns.

International migration framework. There is no agreed international normative framework for the orderly management and protection of people moving across borders. The feasibility of a humane international migration framework should be explored. Such a framework should cover not just the states receiving migrants but also the sending and transit states. Recalling humanity's interdependence, the framework should also strike a careful balance between the security and development needs of receiving states and the human security of people on the move. Such a framework should aim at:

- Progressing towards the orderly and safe movement of people, in part by increasing migratory opportunities and burden-sharing among countries.
- Developing international and regional norms for the movement of people between countries, as well as the rights and obligations of migrants.
- Formulating strategies to combat human trafficking and smuggling, and implementing relevant international and regional conventions, while protecting the rights of victims.
- Protecting migrants against racism and intolerance and other human rights violations.
- Developing an institutional framework.

Therefore, the Commission proposes that a high-level and broad-based task force explore the options and areas of consensus, including alternative institutional arrangements. Parallel to this process, international, regional and national actors should cooperate more on migration issues, with the United Nations taking the lead, in line with the Secretary-General's report on strengthening the organization.[4]

Refugees and internally displaced persons. Protection of refugees and internally displaced persons is a high priority. In particular, the physical security of displaced people needs to be protected by separating armed elements from civilian refugee populations and preventing gender-based violence. Normative frameworks and institutions need to be reinforced. Also required are increased operational involvement and greater predictability in the responses of international agencies.

Concerted efforts should be pursued to identify solutions to displaced populations, whether refugees or internally displaced persons. In the transition from conflict, the voluntary return and integration of displaced people should be a high priority. The needs of displaced people should thus be included in reconstruction and development plans, with burden-sharing by countries and enhanced financial resources from donors.

4. Establishing human security transition funds for post-conflict situations

Cease-fire agreements and peace settlements may mark the end of violent conflict, but they do not automatically imply peace and human security. The responsibility to protect people in conflict should be complemented by a responsibility to rebuild, particularly after an international military intervention. The measure of success is not the cessation of conflict—it is the quality of the peace that is left behind.

A successful transition from conflict to peace and development depends on attaining human security. It is about people reasserting their rights at political, social and economic levels. And one cannot be achieved without the other. But there are gaps in advancing the security of people, in meeting essential needs, in achieving reconciliation and coexistence, in launching reconstruction and development activities and in promoting governance and empowerment. To close these gaps the international community must formulate a new framework and devise a new funding strategy to rebuild conflict-torn states—one that focuses on the protection and empowerment of people.

Such a human security framework would emphasize the linkages among the many issues affecting people, integrating policies and activities and moving beyond simply coordinating sectoral approaches. In the spirit of the Brahimi Report on the reform of peacekeeping operations,[5] it requires setting up unified leadership for all political, military, development and humanitarian actors close to the delivery point of human security, such as in Afghanistan and Timor-Leste. International responses should be driven not by organizational or donor interests, but by the needs of people and communities.

To apply such a framework, a new fundraising strategy is needed for post-conflict situations, at field level, to ensure coherence in the planning, budgeting and implementation of human security activities. The proposal to set up transition funds for each post-conflict situation is a step in this direction. Such funds would finance the activities agreed to under the integrated human security framework, pooling resources for human security activities. The funds could thus address a broader range of human security issues than are addressed today and could focus on chronically underfunded activities, such as

The sequencing of market reforms to promote economic growth must be balanced with investment in social services and human development

education, reconciliation and coexistence, reform of the national security sector and reintegration of displaced people. To allow flexible disbursement, the funds should not be earmarked.

To maintain the confidence of donors and beneficiaries, management of the funds should emphasize transparency and accountability. Participation by national authorities is essential for setting priorities and gaining ownership of the process. To ensure equitable sharing of the benefits of peace, other parties to conflict should also be included to the extent possible.

5. Encouraging fair trade and markets to benefit the extreme poor

Markets and trade are basic to economic growth and have been a source of unprecedented wealth for some. Extensive use of markets will be essential to generate the kinds of growth required to meet the needs of the extreme poor. The central issue from a human security perspective is not whether to use markets—it is how to support a set of diverse and complementary institutions to ensure that markets benefit the extreme poor and enhance people's human security, freedom and rights.

Balance market reform with human security imperatives. The sequencing of market reforms to promote economic growth must be balanced with investment in social services and human development to ensure the well-being of the poorest and most vulnerable. Policymakers should give as much priority to advancing people's security as to reaping benefits from market expansion, foreign investment and growth. Emphasizing the distribution of the benefits of growth and redirecting resources to the extreme poor, especially

women, children, the disabled and the elderly, matter a great deal.

Strengthen social institutions to reach the vulnerable and the extreme poor. Attention must also be paid to strengthening social institutions—such as education, social services, health and community-based care—to complement the market's contribution to human security. For example, women's unequal access to resources, training and education contributes to labour market discrimination against women; prioritizing education for girls and women, and the removal of other structural barriers, can help counteract this discrimination.

Ensure equity in trade arrangements. International trade is crucial for development and growth in all societies. But the efficiency and equity of trade arrangements are important too. Developing countries still face higher barriers against their exports, particularly in agriculture and textiles—labour-intensive industries that are pivotal for equitable growth in many states. Tariffs and quotas for textile imports to rich countries cost developing countries an estimated 27 million jobs.[6] Agricultural protection and subsidies in rich countries cost low- and middle-income countries about $60 billion in rural income a year. Reducing barriers to agricultural and textile trade in developed countries would thus do much to spur the equitable and vigorous economic growth that human security requires.

6. Providing minimum living standards everywhere

A comprehensive approach to work and work-based security is essential to human security. Secure

**A comprehensive approach to
work and work-based security
is essential to human security**

livelihoods depend on finding sustained and creative ways of ensuring both income and meaningful work that build on the capacity and ingenuity of poor people themselves. Critical aspects to be addressed include access to land, credit, training and education, especially for poor women. Also critical are measures to ensure that there is a social and economic minimum for all, including the working poor and those not in paid work. Special measures are needed for those in chronic poverty as well as those who would be most vulnerable to economic hardship during economic downturns, disasters and crises, including women, children, the disabled and the elderly.

At a time when three-quarters of the world's people are not protected by social security measures or do not have secure work or wage work, the first step is to strengthen the commitment to achieving an economic and social minimum, below which no one should fall, by:

- *Promoting, through social dialogue among all actors, investments in minimum economic and social protection measures* that address the needs of the working poor (in the formal and informal sectors), those who provide unskilled migrant labour, those who live in situations of conflict and those working to provide care, especially women.
- *Recognizing that human security entails assigning equal importance to social and economic objectives.* This means that safety nets and social protection systems and programmes need to be in place so that when downturns strike, the negative social impacts are prevented or mitigated.
- *Developing the capacity of governments to raise resources and revenues to finance social programmes*

that address the needs of the poorest and most vulnerable. While social protection policy can enhance opportunities for the poor and vulnerable, it does not deal entirely with issues of equity and attaining minimum living standards.

7. *According high priority to universal access to basic health care*

The world faces multiple health emergencies, above all HIV/AIDS. But tuberculosis, malaria and inadequate coverage of child immunizations also create emergency situations. Poverty-related health threats are perhaps the greatest burden of human insecurity. Most preventable infectious diseases, nutritional deprivation and maternity-related risks are concentrated among the world's poor people. Poverty and disease set up a vicious spiral with negative economic and human consequences. And all forms of violence—collective, interpersonal and self-directed—are public health problems, revealing other links between health and human security. Action to address these emergencies is needed at all levels—community, national and global.

Universal access to basic health care. Health for All has not been realized—unfortunately. The reasons for the failure range from weak political will to economic incapacity. Public systems have not been adequately developed, and private markets in health care have catered to those with money. Progress on universal access to basic health care will require renewed political commitment, translated into sustained investments in the people and infrastructure needed for universal prevention and care. Where possible, civil society and the information media could demand and support political commitments to basic health care.

There is an urgent need for institutional arrangements to make inexpensive and affordable generic drugs available to the developing countries that need them most

Community-based health initiatives. Community-based health care and self-insurance schemes are fundamental to this progress. Although not all sickness can be prevented or treated, all people—including those affected by conflict—should have access to core primary health care services. And all should be protected from the downside risks of devastating illness and catastrophic economic loss. Risk-sharing arrangements that pool membership funds have proven successful, as demonstrated by the pioneering innovation of non-governmental organizations (NGOs), such as the Bangladesh Rural Advancement Committee and Grameen Bank in Bangladesh and the Self Employed Women's Association in India. National and global resources should back community-based insurance systems, financially and organizationally.

Surveillance systems. The world urgently needs primary health services and national disease surveillance systems—formally networked into a global system. Information, data and analysis can help to identify disease outbreaks and strengthen efforts to control their spread. So every country should have primary health services and disease surveillance capacities. Where low incomes preclude adequate local or national systems, international cost-sharing mechanisms should be developed to support a global minimum of health care capacity. These national systems should be linked through networks in a truly global system, to allow for rapid knowledge sharing and rapid responses.

8. Developing an efficient and equitable global system for patent rights

Global flows of knowledge and technology are increasing under the World Trade Organization (WTO). In November 2001, the WTO's Doha Ministerial Declaration recognized the challenges facing developing countries. A number of important drugs do not have patent limitations. But for those that do, current international rules governing intellectual property leave many of the poorest people in the world unable to use the drugs. Because so many lives are at stake, there is an urgent need for institutional arrangements to make inexpensive and affordable generic drugs available to the developing countries that need them most.

Developing countries that currently export generic medicines—such as Brazil, China and India—must fully comply by January 2005 with the WTO requirements that generic medicines be used domestically only. They cannot be exported, even to other countries with similar emergencies that may not be able to produce medicines on their own. If a country has insufficient manufacturing capacity to produce medicines domestically, it will have to rely on expensive patented medicines for health needs—unless, of course, the rules are changed.

On the positive side, the WTO now recognizes public health emergencies as requiring special provisions. The Doha Round affirmed the rights of governments to grant "compulsory licences" allowing the domestic production of essential medicines, even when they are covered by patent, and to purchase "parallel imports" from legitimate international sources during national emergencies, including the HIV/AIDS pandemic. Further, the ministers at Doha agreed that the least developed countries would not be required to offer patent protection on pharmaceutical products until 2016. Because many poor countries do not have sufficient manufacturing capacity, their exercise of compulsory licensing and parallel imports depends on international sources. If other developing countries cannot export essential emergency medicines and vaccines under the WTO, the exercise of emergency measures will be nominal, not real.

Three issues need to be resolved. First is clarifying the definition of "insufficient manufacturing capacity". Second is allowing companies in one country to export inexpensive generic drugs still under patent to other countries. Third is deciding on the measures necessary to prevent the re-export of drugs manufactured under compulsory licences back to the developed world. Addressing these issues and meeting the challenges that the current intellectual property rights regime poses to health security will require new approaches and new thinking about the ownership of knowledge, about health as a human right and about effective market and institutional structures to protect both lives and incentives.

A major objective will be to have intellectual property rights systems that advance human security through the efficient development of appropriate drugs and the facilitation of their extensive use. Any resolution of the current impasse should favour flexibility and overcome import and export controls on the drugs and vaccines needed for emergencies. A balance must be crafted to provide incentives for research and development for both profitable products and technologies to fight diseases of the poor. That balance should also provide equitable access to life-saving essential drugs and vaccines for people unable to purchase technologies from the global marketplace. The balance should recognize the very large public investments in basic research that underlie product development by all manufacturers, including private ones.

9. Empowering all people with universal basic education, through much stronger global and national efforts

Basic education and literacy are vital not only for productivity and job skills but also for empowering students, keeping them safe and giving them a broader world view. Universal primary education, as well as being a fundamental human right, is a tremendously important investment for human security. A basic education contributes to good health and to HIV/AIDS prevention—sometimes even more than health education alone. People who are equipped with information, habits of inquiry and reasoned argument are better equipped to lend their voice to protect human security. And yet schools are sometimes places of human insecurity—when students lack food or suffer violence at school.

Much stronger and sustained global and national commitments are needed for providing universal primary education and eliminating gender disparities in education. That would require action by parents, teachers, education committees, NGOs and social movements, education ministries and political parties, donor governments and such international institutions as the United Nations Children's Fund and the United Nations Educational, Scientific and Cultural Organization.

Some of the most important steps towards achieving universal primary education are well-known: supporting girls' education and making schools adaptable to the needs of girls, committing significant resources to schooling and supporting

Education should promote understanding of people's multiple identities and of the interlinkages within the common global pool of learning

school feeding programmes. To these should be added four additional priorities:

- Expanding the "emergency education" programmes of NGOs and international organizations so that all displaced and crisis-affected children have a basic education.
- Empowering parents and community committees and social movements to hold schools accountable for providing a safe learning environment and a quality education, and urging the information media to fulfil their role as public advocate by focusing attention on improving education systems.
- Encouraging states and school authorities to ensure a safe and secure learning environment for all children, free of discrimination, health hazards and violence.
- Advancing innovative uses of curricula and media (including radio, television, the arts, newspapers and the Internet) to make widely accessible the knowledge and skills needed to improve human security.

10. Clarifying the need for a global human identity

The formation of compassionate attitudes and ethical outlooks is central to empowering communities and furthering human security and deserves far more attention than it generally receives. In a world replete with divisive messages, children and adults will not always adopt the mindset of global citizens in an interdependent world.

To achieve long-term human security, education should promote understanding of people's multiple identities and of the interlinkages within the common global pool of learning. The most effective way to nurture a future generation of educated, empowered and responsible decision-makers—who avert conflict and promote peace and growth—may be to develop methods of teaching that respect diversity.

Schools and their teachers, whether in developed or developing countries, in primary schools or adult literacy classes, can teach mutual respect and solidarity. They can also perpetuate prejudice. Curricula should cultivate respect for other races, faiths, cultures and viewpoints, as well as respect for women. They should also teach students to reason, to consider ethical claims and to understand and work with such fundamental ideas as human rights, human diversity and interdependence.

At the national level, states that champion human security should check that their own curricula cultivate mutual respect and emphasize the multiplicity of identities that people hold. Teacher training institutions and supervision systems should instil the desire to produce open-minded graduates who respect diversity. Particular care should be given to eradicating inflammatory messages in private, religious, and informal education facilities.

The international development institutions that support education—especially those supporting the Education for All campaign—should make additional resources available to governments that wish to undertake such reforms. Promoting education in the short term can avoid undermining human security in the longer term.

Cultivating respect for human rights and diversity also merits special attention among security forces, police, military and others with access to coercive force. More and more these

141

groups are called on to protect human security. Educating them to respect human rights and resist discrimination and prejudice will make the civilians they are expected to protect more secure and reduce the threat of violence to all.

Linking the many initiatives in a global alliance

For each of these agenda items, alliances of key actors should be supported—networks of public, private and civil actors who can develop norms, embark on integrated activities and monitor progress and performance (see the feature on Outreach for human security on page 144). Numerous loose networks, involving a wide range of actors, are already formulating and implementing human security agendas. The Human Security Network links 13 governments. The Canadian Consortium on Human Security brings together academic and activist groups. And tens of thousands of groups are working for peace, governance, human rights, humanitarian assistance, development, poverty reduction and other freedoms that pertain to human security. Specific initiatives, such as the creation of a ministry for human security in Thailand, should be encouraged.

To overcome persistent inequality and insecurities, the efforts, practices and successes of all these groups should be linked in national, regional and global alliances. The goal of these alliances could be to create a kind of horizontal, cross-border source of legitimacy that complements that of traditional vertical and compartmentalized structures of institutions and states. Much of the work of these alliances could be managed over the Internet.[7] These initiatives could begin to give voice to international public opinion on issues of human

security. The success of the international campaign to ban landmines shows the power that such electronic networks can have. It is clear that huge new bureaucracies are not the answer.

The international community should invest more in civil society, including NGOs, reaffirming the role of individuals, corporations, foundations and faith-based organizations in transferring resources to communities and people in need. The international community should also re-examine the compartmentalization of resources as either development assistance or humanitarian relief—and consider integrated investments in human security.

Two examples of resources specifically targeted to promoting human security are the UN Trust Fund for Human Security and the bilateral Grassroots Human Security Grants, both established by the government of Japan. Japan has contributed more than $200 million to the UN trust fund, with plans for more, and all UN agencies are eligible to submit projects for funding. Japan is also providing about $120 million for the bilateral grants in fiscal 2003 to further human security, mainly to local communities and NGOs working in developing countries. To mainstream human security in the UN system—and to integrate fragmented efforts to protect and empower people exposed to severe threats to their survival, livelihoods and dignity—the Commission on Human Security suggests that the donor base of the trust fund be broadened. It also proposes the establishment of an advisory board to guide the trust fund—and more generally to follow up and promote the Commission's conclusions.

A critical initiative—in which a small input of resources might leverage great impact—would be to create a core group that would link disparate human security actors in a strong global alliance around the United Nations and the Bretton Woods organizations. That alliance could in time embrace other networks, especially within the security community, working on related issues. It might also support individuals who champion human security, as well as states that incorporate it into national and foreign policy.

All actors should endeavor to ensure adequate resources for human security. To counter the decline in official development assistance, additional resources and qualitative improvements in the provision of international assistance should be sought. Donors and developing countries should reorient and reallocate their resources to promote human security. Bilateral and multilateral assistance, both humanitarian and development-oriented, should target the protection and empowerment of people.

The Commission concludes its work by calling for integrated action—weaving many threads of work in more comprehensive approaches with wider coverage. It envisions a world that has the capacity to deal with interdependence in a rule-based framework, involving communities and institutions at every level. Multilateralism, far from being an empty vessel, is fundamental to the future of humanity. With a consistent focus on human security, more integrated social arrangements and more integrated global efforts can address the big threats and make people more secure.

Notes

1. Gillian-Borg 2002, pp. 2–6, 407 and table 8A.2.
2. UNDP 1994, p. 54.
3. United Nations 2001.
4. United Nations, General Assembly 2002.
5. United Nations 2000.
6. World Bank 2003.
7. Rischard 2002.

References

Gillian-Borg, Jetta, ed. 2002. *SIPRI Yearbook 2002: Armaments, Disarmament and International Security.* Oxford: Oxford University Press.

Rischard, Jean-Francois. 2002. *High Noon: 20 Global Problems, 20 Years to Solve Them.* New York: Basic.

Sen, Amartya. 2002. "Global Inequality and Persistent Conflicts." Paper presented at the Nobel Awards Conference, Oslo.

UNDP (United Nations Development Programme). 1994. *Human Development Report 1994.* New York: Oxford University Press.

United Nations. 2000. *Report of the Panel on United Nations Peace Operations.* A/55/305–S/2000/809. New York.

———. 2001. *Report of the United Nations Conference on the Illicit Trade in Small Arms and Light Weapons in All Its Aspects.* A/Conf.192/15. New York.

United Nations, General Assembly. 2002. *Strengthening of the United Nations: An Agenda for Further Change: Report of the Secretary-General.* A/57/387. [www.un.org/peace/reports/peace_operations/].

World Bank. 2003. *Global Development Prospects and the Developing Countries 2003.* Washington, D.C.

Outreach for
human security

The Commission on Human Security works through collaborative arrangements, consultations and outreach. It has supported and initiated processes for wide-ranging engagement with civil society, governments and regional and international organizations. Commissioners and members of its Secretariat have organized, hosted and attended public hearings, consultations, symposiums, seminars and roundtable meetings that reached hundreds of people across the world.

The following sections summarize the activities of several of these meetings and present an overview of people's views on human security:

- A symposium on Human Rights and Human Security, convened in San José, Costa Rica, on 1 December 2001.
- A roundtable on Transition and Human Security in Central Asia, convened in Ashgabat, Turkmenistan, on 22–24 April 2002 and attended by representatives of non-governmental organizations, governments in Central Asia and international organizations.
- A symposium on Economic Insecurity in Africa held in Cotonou, Benin, on 24–25 May 2002 and attended by non-governmental and government representatives from West Africa.
- Public hearings at the Global Civic Society Forum in Johannesburg on 27 August 2002 and a meeting on African Civil Society in Pretoria on 15–16 October 2002.

San José Workshop on Human Rights and Human Security

Sonia Picado S., President of the Inter-American Human Rights Institute and a commissioner of the Commission on Human Security, organized a workshop on Human Rights and Human Security in San José, Costa Rica, on 1 December 2001. The meeting was attended by leading human rights activists from Latin America. Bertrand Ramcharan, United Nations Deputy High Commissioner for Human Rights, prepared a background paper for the meeting.

Discussion focused on the relationships between human rights and human security and their importance in conflict and post-conflict situations. The situation in Colombia received particular attention. The workshop concluded with the adoption of a declaration. Some of its key elements:

- We applaud the initiative to generate efforts to determine the meaning and scope of human security and we commit our wholehearted support to the work undertaken by the Commission and to its action mechanisms.
- We reaffirm the conviction that human rights and the attributes stemming from human dignity constitute a normative framework and a conceptual reference point which must necessarily be applied to the construction and putting into practice of the notion of human security. In the same manner, without prejudice to considering the norms and principles of international humanitarian law as essential components for the construction of human security, we emphasize that the latter cannot be restricted to situations of current or past armed conflict, but rather is a generally applicable instrument.
- We recall that the 1993 Vienna Declaration, adopted at the Second World Conference on Human Rights, laid out an unavoidable course when it stipulated the universal and

comprehensive nature of an interdependence among human rights, and when it underlined that the effective exercise of all such rights—civil, political, economic, social and cultural, individually or collectively considered—is a condition for the development of people and for legitimacy of systems of government. This universal, comprehensive nature and interdependence must enrich the concept and practice of human security.

- We call for necessary progress towards ways to promote the enforceability of all human rights, through actions by national institutions, the system of justice, and international protection mechanisms, both universal and regional.
- We maintain that human rights and the effective application of mechanisms for their exercise and protection play a key role in preventing and resolving conflicts.
- We renew our certainty that democracy is an indispensable condition for the effective exercise of human rights and to establish the foundations for harmonious social relations which foster human security. In this regard, we salute, in the Americas, the recent approval of the Inter-American Democratic Charter.
- We affirm that protection of individual and collective security in the face of crime and violence is an essential component of the concept of human security, and it stems from the responsibilities of the state as guarantor of the rights of those who are in its territory. In this same way, we affirm that human security demands public policies that tend to eliminate all forms of exclusion.
- We recall the existence of the right to development stated in the international instruments of the universal system, and we highlight the links among development, effective exercise of human rights, and human security. We underline the importance of globalization taking place under conditions that facilitate the growth of international trade but that also ensure that there is a balance between the interests of producers and those of consumers, between workers and employers, between large and small economies, between investment and job creation, between growth and income distribution. The search for fair terms of trade and the existence of real opportunities for countries' development are significant components of human security at an international level.
- We express our concern over the current scale of growth of poverty and of the phenomenon of migration throughout the word and in the Americas, and especially over the scope of forced internal displacement, and we recognize the importance of the Guiding Principles on Internal Displacement that have resulted from the work of the Special Representative of the Secretary-General of the United Nations.
- We affirm that non-discrimination and respect for diversity are an essential and first-order condition for the effective exercise of human rights and for the achievement of human security. Therefore, overcoming de facto inequalities based on, shielded by, or derived from gender, ethnic identity, religion, language or any other social condition, must be a high priority.

Roundtable on Transition and Human Security in Central Asia

Ten years of independence and the transition to market economies and democratic political systems, against a backdrop of intense geopolitical change, have had deep impacts on the political, economic, social and cultural aspects of people's lives in the five new countries of Central Asia—Kazakhstan, Kyrgyz Republic, Tajikistan, Turkmenistan, and Uzbekistan. Participants deliberated on these impacts during a roundtable meeting organized by the Commission on Human Security in Ashgabat, Turkmenistan, 22–24 April 2002.

The region has experienced some of the most dramatic increases in human insecurities: sudden impoverishment; falling wages; rising inequality, unemployment and under-employment; declining health care and education opportunities; and worsening environmental degradation. The challenge for countries in Central Asia is to regain their former relatively high human development indicators, overcome emerging poverty and maintain social cohesion. This calls for a renewed role for the state and a revision in the responsibilities of civil society and the international aid community. Otherwise, a failed transition in Central Asia will have produced greater human insecurity, rather than security.

Roundtable participants identified a variety of internal and external human insecurities stemming from three sources: chronic threats inherited from the past, new insecurities that appeared during the transition, and threats from geopolitical changes in the region and in the world.

The countries of Central Asia inherited chronic human security threats arising from their history, geography and spatial distribution; the nature of rural and traditional societies and the transformation processes that the countries underwent as part of the Soviet Union. Inherited problems included their landlocked position, isolation and lack of access to global markets, economic dependency, lagging technologies and ecological problems resulting from natural causes and from poor policy choices.

The past decade of transition in Central Asia created multi-dimensional structural changes in society, the economy and the political system. Social and economic policies were exacerbated by the shrinking role of the state in economic activities and social welfare responsibilities. Emerging markets lacked institutional capacity, and civil society organizations failed to effectively fill the vacuum.

Economic insecurity increased, with rising unemployment and under-employment, wage gaps and arrears, high inflation and catastrophic loss of savings. At the state level, economic insecurity was reflected in economic crimes, gray and black economy and corruption. Sudden poverty, inequality and polarization of income appeared, and social safety nets were weakened during a time of massive unemployment and shrinking output. Human resource development declined dramatically, due to declines in the quality of education and health care, infrastructure breakdown, shrinking budgets, poor and outdated technologies and personnel flight. An increase in drug abuse and crime fostered violence in households, mafia structures, criminality in business and politics, and trafficking in goods and people.

In addition, incomplete political changes and democratization led to other problems as countries sought the right balance among democratic pluralism, the sharing of power across political parties and regions, stability, and rights and freedoms for the population. Political reforms suffer from corruption, lack of transparency and lack of capacity to implement the rule of law. Extremism seems to be growing as a reaction to the vacuum left in the wake of the collapse of socialist ideology and in response to repression and violations of human rights in the name of stability.

The changing dynamics within Central Asia and the impacts of conflicts in Afghanistan have further aggravated traditional insecurities, raising fears of an escalation in instability. Uncontrolled borders permit the proliferation of arms, threats of terrorism and extremism, the creation of networks of mafia structures and organized trafficking in arms and drugs, destabilizing states and markets and reducing economic security for people. Patterns of migration in the region and large-scale displacements of populations within the region are manifestations of both traditional and new insecurities.

Addressing human insecurities in Central Asia requires an integrated approach to the identification of the causes and consequences of insecurity—including the threat to national and regional security. Participants called for awareness building through dialogue, for political commitment on behalf of states in conjunction with civil society and for the monitoring of changes through the collection and analysis of qualitative and quantitative data. Ultimately, policy choices must balance short-term needs and long-term preventive policies to avoid negative consequences. Proper financing is needed through prioritization and budgeting and efficient revenue collection. As one participant noted, human security in the region would be greatly improved if expenditures on the military and weapons were redirected to human development. Finally, there is a need for coordination of extra-regional and global efforts to create environments that guarantee security and stability. This point is especially relevant to the situation in Afghanistan and the coordination of efforts on both sides of the border in order to stop the smuggling of weapons, drugs and people. Ultimately, the coordination of the humanitarian, development and political mandates of the United Nations and multilaterals in the region would support an integrated human security approach.

Cotonou symposium on Economic Insecurity in Africa

The onslaught of communicable diseases, economic hardship, and the negative effects of globalization, combined with legacies of past mistakes, make it difficult for a vast majority of people in Africa to feel secure.

Economic insecurity alone, even in the absence of other threats, significantly undermines human security. Precarious economic conditions, fluctuating markets over which producers have no control, chronic unemployment or under-employment and the impact of HIV/AIDS are manifestations of this insecurity. Together they disrupt fragile social services and often threaten efforts at democratization. Some 80% of countries with low human development indexes are in Africa, and 45% of the population subsists on less than $1 a day. In many parts of Africa, open or simmering conflicts place further hardship on people.

In light of these continuing crises, participants at the symposium articulated a vision for an alternative future. Voicing Africans' concerns, participants indicated that the first step towards an alternative vision that promotes human security and enables people to regain some control over their lives is to confront the humiliation of the past. Africa's history, and the internal and external forces that determine its development, are at the root of the continent's structural handicaps. This fight for dignity seeks to promote individual and collective trust in governance processes, crucial for dealing with economic deprivation and human insecurity. Poverty is not a fatal or immutable fact of life for millions, but the result of bad policy choices and practices. That means that people can take actions to alter the conditions that lead to poverty.

While states bear a heavy responsibility for the current situation, they also hold the key to redressing it. But if governments are to resolutely address persistent poverty and growing inequities, they need more and better civil society participation in the political, economic and social sectors. The continuing alienation and exclusion of people from processes of governance must be replaced by conditions that build the capacity and resilience of both the state and the people to protect people in downturns, conflict and in situations of chronic poverty. The precarious situation of women and children in conflict and in chronic poverty is a matter for urgent attention. Emphasis must be placed on the promotion of responsible governance at all levels, from village to nation. As shared during the meeting, there is no substitute for democracy and participation for freeing the creativity of large sectors of the population. The development of human resources through better health, education and social infrastructure can build the capabilities of individuals and communities alike.

To ensure that markets promote pro-poor growth and access for poor countries, Africa needs regional cooperation—despite mixed experience with economic integration. Regional and international cooperation is also needed to harness technical and human resources, to prevent or mitigate conflict, and to address cross-border issues such as migration, forced displacement and the spread of communicable diseases. Development aid is essential to complement internal resource mobilization in reducing human and economic insecurity. Innovative institutional arrangements, such as the New Partnership for Africa's Development, provide opportunities for mainstreaming human security and give Africa greater responsibility for determining its own future. Investment and wider access to markets benefit mainly countries that are able to meet international standards. Countries in which human insecurity is most prevalent are not in this position, and thus may miss new opportunities and sink further into poverty.

The challenge of promoting investment and wider access to markets, dealing with debt and the impacts of structural adjustment, and the complex connections between conflict and poverty require renewed political commitment. Transcending the legacy of humiliation, people and states must forge a new vision of human security.

Public hearings at the Global Civic Society Forum in Johannesburg and a meeting on African Civil Society in Pretoria

Concerns about state security and ongoing conflict cannot be separated from development and poverty.[1] The greatest threat to human security is widespread and endemic poverty and social inequality. Poverty eradication, reconstruction and development, in countries undergoing political and economic transitions as well as in countries experiencing chronic conflict, are long-term processes. They require a multi-faceted and complex range of responses and initiatives to the many and diverse problems that make and keep people insecure. Problems such as poverty, HIV/AIDS, lack of food, unemployment and economic resources are systemic. People often view the inability to respond to such problems as reflecting bad governance, an absence of political will, a lack of democracy and respect for human rights, and fragmented communities fuelled by ethnic hatred, gender discrimination and inequality. Overwhelmingly, the most marginalized of the poor are African women and children living in rural areas without access to basic services.

The problems confronting Africa, such as poverty, ongoing conflict and violence, increasing numbers of displaced people, infectious diseases, lack of water and natural resource management, and environmental destruction are problems that threaten human existence itself.[2] "The search for human security in a debilitating African reality must also be a struggle for the socio-economic transformation of African states. A struggle that overcomes—within the global village—our basic poverty and underdevelopment, and lays the material basis for enduring and stable multi-national commonalities".[3] These were among some of the views of people who participated in the Commission on Human Security's public hearings at the Global Civil Society Forum of the World Summit on Sustainable Development in Johannesburg and a meeting on African Civil

Society in Pretoria. Both events were led by Commissioners Frene Ginwala and Albert Tevoedjre, with support by the Africa Institute of South Africa.

Participants called attention to the huge income gaps in many countries, noting that the inability to control access to resources is a primary cause of human insecurity. This is true not only for those precariously balanced on the threshold of destitution, but for most people living in a demand-driven, capital-based society. Participants called on the Commission and the world community to make human security a reality by addressing poor people's rights to land, to decent work, to health care and to other resources for disabled people, women and other excluded members of society. For many of those who shared their views with the Commission, human security was understood in relation to "the basic needs of life—paid work, housing, health, education, food, water— … that is the primary concern of the security of an average person in the developing world".[4] In addition, environmental security and sustainable development were seen as inextricably linked to human survival, and community management of natural resources was understood to be critical.

The crisis of poverty and unemployment was considered to be one of the most significant sources of insecurity, especially in Africa. Compelling views on the many types of poverty and strategies to deal with them were presented. Many participants illustrated how poverty, through a lack of access to essential services such as health and education, can create untold misery for people. "Insecurity is rooted in a denial of a person's control over access to resources, and in particular, to fundamental necessities including food and basic services. Lack of such control means that people's immediate daily existence is at best precarious."[5] Poverty was also seen as the lack of income generating assets, resulting in an absence of economic and political power. Special emphasis was placed on income poverty and its multiple impacts on poor people, trapping them in a vicious cycle of deprivation and eroding their dignity. Poverty locks people out of the economy, making them vulnerable and placing them at risk of disability, ill health, violence and a range of problems that affect their life and their opportunities to advance.

Weak national economies also contribute to human insecurity. In a weak economy, individuals have low wages, meagre job opportunities, and little access to credit. With few life choices, they must calculate the opportunity cost of meeting basic needs such as nutrition, education and health for themselves and their families.[6] Strategies for responding to these problems, linked to regional and global economic processes, and to the social dimensions of globalization are being debated. Central to the debate is the need to respond to ongoing mass unemployment with some form of universal non-means tested income grant in the absence of other forms of earnings replacement. Called a basic income grant in South Africa and a guaranteed income by the international labour movement, it reflects the need for minimal living standards to be promoted everywhere.[7]

Having grappled with insecurity for many years, people are now coming together to create political space and design ways to resolve their problems.[8] Coalitions of poor people, human rights activists, workers and policy advocates, among others, are promoting the adoption of a tax-funded basic income grant in South Africa and internationally. They view such a grant as a means of assisting people to engage in economic activity, raising the standards of communities and eradicating the most severe forms of poverty. Set at a minimal amount and designed as an incentive for work and household survival, it would not create dependency but be a "leg up" out of poverty. Being universal, such grants would prevent people from falling through the social security net and mitigate the worst effects of economic and political crises, especially during downturns.

Social activism by women, human rights advocates, workers and environmentalists have succeeded in placing some of the most critical and pervasive human problems on the global agenda. But such efforts have yet to lead to concrete change in the lives of the most vulnerable and at risk. For example, despite international human rights instruments, women's rights are violated daily. Without effective protection of women, human security will remain unattainable.

All these aspects highlight the many dimensions to human security and the need for a comprehensive and integrated approach with many actors at all levels. Voicing the sentiments of many, another participant stated: "Human security cannot be achieved unless democratic governments or systems abide by rules and regulations set out in international agreements, conventions and domestic laws observe human rights ... to secure health, to secure education, to secure people's lives and to secure the necessities of life ... It is our duty as civil society ... to protect these rights to see that there is adequate legislation which complies with human rights conventions and agreements".[9]

Notes

1. David Malcolmson, statement made on behalf of the Secretariat of the New Partnership for Africa's Development at the Commission on Human Security public hearings on human security held at the Global Civil Society Forum of the World Summit on Sustainable Development, Johannesburg, 27 August 2002.

2. These views were reinforced at the Commission on Human Security Africa-wide civil society consultative meeting on human security held in Pretoria, 15–16 October 2002.

3. K. David Mafabi, Pan African Movement, October 2002, Pretoria.

4. Nigerian participant, name unknown at the Commission on Human Security public hearings on human security held at the Global Civil Society Forum of the World Summit on Sustainable Development, Johannesburg, 27 August 2002.

5. Isobel Frye, statement made on behalf of the Black Sash, at the Commission on Human Security public hearings on human security held at the Global Civil Society Forum of the World Summit on Sustainable Development, Johannesburg, 27 August 2002.

6. Mansah Prah, Dept. of Sociology, University of Cape Town, statement made at the Commission on Human Security Africa-wide civil society consultative meeting on human security held in Pretoria, 15–16 October 2002.

7. Detailed oral and written statements on economic insecurity and the Basic Income Grant were made by a number of people including Neil Coleman from Congress of South African Trade Union and Ravi Naidoo from the National Labour and Economic Development Institute of South Africa.

8. Reverend Edward Limo, statement made at the Commission on Human Security Africa-wide civil society consultative meeting on human security held in Pretoria, 15–16 October 2002.

9. Halisman, Sudanese Consumer Protection Society at the Commission on Human Security public hearings on human security held at the Global Civil Society Forum of the World Summit on Sustainable Development, Johannesburg, 27 August 2002.

About the Commission on Human Security

The Commission on Human Security was established in response to the UN Secretary-General's call at the Millennium Summit in September 2000 to achieve the twin goals of "freedom from fear" and "freedom from want". Launched in January 2001 and beginning operations in June 2001, the Commission seeks to fulfil three objectives under its two-year mandate:

- Promoting public understanding, engagement and support of human security and its underlying imperatives.
- Developing the concept of human security as an operational tool for policy formulation and implementation.
- Proposing a concrete programme of action to address critical and pervasive threats to human security.

The Commission receives financial support from the Government of Japan, with the continuing assistance of foreign ministers Yoriko Kawaguchi and Makiko Tanaka, and from the Rockefeller Foundation, the World Bank (Africa Region), the Greentree Foundation, the Government of Sweden and the Japan Center for International Exchange.

The Commission works through collaborative arrangements, consultations and outreach.

Collaborative arrangements

To advance an integrated approach for collaborative action, the Commission has drawn widely on other initiatives and endeavours. Its work has benefited greatly from the support of the United Nations High Commissioner for Refugees (UNHCR); the United Nations Development Programme (UNDP), particularly the Human Development Report Office (HDRO); and the United Nations Office for Project Services (UNOPS). The UNHCR provided ongoing guidance with research and other services through Cynthia Burns, Jeff Crisp, Bela Hovy and Kamel Morjane. The HDRO, under the leadership of Sakiko Fukuda-Parr, provided assistance through the services of Tanni Mukhopadhyay, Richard Ponzio, Shahrbanou Tadjbakhsh and others. The UNOPS provided assistance and support through the services of Daniela Costantino and Maria Hemsy.

Two broad areas of research and related consultative processes inform the Commission's deliberations. One area deals with human insecurities resulting from conflict and violence, and the other with the links between human security and development. Together, the two areas address the need for providing effective protection in critical situations.

The project on conflict focuses on individuals or communities facing extreme situations like displacement, discrimination and persecution. It addresses the special security needs of people and the protection of victims, refugees and internally displaced people. It also addresses the interrelations between insecurity and the need to ensure that developmental activities proceed alongside conflict resolution. The project commissioned research, undertook field-based assessments of specific themes and organized a series of events in collaboration with the UNHCR and other partners.

The project on the developmental aspects of human security focuses on insecurities related to poverty, health, education, gender disparities and other types of inequality. It also works on problems that cut across these themes, including institutional arrangements for reducing insecurities and the new vulnerabilities associated with the current global situation. Research papers were commissioned to examine the relationships among these factors and the substantive policy implications of human security. The project convened workshops and hosted monthly seminars to promote policy debate on human security. The Global Equity Initiative, under the leadership of Commissioner Lincoln Chen, provided research support for the Commission through the work of Sudhir Anand, Prea Gulati, Juan Carlos Hincapie, Paula Johnson, Chris Linnane, Sarah Michael, Vasant Narasimhan, Barbara Perlo, Paul Segal, Ellen Seidensticker, Patricia Tyler, Jonathan Welch and Florence Werthmuller.

Consultations and outreach

The Commission has supported and initiated processes for wide-ranging engagement with civil society, governments and regional and international organizations. Commissioners and members of the Secretariat have organized, hosted and attended public hearings, consultations, symposiums, seminars and roundtable meetings that reached hundreds of people across the world.

The Commission has held five general meetings, with associated outreach activities. At the first meeting in New York on 8–10 June 2001, commissioners shared their views on human security and agreed on a plan of work. The second meeting, on 15-17 December 2001 in Tokyo, was convened at the invitation of the Government of Japan, which organized a one-day symposium before the meeting. The third meeting, facilitated by Commissioner Carl Tham, was convened in Stockholm on 8–10 June 2002, with the support of the Government of Sweden. Following that meeting, a roundtable dialogue, sponsored by the International Institute for Democracy and Electoral Assistance, provided for an exchange of views with the commissioners on the relationships among human security, human rights and democracy. The fourth meeting was convened in Bangkok on 8–10 December 2002 with the support of Commissioner Surin Pitsuwan. The Commission also participated in an outreach event organized by Chulalongkorn University. At the fifth meeting in Tokyo on 22–24 February 2003, commissioners discussed and finalized this report and agreed on the next steps. The meeting was followed by a symposium organized by the Ministry of Foreign Affairs.

Public hearings on human security were also convened around the world (see Outreach on page 144). A symposium on Human Rights and Human Security was convened in San José, Costa Rica on 1 December 2001. The meeting was co-organized by the Inter-American Institute for Human Rights, the University for Peace and the Commission's Secretariat.

A roundtable meeting on Transition and Human Security in Central Asia was convened in Ashgabat, Turkmenistan, on 22–24 April 2002 and attended by representatives of non-governmental organizations, governments in Central Asia and international organizations. The UNDP Regional Bureau for Europe and the CIS assisted the Commission in organizing the meeting.

A workshop on Rethinking Peace, Coexistence and Human Security in the Great Lakes was held in Kigali, Rwanda, on 16–19 April 2002. It was organized by the Commission,

154

the UNHCR, the Centre for Conflict Management of the National University of Rwanda and the Center for International Development and Conflict Management of the University of Maryland.

Non-governmental and government representatives from West Africa participated in a symposium on Economic Insecurity in Africa in Cotonou, Benin, on 24–25 May 2002. The UNDP and the Centre PanAfricain de Prospective Sociale assisted in organizing the symposium.

Public hearings on human security were convened at the Global Civil Society Forum of the World Summit on Sustainable Development in Johannesburg on 27 August 2002. The hearings and related activities were organized by the Africa Institute of South Africa for the Commission and cosponsored by the World Bank (Africa Region). Participants from more than 25 countries and five regions made oral and written submissions to the Commission.

An Africa-wide civil society consultative meeting on human security was held in Pretoria on 15–16 October 2002, organized by the Africa Institute of South Africa and sponsored by the World Bank (Africa Region). Participants, representing key sectors of civil society, business, trade unions, development, humanitarian and security fields, shared their perceptions and experiences on human security issues in Africa.

The findings and outcomes of these events have significantly informed the work of the Commission. Reports on the events were prepared and shared. The Commission has made every effort to ensure that this report reflects the many rich insights and experiences shared by the people who attended these meetings.

The Secretariat

The Secretariat works under the direction of François Fouinat (Executive Director) and Viviene Taylor (Deputy Director and project coordinator for development) and included Sabina Alkire (researcher and writer), Johan Cels (project coordinator for conflict), Sumana Raychaudhuri (associate editor), Kazuo Tase (liaison officer from the Government of Japan) and administrative assistants Bonna Mpama, Eucaris Perez-Valero and Karima Zerrou. Research support was provided by Ann Barham, Christine Cheng, Marijke Cortebeeck, Frank Fountain, Julia Gohsing, Ayako Kimura, Ludovica Piacentini and Florence Poli.

General acknowledgements

The work of the Commission was supported by a number of individuals, institutions and organizations representing a wide range of interests and concerns. To all those who provided insights, support and commitment to the promotion of human security, the Commission expresses its gratitude and thanks. The Commission is especially appreciative of the efforts made by the many people representing women, workers, refugees, the landless, the disabled, poor people, young people, and displaced communities, and of the many others who shared their experiences, concerns and aspirations with the Commission.

While many governments recognize the importance of human security, special mention must go to the Japanese. Significant support was provided by Keizo Takemi (Japanese Diet Member) and Tadashi Yamamoto (President of the Japan Center for International Exchange), and by the

Government of Japan: Yukio Sato, Koichi Haraguchi, Yukio Takasu, Koichi Takahashi, Kaoru Ishikawa, Kunio Umeda, Eiichi Oshima, Masaharu Yoshida, Hideki Ito, Jun Shimmi, Naoki Ito, Takeshi Akamatsu, Hiroyuki Uchida, Ryo Nakamura and Akiko Noda.

For the Commission's Stockholm meeting in June 2002, generous support was given by the Swedish government: Jan O. Karlsson, Gun-Britt Andersson, Ingrid Wetterqvist, Karin Snellman, Sara Bertilsson. The Commission especially appreciated the participation of HRH Princess Maha Chakri Sirindhorn of Thailand and Anand Panyarachun at its meeting in Bangkok.

Peter Geithner also contributed advice and guidance to the work of the Commission throughout the process.

Organizations

Numerous international agencies and civil society actors provided assistance. The Commission appreciates their interest in human security and counts on them to translate it into concrete activities improving the plight of people. They include Africa Humanitarian Action, African Union, Amnesty International, Black Sash (South Africa), Brookings Institute, Canadian Consortium for Human Security, Carnegie Endowment for Peace, Center for Conflict Management (National University of Rwanda), Center for International Development and Conflict Management (University of Maryland), Chulalongkorn University, Community Law Centre (University of the Western Cape), Congress of South African Trade Unions, Council on Foreign Relations (USA), Development Alternatives with Women for a New Era (DAWN), Economic Policy Research Institute (South Africa), The Ford Foundation, Human Security Network, ICRC, Institut des Hautes Études Internationales (Geneva), Institute for Democracy and Electoral Assistance (IDEA), Inter-American Institute of Human Rights, Inter-Parliamentary Union International Migration Policy Programme, International Labour Organization (ILO), International Organization for Migration, International Peace Academy, Legal Resources Centre (South Africa), National Labour Economic and Development Institute (NALEDI-South Africa), OAS, OCHA, OSCE, Pratichi Trust (India), Save the Children Fund, Stockholm International Peace Research Institute, Swiss Peace Foundation (Afghan Civil Society Forum), Trilateral Commission, UN High Commissioner for Human Rights, UN Intellectual History Project, UNAIDS, UNESCO, UNICEF, United Nations Secretariat, United Nations University (Japan), UNRWA, World Bank, World Economic Forum, World Food Progamme and the World Health Organization.

Individuals

Alayne Adams (Columbia University), Mahnaz Afkhami (Women's Learning Partnership for Rights, Development and Peace), Nazaré Albuquerque (Catholic Relief Services), Mely Anthony (Nanyang Technological Institute), Peggy Antrobus (DAWN Caribbean), Bertrand Badie (Institut d'Études Politiques, France), Frederick D. Barton (Center for Strategic and International Studies), Linda Basch (National Council for Research on Women, USA), Alaka Basu (Cornell University), Kazem Behbehani (World Health Organization), Susan Beresford (Ford Foundation), Giovanni Berlinguer (Università La Sapienza),

Douglas Bettcher (WHO), Jacqueline Bhabha (Harvard University), Derek Bok (Harvard University), Sissela Bok (Harvard University), Sugata Bose (Harvard University), Claude Bruderlein (Harvard University), Alexander Butchart (WHO), Maria Calivis (UNICEF), Richard Cash (Harvard University), Ewa Charkiewicz (DAWN), Mirai Chaterjee (Self Employed Women's Association, India), Martha Chen (Harvard University), Mushtaque Chowdhury (BRAC), Michele Clark (Johns Hopkins University), William Clark (Harvard University), Sonia Correa (DAWN Latin America), Robert Curvin (Greentree Foundation), Norman Daniels (Harvard University), Susan Davids (ILO), Robert DeVecchi (Council on Foreign Relations), Michael Doyle (UN Secretariat), Jean Drèze (Delhi School of Economics), Paul Evans (University of British Columbia), Timothy Evans (Rockefeller Foundation), Marika Fahlen (UNAIDS), Roya Ghafele (Vienna University), Raimundo Gonzalez-Aninat (Chile), Stephanie Griffith-Jones (University of Sussex), Claudio Grossman (Inter-American Commission of Human Rights), Thomas Hammerberg (Olof Palme Centre), Fen Hampson (Carleton University), Daniel Helle (ICRC), Arthur Helton (Council on Foreign Relations), David Heymann (WHO), Michael Ignatieff (Harvard University), Rolf Jenny (IMP, Geneve), Soren Jessen-Petersen (Stability Pact for South Eastern Europe), Anders Johnsson (Inter-Parliamentary Union), Mats Karlsson (World Bank), Hideko Katsumata (JCIE), Inge Kaul (UNDP), Sanjeev Khagram (Harvard University), Jenny Kimmins (University of Sussex), Gary King (Harvard University), Margaret Kowalsky (Harvard University), K. Shiva Kumar (UNICEF), Frank Laczko (IOM), Melissa Lane (Cambridge University), Jennifer Leaning (Harvard University), Walter Lichem (Federal Ministry of Foreign Affairs, Austria), Frances Lund (University of Natal), Andrew Mack (University of British Columbia), Bene Madunagu (DAWN Africa), Eddy Maloka (Africa Institute, South Africa), David Malone (International Peace Academy), Maria Helena Martinez (Inter-American Institute of Human Rights), David Meddings (ICRC), Martha Minow (Harvard University), Abram L. Mogilevsky (Turkmen National Institute, Turkmenistan), Vanita Muckherjee (DAWN Asia), Christopher Murray (WHO), Izumi Nakamitsu-Lennartsson (IDEA), Kathleen Newland (Migration Policy Institute), Edward Newman (UNU), Pedro Nikken (Inter-American Institute of Human Rights), Herbert S. Okun (USA), Khaled Philby (UNDP), Rajeev Pillay (Abacus International Management), Anne-Marie Pitsch (University of Maryland), Dana Firas Raad (Harvard University), Kent Ransom (Self Employed Women's Association, India), Elisabeth Rasmusson (Internally Displaced Persons Project, Norwegian Refugee Council), Paul Révay (Trilateral Commission), Iqbal Riza (UN Secretariat), Santiago Romero-Perez (Inter-Parliamentary Union), Emma Rothschild (Cambridge University), Barnett Rubin (New York University), Gita Sen (Indian Institute of Management), Kenji Shibuya (WHO), Olive Shisana (Human Sciences Research Council), Noala Skinner (UNICEF), Claire Slatter (DAWN), Fatou Sow (DAWN Africa), Rodolfo Stavenhagen (Inter-American Institute of Human Rights), Thorvald Stoltenberg (IDEA), Jonas Store (ECON, Oslo), Wun' Gaeo Surichai (Chulalongkorn University), Simon Szreter (Cambridge University), Rosemary

Taylor (Tufts University), Antonio Augusto Cançado Trindade (Inter-American Court of Human Rights), Mio Uchida (JCIE), Peter Uvin (Tufts University), Hans van Ginkel (UNU), Anthony van Niewoukerk (Africa Institute, South Africa), Thomas Weiss (New York University), Mary Wilson (Harvard University), Kelly Wong (University of Maryland), and Mark Zacher (University of British Columbia).

Special thanks to the assistants who supported the Co-chairs: Claudia Fletcher, Ruth Easthope, Rosanne Flynn.

Editing and production

Communications Development Incorporated provided overall design direction, editing and layout, led by Bruce Ross-Larson and Meta de Coquereaumont. The editing and production team consisted of Joseph Costello, Wendy Guyette, Elizabeth McCrocklin and Elaine Wilson.

Selected background papers contributed to the Commission

Note: The background papers represent the authors' views and do not necessarily represent the views of the Commission or its members.

Adams, Alayne M., and Mushtaq Chowdhury. "Harnessing Social Capital to Increase Health and Human Security: The Social Action Agenda of an NGO in Bangladesh."

Albuquerque, Nazare. 2002. "The Transition from Relief to Development: A Human Security Gap" May.

Alkire, Sabina. "Conceptual Framework for Human Security."

Armstrong, Andrea C. 2002. "Being Recognized as Citizens: A Human Security Dilemma in Central Asia and the Caucasus."

Bach, Robert. "Global Mobility, Inequality and Security."

Barton, Frederick D., John Hefferman and Andrea Armstrong. 2002. "Being Recognized as Citizens: A Human Security Dilemma in Sub-Saharan Africa, South, Central, and Southeast Asia, the Caucasus and Central and Eastern Europe: Lessons Learned and Policy Recommendations."

Berlinguer, Giovanni. "Bioethics, Human Security, and Global Health."

Bettcher, Douglas, David Meddings and Roya Ghafele. "Human Security, Public Health, and Violence."

Caballero-Anthony, Mely. "Health and Human Security in Asia: Realities and Challenges."

Chatterjee, Mirai, and M. Kent Ranson. "Exploring the Quality and Coverage of Community-based Health Insurance Among the Poor: The SEWA Experience."

Chen, Lincoln, and Vasant Narasimhan. "Human Security: Opportunities for Global Health."

Choduba, Johannes. 2002. "Being Recognized as Citizens: A Human Security Dilemma in Central and Eastern Europe."

Clark, Michele Anne "Trafficking in Persons: An Issue of Human Security."

Coletta, Nat J. "Human Security, Poverty and Conflict: Implications for IFI Reform."

Collins, Kathleen. 2002. "Human Security in Central Asia: Challenges Posed by a Decade of Transition."

Faubert, Carrol. 2002. "Refugee Security in Africa."

Gahr Store, Jonas. "Politics, Policies, and Global Institutions."

Garcia-Moreno, Claudia, and Sonali Johnson. "Gender Insecurity and Health."

Griffith-Jones, Stephanie, and Jenny Kimmis. "International Financial Volatility."

158

Hampson, Fen, and Mark Zacher "Human Security and International Collaboration: Some Lessons from Public Goods Theory."

Heymann, David L. "The Evolving Infectious Disease Threat: Implications for National and Global Security."

Hefferman, John. 2002. "Being Recognized as Citizens: A Human Security Dilemma in South and Southeast Asia."

Instituto Interamericano de Derechos Humanos. 2001. "Relación entre Derechos Humanos y Seguridad Humana."

Khagram, Sanjeev, William C. Clark and Dana Firas Raad. "From the Environment and Human Security to Sustainable Development and Comprehensive Security."

Kirby, Kay. "Displacement as Policy." Prepared in cooperation with the Internally Displaced Persons Project, Norwegian Refugee Council.

Lane, Melissa. "Human Rights and the Private Sector."

Leaning, Jennifer, Sam Arie and Gilbert Holleufer. "Conflict and Human Security."

Michael, Sarah. "The Potential Contribution of NGOs to Achieving Human Security."

Ntegaye, Gloria. 2002. "Being Recognized as Citizens: A Human Security Dilemma in Sub-Saharan Africa."

Ramcharan, Bertrand. 2001. "Human Rights and Human Security."

Schmeidl, Susanne and others. 2002. "The Transition from Relief to Development from a Human Security Perspective: Afghanistan."

Schoettle, Enid. "Three Additional Threats to Human Security: Transnational Organized Crime, Terrorism, and Weapons of Mass Destruction."

Shibuya, Kenji. "Global Health Risks to Human Security: Implications from the Global Burden of Disease 2000 Study."

Shisana, Olive, Nompumelelo Zungu-Dirwayi and William Shisana. "AIDS: A Threat to Human Security."

Szreter, Simon. "Health and Human Security in an Historical Perspective."

Tadjbakhsh, Shahrbanou. 2002. "A Review of National Human Development Report and Implications for Human Security."

Thouez, Colleen. 2002. "Migration and Human Security." Prepared by the International Migration Policy Programme.

Vaux, Tony, and Frances Lund. "Overcoming Crisis: Working Women and Security—Experiences of the Self Employed Women's Association (SEWA), Gujarat, India."

Wilson, Mary E. "Globalization of Infectious Diseases."